NEW CENTURY COMMENT

General Editors

RONALD E. CLEMENTS
(Old Testament)

MATTHEW BLACK
(New Testament)

EPHESIANS

THE NEW CENTURY BIBLE COMMENTARIES

EXODUS (J. P. Hyatt)
LEVITICUS AND NUMBERS (N. H. Snaith)*
DEUTERONOMY (A. D. H. Mayes)
JOSHUA, JUDGES, AND RUTH (John Gray)*
EZRA, NEHEMIAH, AND ESTHER (L. H. Brockington)*
JOB (H. H. Rowley)
PSALMS Volumes 1 and 2 (A. A. Anderson)
ISAIAH 1-39 (R. E. Clements)
ISAIAH 40-66 (R. N. Whybray)
EZEKIEL (John W. Wevers)*
THE GOSPEL OF MATTHEW (David Hill)
THE GOSPEL OF MARK (Hugh Anderson)
THE GOSPEL OF LUKE (E. Earle Ellis)
THE GOSPEL OF JOHN (Barnabas Lindars)
THE ACTS OF THE APOSTLES (William Neil)
ROMANS (Matthew Black)
1 and 2 CORINTHIANS (F. F. Bruce)
GALATIANS (Donald Guthrie)
EPHESIANS (C. Leslie Mitton)
PHILIPPIANS (Ralph P. Martin)
COLOSSIANS AND PHILEMON (Ralph P. Martin)
1 PETER (Ernest Best)*
THE BOOK OF REVELATION (G. R. Beasley-Murray)

*Not yet available in paperback
Other titles are in preparation

NEW CENTURY BIBLE
COMMENTARY

Based on the Revised Standard Version

EPHESIANS

C. LESLIE MITTON

WM. B. EERDMANS PUBL. CO., GRAND RAPIDS

MARSHALL, MORGAN & SCOTT PUBL. LTD., LONDON

Copyright © Marshall, Morgan & Scott 1973
First published 1973 by Marshall, Morgan & Scott, England
Softback edition published 1981

for
Wm. B. Eerdmans Publishing Company
255 Jefferson Ave. S.E., Grand Rapids, Mich. 49503
and
Marshall, Morgan & Scott
1 Bath Street, London EC1V 9LB
ISBN 0 551 009 09 8

Library of Congress Cataloging in Publication Data

Mitton, C. Leslie.
Ephesians.

(New century Bible commentary)
Reprint. Originally published: London: Oliphants,
c1976. (New century Bible)
Bibliography: p. xiii
Includes indexes.
1. Bible. N.T. Ephesians — Commentaries. I. Title.
II. Series. III. Series: New century Bible.
BS2695.3.M57 1981 227'.507 81-5568
ISBN 0-8028-1907-9 (pbk.) AACR2

In gratitude to
Margaret,
Joan and John
and
Ian,
friends as well as family

CONTENTS

EDITOR'S NOTE

This New Century Bible *Ephesians* by Dr C. Leslie Mitton follows the plan, announced in the foreword to *Colossians and Philemon*, to replace the single volume *Ephesians, Philippians, Colossians and Philemon*, modelled on the old series and now out of print, by three separate volumes on Ephesians, Colossians and Philemon, and Philippians.

MATTHEW BLACK

ABBREVIATIONS

BIBLICAL

OLD TESTAMENT (OT)

Gen.	Jg.	1 Chr.	Ps.	Lam.	Ob.	Hag.
Exod.	Ru.	2 Chr.	Prov.	Ezek.	Jon.	Zech.
Lev.	1 Sam.	Ezr.	Ec.	Dan.	Mic.	Mal.
Num.	2 Sam.	Neh.	Ca.	Hos.	Nah.	
Dt.	1 Kg.	Est.	Isa.	Jl	Hab.	
Jos.	2 Kg.	Job	Jer.	Am.	Zeph.	

APOCRYPHA (Apoc.)

1 Esd.	Tob.	Ad. Est.	Sir.	S 3 Ch.	Bel	1 Mac.
2 Esd.	Jdt.	Wis.	Bar.	Sus.	Man.	2 Mac.
			Ep. Jer.			

NEW TESTAMENT (NT)

Mt.	Ac.	Gal.	1 Th.	Tit.	1 Pet.	3 Jn
Mk	Rom.	Eph.	2 Th.	Phm.	2 Pet.	Jude
Lk.	1 C.	Phil.	1 Tim.	Heb.	1 Jn	Rev.
Jn	2 C.	Col.	2 Tim.	Jas	2 Jn	

OTHER ABBREVIATIONS

AV   *Authorised Version* (King James' Version, 1611).

EE   *The Epistle to the Ephesians: Its Authorship, Origin and Purpose*, C. L. Mitton (Oxford, 1951).

ER   *The Epistle to the Romans (ICC)*, W. Sanday and A. C. Headlam (T. and T. Clark, Edinburgh, 1895).

ExpT   *Expository Times*.

ICC   *International Critical Commentary*.

LXX   Septuagint (Greek Old Testament).

MS   manuscript.

NEB   *The New English Bible* (1970).

NTAP   *The New Testament in the Apostolic Fathers*, Oxford Society (1905).

writer is most successfully reproducing the essential Pauline teaching. At other points I have felt the epistle laboured and a little artificial, and it is these passages which on other grounds also have been regarded as non-Pauline—passages in which the writer is adapting or developing Paul's teaching to make it applicable to the needs of his own later time.

One effect of this further study of Ephesians has been to make me feel that for many readers its emphasis on the Church has led to the neglect of other parts—far the greater part of the epistle— which do not deal with the Church. These include some splendid affirmations of Christian faith and experience. I have also felt that the sections on the Church, though they have been greatly valued in past centuries, do not emphasise those aspects of the Church's life which seem most important in the life of today.

I should like to take this opportunity to express my deep sense of gratitude to the Methodist Church for giving me the immense privilege of being a minister in its ranks, for twenty years in the practical work of the circuits, and for twenty years as a teacher of the New Testament in one of its theological colleges. The passing years have also brought a deepening sense of gratitude to my immediate family, for providing a healing centre of friendship from which to face life's duties. To them I dedicate this book.

C. Leslie Mitton

PREFACE

2 left this,

It has been an interesting experience to return to the detailed study of 'Ephesians' after an interval of more than twenty years. My first major piece of New Testament research was into the question of the authorship, origin, and purpose of this epistle, particularly in relation to E. J. Goodspeed's theory about it. This theory on first acquaintance had intrigued me, without fully convincing me. The aim of my research was to determine how far it was securely based, and after two or three years of detailed study I reached the conclusion that Goodspeed was in the main right, and that the most significant feature of Ephesians was its dependence on Paul's other letters, and especially on Colossians. Moreover, this dependence was of a kind which could not be reconciled with Pauline authorship. The post-Pauline author who produced 'Ephesians' must have done so in the presence of written copies of Paul's letters, and his intention was to produce a kind of comprehensive summary of Paul's teaching, at the same time adapting it to the needs of a later generation of Christians. The result of this research was published in my book *The Epistle to the Ephesians: Its Authorship, Origin and Purpose* (1951).

Since then my interests have been taken up by other parts of the *NT*, especially the Synoptic Gospels and the Pauline letters. Ephesians has not remained the focus of my attention, though I have tried to keep abreast of scholarly studies on it. In recent times these have been concerned mainly with its connexion with the liturgical life of the early Church, and also with the writings of the Qumran community. In the meantime my own studies have involved me in a close acquaintance with such Pauline letters as Romans, 1 and 2 Corinthians, and Galatians, and I find myself acknowledging a deep sense of personal indebtedness to Paul and an eager rapport with him as an interpreter of Christian faith and experience.

In view of this, when I was invited to write a commentary on Ephesians, I found myself wondering how far I should find my earlier conclusions corroborated or undermined by a devotional and theological approach to the text, rather than a largely critical one. The work, however, has confirmed the earlier conclusions. There is much in Ephesians to which I find myself responding with eagerness and excitement, and it is here that the

NTS   *New Testament Studies.*

PRE   *Prolegomena to St Paul's Epistles to the Romans and Ephesians,*
         F. J. A. Hort (1895).

RSV   *Revised Standard Version* (*NT*, 1946; *OT*, 1952; rev. edn.
         1973).

RV   *Revised Version* (*NT*, 1880; *OT*, 1884).

TDNT   *Theological Dictionary of the New Testament,* ed. G. Kittel
         and G. Friedrich (ET 1964–1975).

TEV   *Today's English Version* (*Good News for Modern Man*) (*NT*,
         1966).

ZNW   *Zeitschrift für die neutestamentliche Wissenschaft.*

SELECT BIBLIOGRAPHY

Abbott, T. K. *The Epistles to the Ephesians and the Colossians (ICC)*, T. and T. Clark, Edinburgh, 1899.

Abbott-Smith, G. *A Manual Greek Lexicon of the New Testament*, T. and T. Clark, Edinburgh, 1923.

Allan, J. A. *Ephesians (Torch Commentary)*, SCM, London, 1959.

Beare, F. W. *The Epistle to the Ephesians (Interpreter's Bible Commentary)*, Abingdon, Nashville, 1953.

Chadwick, H. 'Die Absicht des Epheserbriefes', *ZNW* 51 (1960), pp. 145–53.

Common Bible. A revision of the *RSV*, Collins, London, 1973.

Dibelius, M. *Handbuch zum Neuen Testament*, 1953.

Dodd, C. H. *The Epistle of Paul to the Romans (Moffatt Commentary)*, Hodder and Stoughton, London, 1932.

Dunn, J. D. G. *Baptism in the Holy Spirit*, SCM, London, 1970.

Goodspeed, E. J. *The Meaning of Ephesians*, Chicago, 1933.

Houlden, J. H. *Philippians, Colossians, Philemon, and Ephesians*, Pelican, Harmondsworth, 1970.

Hunter, A. M. *Paul and his Predecessors*, SCM, London, 1940, 1961.

Jeremias, J. *The Central Message of the New Testament*, SCM, London, 1965.

Keck, L. E., and Martyn, J. L. (eds.) *Studies in Luke–Acts*, Abingdon, Nashville, 1966.

Kirby, J. C. *Ephesians: Baptism and Pentecost*, SPCK, London, 1968.

Kümmel, W. G. *Introduction to the New Testament*, SCM, London, 1965.

Masson, C. *L'Épitre de Saint Paul aux Éphésiens*, Delachaux Niestlé, Neuchâtel, 1953.

Mitton, C. L. *The Epistle to the Ephesians: Its Authorship, Origin and Purpose*, Oxford, 1951.

Mitton, C. L. *The Formation of the Pauline Corpus of Letters*, Epworth, London, 1955.

Moffat, J. *Introduction to the Literature of the New Testament*, T. and T. Clark, Edinburgh, 1910.

Moule, C. F. D. *The Birth of the New Testament*, A. and C. Black, London, 1962.

Moule, C. F. D. *The Epistles to the Colossians and Philemon*, Cambridge UP, 1955.

Mussner, F. *Christus, das All und die Kirche*, Paulinus Verlag, Trier, 1955.

Percy, E. *Die Probleme der Kolosser- und Epheserbriefe*, Gleerup, Lund, 1946.

Sampley, J. P. '*And the Two Shall Become One Flesh*': *A Study of Traditions in Ephesians 5: 21–33*, Cambridge UP, 1971.

Scott, E. F. *The Epistles of Paul to the Colossians, to Philemon, and to the Ephesians (Moffatt Commentary)*, Hodder and Stoughton, London, 1930.

Taylor, J. V., *The Go-Between God*, SCM, London, 1972.

Vermes, G. *The Dead Sea Scrolls in English*, Pelican, Harmondsworth, 1962.

INTRODUCTION

to

Ephesians

INTRODUCTION

The Epistle to the Ephesians ranks high among the letters of the Pauline corpus. Luther included it in the select group of writings which he designated 'the true kernel and marrow' of the books of the New Testament. Hort and Dodd both described it as 'the crown of the Pauline writings'; and A. S. Peake and F. F. Bruce both called it 'the quintessence of Paulinism'. It is the 'quintessence of Paulinism' because all the essential elements of Paul's teaching are included in it, expressed with a maturity and comprehensiveness not always found in the earlier letters. It is 'the crown of Pauline writings' because here Paul's theological thought, especially about the Church, reaches a stage of development which exceeds all that preceded it. Some of the vigour and depth of feeling found in Galatians and Corinthians is missing, but this lack is compensated by the sense of balance and quiet assurance which is characteristic of Ephesians.

Indeed balance, comprehensiveness and confident serenity are the special features of this epistle. No major enduring element in Paul's teaching is missing from it, and parts of the teaching are carried forward to a more developed form and combined in a systematic whole. There is a complete absence of any discordant note. Even happy letters like Philippians contain some echoes of dissension; but here the atmosphere of reconciliation and unity is uninterrupted. It is as though the writer deliberately stands aside from the actual issues on which Christians may find themselves divided, and concentrates entirely on the positive affirmation of those enduring truths which bring healing and concord within the Christian community.

1. AUTHENTICITY AND AUTHORSHIP

From earliest days Ephesians held an acknowledged place in the Pauline corpus of letters. It is present among Paul's letters in every known manuscript, even in the Chester Beatty MS which omits the Pastoral epistles. It bears Paul's name not only in the title and opening address, but also in the body of the epistle itself. In the Muratorian Canon, one of the earliest lists representing a period before the canon of the NT had been finalised, it was accorded a

2

secure place. In the early centuries its claim to Pauline authorship remained unquestioned.

Moreover, it is quoted from an early date in other Christian writings. Some apparent echoes of it are to be found in *1 Clement* (*c.* AD 90), though they are insufficient to prove literary dependence. But there can be no reasonable doubt that both Polycarp and Ignatius (*c.* AD 110) use words borrowed from it (see *EE*, pp. 160ff.), and after their time it is quoted constantly. It was in fact consistently treated as a genuinely Pauline letter without any hint of doubt or uncertainty until the end of the eighteenth century, apart from one single tentative hint from Erasmus who speculated that in view of its many differences from other Pauline letters it could conceivably have been written by someone other than Paul.

Generally speaking its authorship was not even questioned. Scholars, however, did note peculiarities about it which made it different from other letters by Paul. For instance, it was not clear to whom it was addressed. The words 'in Ephesus' (1:1), describing the church to which it is sent, are missing from some of the earliest and most reliable MSS, and do not appear in the *RSV*. No church is named and an awkward gap is left in the sentence. In any case Ephesus does not provide a convincing destination for this letter, because the letter makes it clear that the writer and the readers were unknown to each other (1:15, 3:2). Ephesus, however, was a city where Paul had spent an unusually long period of ministry, and where he was well known. A widely accepted explanation of these apparently inconsistent features was that the letter was in fact originally intended as a circular letter, of which many copies had been made, but with the place for the name of the church addressed left blank for a later appropriate insertion. Such a theory might explain why Marcion knew this letter but referred to it as one addressed to the Laodiceans. Moreover, the cautiously impersonal nature of the letter lent support to such an interpretation. It was noted that even the references to Paul himself (3:1–4, 3:7, 4:1) were very formal, almost artificial. Indeed, it appeared, as H. Chadwick shrewdly commented, to be a letter which was addressed to everyone in general and no one in particular. There is little or nothing which can be learned from it about the people to whom it is being sent.

By the end of the eighteenth century, however, particularly in

Germany, the identification of more and more points where Ephesians was different from the other Pauline letters began to lead to doubts about its supposed Pauline authorship. These misgivings continued to increase until by the end of the nineteenth century it is probably true to say that most German scholars not only had begun to question its Pauline authorship, but even to deny it outright. These misgivings affected British scholarship also, but up to the outbreak of war in 1939 most British scholars still held to Pauline authorship, though they now realised that it was a vulnerable position in constant need of defence. It could no longer be assumed without question.

The considerations which told against Pauline authorship were as follows:

(1) *Linguistic Arguments*

About ninety words in Ephesians are not used elsewhere in Pauline letters, although, significantly, some of them were in common use in writings dated towards the end of the century. One such word is *diabolos* meaning devil. Paul never uses it, always preferring to speak of Satan. There is also the strange phrase 'in the heavenly (places)', five times in Ephesians, and not at all in Paul's other letters.

(2) *Stylistic Arguments*

Sanday and Headlam (*ER*, p. lv) analysed the stylistic differences by noting that Paul's style could normally be described as marked by 'energy and vivacity', a 'rush of words', and language which is 'rapid, terse and incisive'. By contrast in Ephesians we meet sentences which are abnormally long and slow-moving. Measuring the length of sentence in Westcott and Hort's Greek Testament they calculated that the average length of sentence in Romans is 1·4 lines, whereas in Ephesians it is 3 lines. In Romans there is a question mark for each 65 lines; in Ephesians only one in 270 lines. Jülicher also noted 'the unwonted stiffness of the style' in Ephesians, 'the cumbrous chains of sentences, full of participles and relative pronouns', and 'the numerous lengthy passages each consisting in reality of a single sentence' (1:3–14, 1:15–23, 2:1–10, 3:1–9). According to Moffatt, 'in Paul's letters there is

always something of a casca   Ephesians we have a slow
bright stream which brims its   ks' (p. 389).

(3) *Literary Arguments*

There is a curiously large measure of interdependence between
Ephesians and Colossians. Almost universally it is agreed that
Colossians is the earlier of the two. If so, then more than one
quarter of the words in Ephesians appear to be directly borrowed
from Colossians; and more than one third of the words in Colossians are reproduced in Ephesians. But what makes this unusual
relationship very hard to reconcile with the Pauline authorship
of Ephesians is that some of the words taken over from Colossians
are used in Ephesians in a strikingly different sense. Such words
include 'mystery', *oikonomia*, *plērōma*.

Many scholars have felt also that the personal references to
Paul himself in Ephesians sound rather artificial, and not at all
like Paul's references to himself in other letters (see 3:2, 3:4, 3:8).

(4) *Historical Arguments*

Some of the elements in Ephesians appear to reflect a condition of
community life in the Church later than the time of Paul. In particular, the issue about the conditions on which Gentiles may come
into the Church along with Jews is over and done with, whereas in
Paul's day it was a constant and painful bone of contention.

(5) *Doctrinal Arguments*

In matters of doctrine Ephesians reflects a later point of view than
that found in Paul's letters. This group of arguments certainly
needs to be treated with caution because a man's own thought
may change considerably, even over a short period of time,
especially when he finds himself confronted with an entirely new
set of circumstances. But some of these changes in Ephesians have
been felt to be so striking that they are hard to reconcile with
changes within the same person's mind over a comparatively short
period of time:

(a) In Ephesians the Church is always, without exception, the
one universal Church, never the local congregation, as it

normally is in Paul's letters, and is accorded a depth of reverence not found elsewhere, e.g., as the 'bride of Christ'. The controversy about the suitability of uncircumcised Gentiles taking an equal place with Jews within the Church has been totally resolved, but there is repeated emphasis on the need for unity within the Church.

(b) The deferential reference to 'apostles and prophets' as the foundation of the Church (2:20) is strikingly at variance with Paul's emphatic declaration that the Church's one and only foundation is Christ himself (1 C. 3:3). Moreover, it seems unlikely that Paul who firmly claimed for himself the right to be known as an apostle would have so referred to a group which included himself.

(c) The second coming of Christ, which plays a prominent part in all Paul's thinking and is mentioned in every one of his letters, is totally absent from Ephesians. In contrast, a long future is now expected for the Church (2:7, 4:13, 3:21).

(d) In Paul's letters, in view of the expected nearness of the end of all things, entry into marriage by Christians is not encouraged (although it is not actually forbidden). In Ephesians, however, marriage is accorded the highest honour and is even acclaimed as a worthy symbol for the relationship between Christ and his Church. In Ephesians also we find a new sense of the importance of a careful and appropriate upbringing for the children of Christian parents.

These five groups of arguments are further elaborated in *EE*, pp. 7–24.

Cumulatively these arguments were impressive, but as late as the 1930s they were not regarded by most British scholars as strong enough to cause them to abandon belief in Pauline authorship. It was felt that the surrender of Pauline authorship would greatly lessen the value of the letter. If it was not by Paul, then it could be described as a plain 'forgery' or 'fake', and as such quite unworthy of a place in Christian Scripture. It was also contended that it was most improbable that there was in the early Church an unknown Christian of such refined spiritual gifts as to be able to write such a spiritual classic as Ephesians.

These, however, were emotional appeals rather than rational

traditional rebuttal to anti Pauline arguments

arguments. But valid arguments also were brought forward. It was
pointed out that some undoubtedly genuine Pauline letters con-
taine1 a large number of words not found in the other letters. The
stylistic differences in Ephesians could be explained by the special
circumstances of the letter: Paul was older; he was spending a long
period of enforced inactivity in a Roman prison, and in consequence his mind adopted a more contemplative mode. Moreover,
it was claimed that the writing was not really a letter at all but
a kind of 'poem in prose' (McNeile), or a prolonged prayer.
The interdependence between Ephesians and Colossians, it was
argued, favoured Pauline authorship, since an independent compiler would have reproduced the words from Colossians in a much
less flexible way. The masterly freedom with which material from
Colossians is used in Ephesians seemed more appropriate to Paul
himself. Moreover, why would an imitator choose Colossians, a
relatively unimportant letter, for this special degree of attention?
Concerning doctrinal variation it was claimed that a mind so agile
and versatile as Paul's cannot be expected merely to reproduce
what he has thought and said before; in the face of new situations
he was quite capable of moving to new theological insights.

Perhaps, however, there was no single consideration which so
influenced scholars to hold to Pauline authorship as the fact that
no one had been able to suggest why anyone other than Paul
should produce a writing such as Ephesians and ascribe it to Paul.
The complete lack of any convincing *Sitz-im-Leben* was for many
the decisive consideration which led to their refusal to abandon
Pauline authorship.

It was to the credit of E. J. Goodspeed, the American scholar,
that he addressed himself to this crucial issue and proposed a very
persuasive reconstruction of a post-Pauline situation which might
have produced Ephesians. His theory was based on a most careful
study of Ephesians, first, in its intimate relation to Colossians, and,
secondly, in its relation to the other Pauline letters. He showed
that the curious degree of interdependence with Colossians and the
manner of it is best to be explained as the work of someone other
than Paul himself, but it must have been someone who knew
Colossians very well, indeed almost by heart, and who borrowed
from it as a result of his intimate knowledge and appreciation of it.
It was not at all the kind of borrowing which could be explained
either as the work of Paul himself or of one who copied slavishly

from a document in front of him. Goodspeed also demonstrated
that Ephesians, to a degree not found in any other of the letters,
incorporated precise words and phrases from all the other Pauline
letters. By a series of underlinings where such borrowings occurred
he was able to demonstrate the remarkable extent to which
words from other letters were echoed in Ephesians. Again, the
explanation that it was Paul simply using his own Pauline phrases
a second time is unacceptable, since no other Pauline letter shows
anything like the same degree of interdependence; it must be the
work of a later Paulinist whose mind was intimately familiar with
the contents of the other letters, and who was seeking to express
Paul's thoughts by using as far as possible Paul's own words.

Goodspeed's theory was argued in his book *The Meaning of
Ephesians* in 1933, but owing to war conditions prevailing from
1939 to 1945 did not become well known in Britain till some years
after 1945. My own book on Ephesians arose from a careful
examination of Goodspeed's arguments and conclusions. At first
I had been intrigued by them; then followed a period of scep-
ticism; this led me to carry through a most careful investigation
of all the factors Goodspeed had relied on, and the result was that
I came to be persuaded of the basic validity of much of his theory.

His theory was briefly this: Paul's letters to individual churches
were largely forgotten after they had been read. Only some of
them survived in the store-cupboards of churches or in the possession of interested individuals. Clear evidence of this is provided
in the most surprising fact that Acts shows no knowledge at all of
any letters written by Paul to his churches. It can only mean that
when Acts was written, the letters had not gained any kind of
publicity or recognition in the Church. In some churches, however, Paul was remembered with gratitude by personal friends
who regretted the degree to which he was now largely ignored by
Christians in general. One such friend knew of one letter which
Paul had written, that to Colossae, and read and re-read it till he
knew it almost by heart. When Acts was published it told of
Paul's visits to many Christian churches, and this friend realised
that these other churches might conceivably possess letters from
Paul as the church at Colossae did. Using the information in Acts
he approached the churches which Paul had visited on his
journeys as described there, and to his delight found that some did
still possess letters or parts of letters which they had received from

Paul years before. The information in Acts would lead him to Galatia, Philippi, Thessalonica, Corinth, and Rome, where he secured copies of Paul's letters to the churches there. As he read these collected letters, he realised what a vast treasure for the Church was represented in them. Together with the stories in Acts they brought Paul to life again and enabled him to speak to a new generation of Christians for many of whom he was now just a name from the past.

The great disadvantage was that each surviving letter was addressed to a particular locality and to a particular situation now in the past. There was no one letter which gave a comprehensive statement of Paul's teaching, in such a way as to make it sound relevant and applicable to this new generation and its own pressing needs. So this friend set himself to prepare such a document. So far as he could, he used Pauline phrases from the other letters, so that Paul would speak for himself as much as possible. Since Colossians had been so long familiar to him, inevitably its phrases provided the bulk of his material. In his selection of material he gave special emphasis to those aspects of Paul's teaching which he felt to be appropriate to the needs of his own day.

Goodspeed speculated that such a compilation might well have been originally intended to serve as an introductory letter to the whole published corpus of letters and guessed that the compiler of Ephesians (and collector of the individual letters) was none other than Onesimus, Philemon's runaway slave. This Onesimus was identified (with good arguments provided) with the Onesimus who was bishop of Ephesus in the last decade of the first century. It is significant that Onesimus was named in Col. 4:9, lived in the neighbourhood of Colossae, and would, therefore, know Paul's letter to Colossae. He also had very strong personal reasons for a lasting gratitude to Paul.

There are some features of Goodspeed's theory which may be regarded as of peripheral significance—the suggestion that Ephesians once stood as an 'Introduction' to the first published Pauline corpus, that Acts actually provided hitherto unknown information about the churches where Paul had worked, and that Onesimus was the collector of the letters and the compiler of Ephesians. But there are other features which appear to be well established. The relationship of Ephesians to Colossians supports the idea that the writer was not Paul himself, but one who knew

Colossians intimately, and who when using its phrases was quite capable of using them in new and un-Pauline ways. The unique way (among Pauline letters) in which other letters are echoed indicates that Ephesians was written in the presence of these other letters (that is, after they had been collected) and with a deliberate intention of incorporating phrases and ideas from them. The fact that the emphases present are particularly appropriate to the life of the Church about AD 90 shows that he is not just reproducing Paul as he was, but seeking to let Paul speak to a later generation and adapting his words to this purpose. 'Paul's Message for Today' might have been the title of Ephesians had not the circumstances of that day made it more suitable to produce an *epistle*, similar in form to Paul's epistles, and to put it forward under Paul's own name.

The fullest defence of the Pauline authorship of Ephesians, since the publication of Goodspeed's theory, is a book written in German by a Scandinavian scholar. It is *Die Probleme der Kolosser- und Epheserbriefe* by Ernst Percy, a most detailed and exhaustive study of the whole subject. Unfortunately this book has not been translated into English. Dr Percy recognises quite frankly the features in Ephesians which have led some to abandon Pauline authorship, but his own conclusion is that the difficulties involved in abandoning Pauline authorship are even greater than the difficulties in retaining it. There are three features of Ephesians which for him are decisive in favour of Pauline authorship. They are (i) the remarkable similarities between Ephesians and the undoubtedly genuine Pauline letters; (ii) the explicit personal authentication of the letter in Eph. 3:1-13; and (iii) the difficulty of discovering any satisfactory aim for the letter in a post-Pauline situation. (Percy is not persuaded by Goodspeed's reconstruction of such a situation.)

With engaging frankness, however, Percy does allow that some features in Ephesians do in fact stubbornly refuse to be fitted into an assumption of Pauline authorship. These include 2:20 (the description of the Church as built on the foundation of apostles and prophets), 3:5 (another reference to 'the holy apostles and prophets'), and 5:28-29 (the passage about the relationship between Christ and his Church being similar to marriage). He also confesses himself embarrassed by some of the modifications of meaning introduced into words from Colossians when they are

yes, the apostle who in I Cor. talked marriage down — now sees it as so sublime as to be almost divine.

incorporated into Ephesians, e.g., 5:22–33 (cf. Col. 3:18), 6:8
(cf. Col. 3:24), 4:3–4 (cf. Col. 3:14f.), 5:20 (cf. Col. 3:17).
Nevertheless, his final conclusion is: 'The assumption of a post-
Pauline origin will present us with greater difficulties than the
assumption of its genuineness.' To me, however, it seems to be the
other way round; the difficulties presented by an assumption of the
direct Pauline authorship of Ephesians appear insuperable. This
does not, however, make the work un-Pauline. On the contrary,
the author has presented us in Ephesians with a brilliant and
comprehensive summary of Paul's main theological emphases,
though he has, where necessary, adapted and interpreted them
for the needs of a new situation. Published about a generation
after Paul's death, it is as it were, 'Paul's Message for Today'.

he feels all his doing is updating Paul, so as Paul speaks?

2. THE RELATIONSHIP OF EPHESIANS TO OTHER NT WRITINGS

More than any other writing in the *NT* Ephesians has close literary
relationships with other *NT* writings, and since this complicated
relationship has great significance for any assessment of the
situation for which Ephesians was written, it is right to examine it
more closely. The closest of these relationships is with the epistle
to the Colossians.

Ephesians and Colossians

More than one third of the words in Colossians re-appear in
Ephesians. At only one point, however, is there any long continuous quotation of identical words. This is found at Eph.
6:21–22, where as many as thirty-two consecutive words (apart
from an omission of two words) are repeated exactly from Col.
4:7–8. Clearly at this point the writer of Ephesians has referred
to the earlier text and, for some reason, copied out verbatim what
he found there. Elsewhere, however, though Ephesians is often
dealing with the same theme as Colossians and in similar words,
never more than seven or eight identical words, at most, are repeated in the same sequence, and only rarely so many. A few
instances (out of many) of the closest parallels may be found at
Eph. 1:4 = Col. 1:22; Eph. 1:7 = Col. 1:14; Eph. 2:5 = Col.
2:13; Eph. 3:2 = Col. 1:25; Eph. 4:2 = Col. 3:12.

Another feature of this relationship is that Ephesians combines in a single unit groups of words taken from different contexts in Colossians; for instance, Eph. 2:1–5 brings together words taken from both Col. 2:13 and 3:6. This suggests that the writer of Ephesians was intimately familiar with Colossians, knowing it almost by heart and able to recall parts of it from memory. It does not suggest that he was copying word for word the text of Colossians open in front of him (apart from the one lengthy quotation just mentioned). This relationship could be explained on the basis either of Pauline or non-Pauline authorship.

There are, however, two features which tell against Pauline authorship at this point. The first is the curiously mechanical way in which words, which were merely adjacent to each other in Colossians, but not related in sense, are associated in Ephesians within a new relationship of meaning. For instance, in Col. 3:17 the phrase 'in the name of the Lord Jesus' qualifies the words 'do all', and the word for 'giving thanks', though not far away, has no immediate relationship with it. In Eph. 5:20, however, 'in the name of the Lord Jesus' has been transferred to the words 'giving thanks', with which it had nothing at all to do in Colossians. Paul himself would hardly have been likely to make such an odd switch of meaning, though another person whose mind was full of the words of Colossians, but who had not written them, could conceivably make this new link.

The second feature which tells here against Pauline authorship is that when a significant word is taken from Colossians into Ephesians, sometimes its meaning undergoes a striking change. In Colossians, for instance, the 'mystery' (as used in 1:26–27, 2:2, 4:3) consists of Christ himself, God's unexpected answer to human need, a secret which no one in advance could have guessed or anticipated at all. In Ephesians, however, the 'mystery' is no longer Christ himself but God's purpose, through Christ, to 're-unite all things' and particularly to unite Jews and Gentiles within the life of the Church. Also, in Colossians, as in other Pauline writings, the Greek word *oikonomia* is used to mean 'stewardship' or 'an assignment', a special task entrusted to someone. In Ephesians, however, it is used quite differently to mean 'God's own strategy', his broad statesmanship.

Ephesians, if it was by Paul, was sent at the same time and by the same messenger as Colossians (the identity of Eph. 6:21–22

and Col. 4:7–8 indicates this). It must, therefore, have been
written very soon after Colossians while its phraseology and the
meaning of its words were still fresh in his mind. These divergences
of meaning in important words and expressions, therefore, point
clearly to a non-Pauline author.

Ephesians and the Other Pauline Epistles (apart from Colossians)

It is not only from Colossians that the writer of Ephesians borrows.
He avails himself also of words and phrases from the other
Pauline letters. In the process he sometimes conflates groups of
words from different epistles into a single unit of teaching, as, for
instance, at Eph. 3:7, where there are borrowings from both
Rom. 5:15 and 1 C. 3:10; similarly Eph. 1:13–14 combines
elements from both 2 C. 1:22 and Gal. 3:14.

Sometimes the conflation is elaborated to such an extent that
what appears in Ephesians reads like a deliberate attempt to provide a comprehensive summary of Paul's previous teaching on a
particular subject. Eph. 1:21 is one instance of this. We print the
text of the verse in full and indicate in brackets after each word
where that word is used in a similar context in another letter of
Paul:

> Above (Phil. 2:9) all (1 C. 5:24) rule (1 C. 15:24, Col. 1:16),
> authority (Col. :16, 1 C. 15:24), power (1 C. 15:24), dominion
> (Col. 1:16) and every name (Phil. 2:9) . . .

Eph. 1:21 is thus seen to be composed of elements from Col. 1:16,
1 C. 15:24, and Phil. 2:9.

Another instance is to be found in Eph. 2:8–9, though here it is
not only the comprehensive summary of Pauline teaching which is
impressive, but also the interpretative modifications which are
introduced to make the affirmations more intelligible and relevant
to the later situation addressed in Ephesians.

By grace	Rom. 3:24, 11:6.
you have been saved	'they are justified' in Rom. 3:24; Gal. 2:6; cf. also 'having been justified' in Rom. 5:1 and 5:9. See note below on the change of word.
through faith	Gal. 2:16 (cf. Rom. 11:6).

and this is not your own doing	cf. 'not as a result of the law' (Rom. 4:16).
it is the gift of God	'as a gift' (Rom. 3:24).
not because of works	Rom. 11:6, Gal. 2:16, Rom. 3:20, Rom. 4:2.
lest any man should boast	1 C. 1:29.

These two verses in Ephesians have often been described as a most complete summary of Paul's theology of salvation, with the emphasis on its source in the grace of God and its appropriation in human life through faith in Christ, and not at all by human achievement. It is true that in Paul's letters it is not the word 'save' which is used, but rather 'justify'. The word 'justify', how-ever, is used in connexion with Paul's arguments with Judaising Christians, and would not be readily intelligible to Gentiles, unless they had first come under the influence of Jewish teaching. The word 'save', as used by Gentile Christians, would have a similar meaning to that of 'justify', as used by Jewish Christians, and the change is probably made here because the writer is not only reproducing Paul's teaching but also interpreting it in a new and mainly Gentile situation.

'It is not your own doing' is not precisely a Pauline phrase either, but the same meaning is expressed in Romans by the words: 'Not as a result of keeping the law'. This reference to the law, however, would have little meaning to Gentile Christians of AD 90. So the writer expresses the meaning of the earlier Pauline phrase in words which the Gentile Christian of a generation later than Paul would immediately understand. The essence of salva-tion from the Pharisaic point of view was achieved through keep-ing the law, through obedience to known commands. But for the Christian true salvation does not come this way; it is not a result of 'keeping the law'; or, to put it another way, 'it is not your own doing'.

Another passage which reads like an intentional, comprehensive summary of Paul's teaching on another subject, as found in his other letters, is Eph. 4:4-6, where all the elements which make for the unity of the Church are carefully assembled:

one body	Rom. 12:5; 1 C. 10:17, 12:12
one Spirit	1 C. 12:4, 13.
(just as) you were called	1 C. 7:20

(to the one hope)	? 1 C. 13:13
that belongs to your call	1 C. 7:20
one Lord	1 C. 8:6, 12:5
one faith	? 1 C. 13:13
one baptism	1 C. 12:13
one God	1 C. 6:6, 12:6
Father of us all	1 C. 8:6; cf. Rom. 9:5
above all	Rom. 9:5; cf. Rom. 11:36
through all	Rom. 11:36
in all	Rom. 11:36; 1 C. 12:6

In Ephesians, therefore, we meet instances where material from Paul's other letters is reproduced, where elements from different letters are conflated, and where a comprehensive summary of Paul's teaching on some particular subject (for instance, salvation and the unity of the Church) is sometimes provided. Moreover, into these borrowings an element of unobtrusive interpretation of Pauline phrases, not immediately intelligible to Gentile readers, is introduced. It may be argued that this is what you would expect in one of Paul's own later letters, but in fact this proves not to be the case. There is no other letter of Paul's which shows any of this same degree of overlapping with phrases from his other letters. See the study of Philippians from this point of view in *EE*, pp. 107–11. These features are, however, appropriate to a work by a later Paulinist, as he seeks both to represent Paul's teaching to a later generation and at the same time to adapt his words as necessary to make them immediately intelligible to people of a later time and of Gentile origin.

Ephesians and Luke–Acts

The second half of Acts is almost entirely about Paul and his missionary work. Yet, very strangely, there is no hint whatever in these chapters that he ever wrote a letter to one of his churches. It is almost inconceivable that the author could have failed to mention the letters at all, if they had occupied the position in the life of the Church which they achieved later. Indeed, this totally unpredictable omission gives the impression that Luke, when he wrote Acts, was himself wholly unaware of Paul's letters. Moreover, it is argued by such scholars as Moffatt, Peake, and Goodspeed, that none of Paul's characteristic phrases is reflected in

Acts. Even Paul's speeches in Acts (apart from that in Ac. 20) are oddly non-Pauline both in content and in vocabulary.

Between Acts and the Pauline letters there seems to be an almost total absence of literary interconnexion. The same, however, is not true of the relation between Acts and Ephesians. Here there are numerous links both in phraseology and in theological outlook.

In phraseology, there are ten words which appear in Ephesians and Luke–Acts which are not found anywhere else in the *NT*. Moreover, there are some unusual words found in both documents: e.g., *diabolos* (devil) (Eph. 4:27; Acts 13:10); shepherds (pastors) (Eph. 4:11; Ac. 20:28); evangelist (Eph. 4:11; Ac. 21:8). Other striking similarities are: 'in holiness and righteousness' (Lk. 1:75; Eph. 4:24); 'your loins girded' (Eph. 6:14; Lk. 12:35); 'able to withstand' (Eph. 6:13; Lk. 21:15); 'serving the Lord' (Eph. 6:7; Ac. 20:28); 'with all humility' (Eph. 4:2; Ac. 20:28); 'inheritance among the saints' (Eph. 1:18; Ac. 20:32). In addition, the resurrection of Christ is emphasised in both writings, and also his ascension to the right hand of God (Eph. 1:20; Ac. 2:32–35, 7:55); and the unexpected exhortation in Eph. 5:18, 'Be not drunk with wine, but be filled with the Spirit', bears a curious resemblance to the story in Ac. 2:4 and 15, where the apostles are filled with the Spirit, but accused of being drunk.

There is an unusual degree of correspondence between Ephesians and the speech of Paul in Ac. 20 to the Ephesian elders who have been called to meet him for what he regards as a final farewell. Those who accept Pauline authorship of Ephesians would explain this by arguing that Luke was present on this particular occasion (it is in the so-called 'we-sections' of Acts) and, sensing its importance even at the time, took careful notes, and so was able on this occasion at least to reproduce Paul's own words with some degree of accuracy. Those who take a non-Pauline view of authorship will see in this speech in Acts an episode which for one reason or another the writer of Ephesians specially treasured, when he found it in Acts, and memorised much of it so that he could incorporate elements from it in his epistle. The fact that the speech was delivered to people from Ephesus may provide the reason.

When we turn from similarities of phraseology to similarities of outlook here too we find much in common between the two writings. For instance, both are greatly concerned about the unity of the Church, the fact of the Church's roots being within the people of Israel, the importance of the apostles as the founding fathers of the Church, and the expected continuance of the Church's life far into the future (no longer soon to be cut short by an imminent second coming). There are many features to suggest that both writings come from the same period of the Church's advancing life and represent the same basic concerns. Indeed Professor R. P. Martin finds himself so impressed by these similarities that he argues from them that Luke himself should probably be regarded as the author of Ephesians as well as of Luke–Acts (*ExpT* 79, (1967–8), p. 296). He believes that these similarities (the ones we have named and others) justify him in the conclusion that 'the extraordinary literary artist' who wrote Ephesians was none other than Luke, the New Testament theologian of *ecclesia una, sancta, catholica et apostolica*'. He adds: 'Luke has offered in his master's name and by the incorporation of his prayers and teaching an exalted meditation on the great theme of Christ and his Church. The motifs which run through the narratives and speeches of Acts are here transposed into a liturgical–catechetical form.'

If the writer of Ephesians is in fact one who is named elsewhere in the *NT* the guess that it may have been Luke deserves to be given consideration. But there are difficulties in the hypothesis. Why does Acts show no knowledge of Paul's letters when Ephesians is clearly written in full knowledge of them? Why is it that in Acts all except one of Paul's speeches reflect Paul's theology so inadequately, when Ephesians reflects it so well? One further suggestion of Professor Martin is that Luke may have written Ephesians 'during Paul's final imprisonment'; this, however, seems impossible. Ephesians was written in the presence of Paul's collected letters, and Paul's letters were not collected until much later than this.

Ephesians and I Peter

Another *NT* writing with which Ephesians has close literary links is 1 Peter. This is a fact not in dispute. It is the explanation of the similarities which varies.

Passages in the two letters which have correspondences too close

B

to be explained as merely a matter of chance include the following:
(a) 1 Pet. 1:3, cf. Eph. 1:3. (b) 1 Pet. 1:10–12, cf. Eph. 3:2–6
(= Col. 1:26–27). (c) 1 Pet. 2:2–6, cf. Eph. 2:18–22 (= Col. 2:7,
19). (d) 1 Pet. 3:22, cf. Eph. 1:20–21 (= Col. 1:16, 2:12, 3:1).

There are three possible explanations of this relationship:

(1) The writer of Ephesians knew 1 Peter and reproduced ideas
and phrases from it.

(2) The writer of 1 Peter knew Ephesians and reproduced ideas
and phrases from it.

(3) Both writers were quite independent of each other, but
both knew the same liturgical tradition in the Church, and incorporated some of the same material from it into their books.
This third approach was pioneered and expounded by E. G.
Selwyn in an appendix to his commentary on 1 Peter.

It is part of the attraction of (3) that it makes possible the reten-
tion of the Petrine authorship of 1 Peter and the Pauline authorship of Ephesians, whereas (1) and (2) raise real problems for
apostolic authorship in one case or the other.

It is almost certain, however, that the right explanation is to be
found in (2). This can be demonstrated by comparing those passages in 1 Peter and Ephesians where there is not only much
similarity between them, but where, at the same time, Ephesians
is even more closely similar to Colossians. In these passages
Ephesians is reproducing Colossians, as it does in many other
places also. It cannot, therefore, be copying from 1 Peter, nor even
for that matter drawing on an unknown liturgical tradition. It
cannot however, be argued that it is on Colossians that 1 Peter
is dependent, because where Ephesians diverges slightly from
Colossians (in these passages), it is the variant in Ephesians which
1 Peter reproduces rather than the original words of Colossians.
This conclusion has been argued in detail in an article by me in
the *Journal of Theological Studies* of April 1950, and also in *EE*,
pp. 176ff.

3. EPHESIANS AND THE QUMRAN COMMUNITY

The Dead Sea Scrolls were discovered in 1947 and a little later
were identified as part of the library which had been originally
housed in the buildings of the Qumran community on the western
shores of the Dead Sea, before being dispersed and hidden in the

caves of the neighbourhood. The Scrolls were written mainly in Hebrew, but some are in Aramaic. Many of them are copies of books of the *OT*, and others deal with the discipline and beliefs of the community. Since they could be dated as written in the first century AD, they had obvious affinities in language, time, and place to the earliest traditions about Jesus. Early attempts were made to establish links between the community and Jesus. At first some of the claims were greatly exaggerated. Now, however, most scholars agree that there is nothing in the Scrolls to indicate any actual link between them and Jesus (though some have argued for a possible link between John the Baptist and the community; but even this is highly speculative).

The Scrolls have been examined very closely by *NT* scholars to discover any links there may be between them and the various books of the *NT*, whether in ideas or in language. Linguistic similarities are hard to establish since the language of the relevant scrolls is Aramaic and the writings of the *NT* are all in Greek. An influential article on the subject is one by K. G. Kuhn in *NTS* 7 (1960–1), pp. 334–46 entitled 'Der Epheserbrief im Lichte der Qumrantexte'. The conclusion he reaches (p. 345) is that the parallels indicate that 'Ephesians has a definite relationship with the Essene community of Qumran'. Kümmel, however, in his *Introduction to the New Testament*, is content with a verdict much less precise: 'There comes to light in the religious terminology as well as in the paraenesis a striking parallel with the literature of the sect from Qumran.' It is safer to note, with Kümmel, the fact of such parallels as there are than to draw a firm conclusion that this proves any actual dependence. Indeed, the explanation of these parallels may be that the concerns from which the Qumran community sprang and the thought-forms in which they were expressed were widespread in the ancient world.

The kind of similarities which have been noted are as follows: Both documents use the contrast between light and darkness, and the scrolls use the phrases 'sons of darkness' and 'children of light' (cf. Eph. 5:8). The scrolls speak of 'sharing the lot of the holy beings'; cf. 'fellow-citizens of the holy ones' ('saints'), Eph. 2:19. The scrolls refer to the community as a 'temple of God, a true holy of holies'; cf. 'a holy temple in the Lord', Eph. 2:21. Both speak of 'God's secret purpose' (mystery), and both are aware of vast demonic and angelic forces in the regions between man and

God. Both are fond of such tautological phrases as 'the might of his power', and 'the wealth of his grace', and also the piling up of synonyms. Ephesians uses Semitic forms of expressions like 'sons of disobedience', which are common in the scrolls. Kuhn argues that the somewhat problematical meaning of *elenchein* in Eph. 5:11 (translated by *RSV* as 'expose') is clarified by the requirement in the scrolls that a member of the Qumran community, detecting a fellow-member in some doubtful conduct, is required to 'challenge' him with the words: 'This is not right before God.'

It is doubtful if these similarities are strong enough to indicate any direct literary connexion; and even if there is some such connexion, no one has yet suggested any probable explanation of it. Even the argument that the Semitic expressions suggest that the author of Ephesians is of Semitic origin is less than convincing, since the first two chapters of Luke's Gospel have many *Semitisms* in them. These, however, are usually explained as due to a deliberate attempt by Luke to reproduce a style similar to that of the Septuagint.

4. EPHESIANS AND THE GNOSTICS

In the second century AD Gnostic types of thinking posed a serious threat to the Christian Church and its traditional ways of thought. The Church Fathers of that time went to great lengths in denouncing the errors in Gnostic teaching and defending their own theology against Gnostic attacks. In general, Gnostics tended to be people who felt themselves to be more intellectual than ordinary Christians. They interpreted 'reality' as consisting of various grades; besides God and man there were all kinds of intermediate spiritual powers, whom one had to know how to conciliate and use; human beings were divided into higher and lower groups, according to their intellectual and spiritual perception, the 'Gnostics' being the only ones with real insight into truth. For them, physical matter, including the human body, was evil; hence, the human body and its appetites were degrading. In consequence some adopted a very strict attitude of abstinence towards them, but others argued that, provided the spirit of a man was kept in tune with reality, it did not matter at all what he did with his wretched body. This sometimes led to an attitude of careless unconcern about what, to the traditional Christian, was

grossly immoral conduct. Gnosticism, therefore, offered the fullness of Christian experience only to the intellectually élite, and
sometimes showed itself casually indifferent to the control of
physical appetites. In addition, it usually treated the historical
person of Jesus as unimportant or even illusory, finding important
only the eternal spiritual truths which came to light in the eternal
Christ.

Gnosticism did not become a coherent system until the second
century (and even then took many forms), but there is little doubt
that Gnostic ways of thinking were already widespread in the later
part of the first century. They were to be found not only in Greek-
speaking areas, but also among the Jews. Those who had been
influenced by this kind of thinking before they became Christians
tended to interpret their Christian faith along similar lines, and in
some of his letters Paul seems to be seeking to counteract wrong
thinking of this kind. This is certainly true of Colossians, but may
also apply to 1 and 2 Corinthians as well.

Some scholars (e.g., H. Schlier and E. Käsemann) have argued
that Ephesians betrays the influence of Gnostic ideas. Certainly
there are words in Ephesians which Gnostics might well have used:
e.g., knowledge, fullness, mystery, perfect, body, new man. But
though the writer does not shrink from using Gnostic words, there
is little evidence that he shares any of the specifically Gnostic
ways of thinking. He uses the words they use, but fills them
with orthodox Christian significance. Kümmel acknowledges the
Gnostic influence, and writes of Ephesians: 'The shaping of the
Christology and ecclesiology, especially the conceptions of Christ
as the primitive man (*Urmensch*), of the syzygy between Christ and
the church, and of the church as the body of Christ the head,
can be made understandable only against the background of
Christianised, mythological Gnosticism.' F. Mussner in *Christus,
das All und die Kirche*, which is a careful study of the theology of
Ephesians, gives special care to the accusation that Ephesians has
been unduly influenced by Gnostic teaching, especially where
Gnostic words are used, and his conclusion is that the writer 'ignores
their old sense and pours into them a sense of his own'. That is, the
writer acts like a missionary who does not shrink from borrowing
the religious words of the people among whom he works in order
to establish a point of contact with them, but he fills them with a
truly Christian significance.

5. EPHESIANS AND LITURGY

In recent years throughout the various denominations there has been a great upsurge of interest in liturgy. Among students of the *NT* one result of this has been an eager research into the documents of the *NT* to discover passages which have been shaped under the influence of liturgical forms current in the Church at that time, or where the books themselves may have been written, in whole or in part, to provide liturgical material for use in the worship of the Church. In some respects this has helped to provide a broader understanding of the influences which helped to mould the work of the *NT* writers. There is, however, also the danger that this very eagerness to detect liturgical survivals leads to their being suspected or claimed in most improbable places. There is a further danger to be guarded against. In discussing 'liturgical influences' there is not always a clear distinction between an author's use of already existing liturgical material, and the suggestion that the author in his writing was himself seeking to provide liturgical material for others to use.

Prior to about 1960 discussions of Ephesians rarely refer to liturgy. Since that time it has assumed a prominent part. Käsemann was one of the first to argue that liturgical interest played a large part in the production of Ephesians, and his approach is conveniently accessible to English readers in his essay on Ephesians in *Studies in Luke–Acts* edited by Keck and Martyn. His conclusion there is: 'The entire letter appears to be a mosaic composed of extensive as well as tiny fragments of tradition, and the author's skill lies chiefly in the selection and ordering of the material available to him.' One should note that Käsemann here writes 'appears to be'. His opinion is speculative, and is not supported by any strong degree of proof. Indeed, any judgment on this issue is inevitably very subjective, since there are no survivals of Christian liturgy from that early date to provide facts on which an objective judgment may be formed. The fact that parts of Ephesians have a liturgical ring about them does not mean that the author is borrowing from existing liturgies, nor even that he is deliberately composing material for use in public worship. It may be merely that this is the style in which he wrote, especially in the knowledge that his letter would probably be read in the context of people gathered for fellowship or worship.

It is true that the words of 5:14 seem to be words from a hymn, but it is much less likely that 1:5-8 or 1:9-12 are derived from a hymn, though Marxsen claims that this is so. The writer of Ephesians would know that the most likely circumstances in which his composition would be read would be in a meeting of Christian people gathered for fellowship and worship. He would, therefore, address himself to a situation in which the attitude of worship was predominant. What, however, tells most strongly against the idea that Ephesians borrowed largely from liturgical materials is the fact that it can be shown that Ephesians is in fact borrowed largely from the Pauline letters, especially Colossians (see further note at Eph. 1:15). It is very difficult to construct a theory which gives an adequate account of this dependence on the other letters and at the same time accounts for it as derived from liturgical materials. Another ground for misgiving is the uncertainty whether the early Church before the end of the first century had the inclination to construct official and prescribed liturgies or possessed buildings suitable for their use. There is great force in the affirmation of Conzelmann (*History of Primitive Christianity*, p. 54) that 'the primitive Church had other concerns than the construction of a liturgy. It concealed within itself tremendous energies that could not be fettered in fixed forms.'

Those, however, who wish to pursue this enquiry into liturgical influences in Ephesians will find two books in English which represent this approach and believe strongly in its validity. *Ephesians: Baptism and Pentecost*, by J. C. Kirby (1968), argues that chapters 1–3 in Ephesians are 'a *berakhah* for use in public worship, possibly at the Eucharist'. At the same time Dahl's claim is accepted that 'Ephesians is intimately connected with baptism'. Close links are also found with the formal celebration of Pentecost, ascension, and and the gift of the Spirit. It is argued that the specifically epistolary parts of Ephesians (e.g., 1:15–19 and 3:1–13) were added at a later time when it was desired to give the document the appearance of a letter sent by Paul. This, however, founders on an insuperable obstacle: in that case how is it that both the so-called liturgical and epistolary parts of the writing show a similar dependence on Paul's letters? Professor Kirby seeks to explain the Pauline echoes in the liturgical parts by the following suggestion: 'Ephesians' does in fact come *from* Ephesus, and the form of liturgy used in that church came from what Paul had taught during his ministry in that city. Since it was derived from Paul it inevitably showed some similarity to material which Paul had written in his letters. Therefore, the liturgical material which Ephesians took over from the liturgy in use at Ephesus has the appearance of being material borrowed from Paul's letters. This explanation, however, does not commend itself as at all a probable one. (See also pp. 65–6.)

A more recent book with a similar interest is 'And the Two shall become One Flesh': A Study of the Traditions in Eph. 5:21–31, by J. P. Sampley (1971). He argues that this passage reveals (and also pre-supposes in its readers) a knowledge of the following 'traditional' items: (1) standardised rules of behaviour within the Christian family; (2) the 'love thy neighbour' command from Lev. 19:18; (3) the idea of the 'sacred marriage' between Yahweh and the people of Israel; (4) the words from Gen. 2:24 about the 'two becoming one flesh'; (5) the terminology of head, body, and members; (6) traditions about purity (Eph. 5:27). Professor Sampley contends that all these materials came to the writer through 'traditional materials in the worship of the Church'. Certainly these materials were available in the thought-forms of the time or of the past, but there is really no proof that the writer of Ephesians derived them from liturgical forms already in use in Christian worship.

6. THE DATE OF EPHESIANS

Those who regard Ephesians as Pauline usually date it as the last of his letters and place it as near the end of his life as possible. The differences in style and the highly developed theology of the Church (as compared with the earlier letters) make necessary the latest date possible. Since it is presented as written from imprisonment, this is understood as the imprisonment in Rome.

Those who abandon Pauline authorship usually agree with Kümmel's judgment that its production must lie within the period between AD 80 and 100. Kümmel doubts if we have the means of being more precise. Marxsen is content to allocate it to the 'early post-apostolic period'. There is evidence, however, which points to about AD 90, rather than ten years earlier or later. It is highly probable that the letters of Ignatius reveal a knowledge of Ephesians. If the date of these letters is about AD 110, then

Ephesians must have been written some time before. It is also likely that 1 Clement reflects some acquaintance with Ephesians. If the date of this letter was c. AD 96, then Ephesians must be prior to that. The evidence for this literary dependence is stated in *EE*, pp. 160–9. Hort, whose judgment in these matters is greatly to be respected, gave it as his opinion that 'it is all but certain that on this (i.e., Patristic) evidence Ephesians was in existence by AD 95' (*PRE*, p. 118). R. H. Charles in his commentary on Revelation (*ICC*) gave it as his opinion that the writer of Revelation knew Ephesians. The date of Revelation is itself unsure, but on the whole this evidence in favour of Ephesians being earlier than Revelation would support a date not much later than AD 90. The evidence is not conclusive, but points to a time between AD 85 and 95, probably quite near to AD 90. The date cannot be much earlier than AD 90, since Ephesians was included in the Pauline corpus of letters, and this corpus was apparently not known to the author of Acts.

7. OCCASION AND PURPOSE OF EPHESIANS

One of the chief reasons why scholars hesitated to ascribe Ephesians to a post-Pauline writer was the difficulty of suggesting any occasion in the post-Pauline Church which would be likely to produce such a writing. The first to succeed in providing a convincing theory to supply this lack was Goodspeed. He showed that in Ephesians there are quotations from every Pauline letter, and argued from this that it had been written in the presence of the collected letters of Paul. Indeed, Goodspeed argued that its author was the actual collector of Paul's letters, and that Ephesians had been written to provide an introduction to the corpus. In the supposed 'introduction' Paul's teaching was presented in a form which set it free from the restricting local circumstances to which it was tied in the original letters. This theory won much support on the American continent, and in particular John Knox vigorously sponsored it and wrote in support of it. F. W. Beare in *The Interpreter's Bible Commentary* seems also to adopt substantially this point of view. He writes: 'Ephesians is, and is meant by the author to be, a commendation of Paul's theology to the Church of another generation. No other intelligible construction can be put on the opening verses of chapter 3.' Lest one should imagine, however, that Ephesians is merely an unimaginative repetition of Paul's words and sentences, he adds: 'The writer is a great theologian in his own right,' with his main stress upon Christ as the centre towards which all things move to an ultimate unity and on the Church as the agent of this purpose. Beare goes on: 'We shall not find it necessary to seek for a special occasion for its publication.' Probably, however, he would agree that the writer felt that the times in which he lived required this re-presentation of Paul's teaching.

Since Goodspeed, others have made suggestions about the purposes which prompted the writing of Ephesians, sometimes elaborating or qualifying what he had proposed. Henry Chadwick, for instance, in 1960 wrote what has proved to be a very influential article entitled 'Die Absicht des Epheserbriefes' in ZNW 51 (1960). He argued that the author of Ephesians was primarily concerned to insist on the essential continuity between the original Church at Jerusalem, composed of Jewish Christians, and the predominantly Gentile Church of Paul's mission. In spite of the particularity of its origin in time and locality, this Church in its true nature is universal. It is not just a historical phenomenon; it has a metaphysical dimension as well. This Church which has grown from small beginnings in Judea is destined to grow still further until it becomes a centre of unity for the estranged races of mankind, a reminder that God's purpose for mankind is unity. The epistle was written at a time when these truths were in great danger of being ignored.

A little later Käsemann began to emphasise the importance of taking into one's reckoning the liturgical interests in the mind of the author of Ephesians. He sees Ephesians as itself a construction built up out of liturgical materials already available in the Church, and in its completed form itself providing a great enrichment of that material for future use within the Church.

Martin has argued that both Ephesians and Luke–Acts were written to oppose Gnostic influences with their casual attitude to moral conduct, and at the same time to insist that Gentile Christians of their own day remember the great debt they owed to the Jewish past of Christianity, and not to disown their rich heritage. He believes indeed that Luke was the author of Ephesians as well as of Luke–Acts.

Each of these contributions may have some aspect of truth to contribute to the final solution, but in itself none of them offers an explanation of the many echoes of Paul's letters to be heard in Ephesians, and of the particularly close relationship with Colossians. Only Goodspeed's theory does justice to these features.

Before ourselves seeking to offer a description of the situation from which Ephesians arose and the purposes for which it was written, it is appropriate to recall those aspects of the epistle which may throw light on the occasion which led to its compilation.

1. We note first its close dependence on Colossians. What the writer incorporates from Colossians helps to form the character of Ephesians and further reference will be made to this later. It may not be irrelevant, however, to note the elements in Colossians which Ephesians refrains from borrowing. (a) Not surprisingly there is a total omission of the particular aspects of the Colossians 'heresy' against which Paul made vigorous protest, e.g., in 2:8, 11–12, 14–18, 20, 23. (b) The reference in Col. 3:4 to the parousia is omitted, and so also is the affirmation in Col. 1:5 to our 'hope' as 'laid up in heaven'. This serves to make us notice that the imminence of the second coming is absent from Ephesians, and perhaps there is also less emphasis on the future life of heaven. Where it is mentioned in Eph. 1:14, the emphasis is not so much on heaven itself as on the reality, here and now, of the gift of the Spirit which provides a foretaste and guarantee of heaven hereafter. (c) The great affirmations in Colossians about Christ's nature and his inward relationship to God are omitted (e.g., Col. 1:14: 'He is the image of God', and Col. 1:17–18). The assertion of his pre-existence as an agent of creation is also omitted (Col. 1:16–17). Christ, it is true, is central in Ephesians. His greatness could hardly be more emphatically stated. But the whole stress is on what he has done and can and will do for his Christian people rather than on any theoretical christological statement about who or what he is. This may be in part a reaction against Gnostic influences which over-stressed the importance of right knowledge. The writer insists that the essence of Christian faith lies not in theoretical knowledge but in an appropriation, here and now, of all the gifts which God offers to men in Christ.

2. There is also the close dependence of Ephesians on all the other Pauline letters. This means that he writes in the presence of the Pauline corpus (excluding, of course, the Pastoral epistles).

The letters have been collected. He writes in Paul's name, which means that he sets himself firmly among those who are devoted to Paul and his memory, and to all that he stood for. The constant use of phrases from the other letters must have been the result of a deliberate intention to communicate Paul's teaching as far as possible in Paul's own words.

(3.) The style of the epistle is described as liturgical. It cannot be proved that the author borrowed from already existing liturgical materials, or had any intention of providing liturgical material for others. But there can be little doubt that he visualised his writing being read aloud in a context of Christian fellowship and worship, and this influenced the way he wrote.

(4.) The writer insists that the Church serves an essential purpose in the plans of God for mankind, and regards the function of the Church as continuing far into the future. In this Church former Gentiles have as sure a place as those who were formerly Jews, and the two races have been welded into an indissoluble unity. The Gentiles who are Christians are 'fellow-heirs' with Christian Jews (2:13–18, 3:6). They are 'fellow-citizens with the saints and members of the household of God'.

(5.) The Gentile Christians are reminded that though they are now securely within the Church, and indeed predominant in it, they owe their origin to the apostles, who were Jews, and to the community of converted Jews who first believed in Jesus and were the first nucleus of the Church. In this the writer confidently believes that he is stating what Paul himself had insisted on (though in his lifetime the emphasis had had to be placed differently). In Gal. 2:9, for instance, though his prime concern is to assert his own independence of other apostles, Paul nevertheless openly admits how much he valued the knowledge that James, Peter, and John supported the steps he had taken. Moreover, his readiness to carry the contribution of the Gentile churches to the needy Jerusalem community, even though he clearly knew that danger and perhaps death awaited him in Jerusalem, shows how deeply he valued the link of the present with the past. So Ephesians emphasises that the Church is built on the foundation of the apostles (2:20, 3:5).

(6.) The Church for which Ephesians is written has lost all sense of the imminence of the end of all things and the awesome shortness of its own life (in contrast with Paul's own vivid conviction

that 'the time has been cut short', 1 C. 7:29). The Church is now
preparing itself for 'the coming ages' (Eph. 1:17) in which it will
be the instrument for the fulfilment of God's purposes in the world
(2:21, 3:10, 4:13, 4:16, 5:27).

7. In the opening passages of Ephesians there is a recurring
emphasis on the Christian life as wholly the gift of God to man
through Christ. It is all of grace, God's doing, not man's achievement. One suspects that this emphasis may be called forth by the
writer's apprehension about a new kind of moralism developing
with the church, such as later became evident in some of the
apostolic fathers (see *EE*, pp. 274–6).

Such are the features of Ephesians to which justice must be
done in any attempt to reconstruct the situation out of which
Ephesians may have sprung. The one most clear and objective
feature which must be accounted for is the fact that the other
Pauline letters, and especially Colossians, are echoed in it. It is
written by one who had access to and knew intimately all these
letters. It aims to present Pauline teaching in its universal and
eternal aspects. This feature fits in well with the suggestion that it
was written as a result of a close relation to the first collection of
the Pauline corpus. Its aim is to present the abiding truths of the
Christian gospel as they are to be found in Paul's letters. Its
special use of Colossians may well mean, as Goodspeed suggested,
that the writer had known it longest of all the letters, and even had
a close personal link with it. This explanation best accounts for the
unusual degree and manner of the interdependence between the
two letters. It may be possible, also, that the writer found material
in Colossians that was specially congenial to his purposes in
Ephesians. Liturgical explanations of the origin of Ephesians are
based on much less objective tests than one which takes with the
utmost seriousness the relationship of Ephesians to the Pauline
corpus of letters. It may be difficult to maintain with Goodspeed
that Ephesians was actually intended to serve as an 'introduction'
to the corpus; but that it sprang from a relationship with the corpus and from an intention to present the message of the recently
assembled Pauline letters comprehensively to a new generation of
Christians is quite the most probable description of the historical
setting out of which it arose.

The writer was, however, well aware that the context in which

Idea for a base for "Scrip reading" i.e. responsive use.

most Christians would hear the contents of Ephesians in the first place would be a meeting of the Christian congregation for fellowship. Those gathered together would hear it read aloud in a context of worship and prayer. Very few at first would read it privately as we read a book. Hence he phrased what he wrote in a style suitable for the hearer and the worshipper rather than the private reader. This would lead him to use a declaratory style— what today is often called a liturgical style. It would not be surprising if he incorporated here and there snatches from a familiar hymn or a phrase from a credal affirmation; but the liturgical style comes not so much from his borrowings as from his awareness of the context in which the writing would be used.

Since he wrote for Christians about the year AD 90, to whom for the most part the name of Paul had become a somewhat vague memory from the past, he would understandably wish to emphasise those elements in Paul's teaching which gave expression to the enduring truths of the gospel. But he would also wish to underline aspects of the message which were particularly relevant to his own day. One such issue arose from the fact that there had been no immediate parousia, as Paul had expected, and anticipation of its nearness had ceased to be an important part of the life of the Church—or in the mind of this particular writer. The second coming of Christ, and with it the end of all things, was no longer a matter of urgent concern. This meant that the Church itself took on an entirely new significance. For Paul and his immediate followers it consisted of the company of Christians within whose fellowship the individual Christian could be sustained in his faith, and through which they sought to witness to Christ and win others to faith in him. But its significance was only for the short interval between the resurrection and the parousia. Now, however, the Church faced an indefinitely long future. What were its responsibilities in this unexpected situation? What was God's purpose for it? How could its new significance best be expressed? These issues are clearly prominent in the thought of this writer and his answers have served the Church down the centuries.

The Church, however, was now predominantly Gentile. The old point of contention as to whether Gentiles could become full members of the Church without first accepting circumcision had been settled and almost forgotten. The great threat now was that the Gentiles would impatiently disown their Jewish origins as of

no importance and, following Gnostic counsels, depend wholly
on the spiritual truth within their hearts. There was a real danger
of the Gentile section of the Church becoming a separate denomination only too ready to forget the embarrassing fact that
their faith had, humanly speaking, all begun in Judea, and that
the first group of Christians had been Jewish. The writer of
Ephesians saw any racial or nationalistic division within the
Church as disastrous, something utterly alien to all it was meant
to stand for in the world. To counter it he seeks to emphasise the
continuing oneness of the Church with its Jewish origins and with
the apostles as its foundation, and the indivisible unity within it of
Christians whatever their origin, whether Jew or Gentile. The
Church must be not only happy in its present and confident in
face of the future, but also proud of its past and loyal to it. Hence
the Church, the continuing body through whom Christ works in
the world, emerges as a factor of central importance in the letter,
almost a mystical or metaphysical reality as well as a plain
historical fact.

The current Gnostic threat is also present in the writer's mind.
His insistence on the importance of the historical past of the
Church is one of his moves to counter it. Another move is in his
strong insistence on the essential importance of the moral qualities involved in Christian living. He agrees with the Gnostics in
their insistence on the importance that each Christian should himself know the inward transforming experience of the living Christ;
the Christian even now can be, as it were, 'risen with Christ' and
even 'ascended with Christ'. But with this must be combined
loyalty to the past and loyalty to the community of Christians and
loyalty to the moral obligations involved in being a Christian.
Moreover, the writer's insistence is that all our knowledge of
Christ and the change in human life that follows is ours as the gift
of God. It is ours to accept humbly. It does not come through
high spiritual perceptiveness or intellectual superiority.

There is another danger, besides that of Gnosticism, the writer
seeks to counter. At the opposite end of the spectrum, perhaps
partly roused by the excesses of Gnosticism at the other end, was
a new moralism. The fact that moral living was necessary for the
Christian came to be expressed as though moral goodness were the
prequisite to spiritual experience. Salvation was made to depend
on goodness. To counter this danger the writer recalls Paul's

teaching on the grace of God through Christ as the only means of man's salvation. The Christian life, from beginning to end, is the gift of God by which human life, both in its inward experience and outward behaviour, is transformed. It is neither a pedestrian moralism nor a superior style of mystical illumination.

This is the composite situation out of which Ephesians sprang, reflecting an enthusiastic loyalty to Paul's message and an intense determination to show that what Paul stood for offered real guidance in the urgent problems of a new generation of Christians.

8. THE CONTENTS OF EPHESIANS

It is possible to draw up an outline of Ephesians, but we do not find in it any developing pattern of argument as in Romans, nor any orderly treatment of a succession of issues, as in 1 Corinthians. Points already emphasised are later taken up and emphasised again, so that it is not possible to discern any logical or orderly progression. There is a similarity in the general plan to that found in some of Paul's letters, in that in the early chapters the writer is mainly affirming Christian truths of belief or experience, while the later chapters (4 to 6) consist largely of exhortations to conduct worthy of those who hold such beliefs.

The epistle is famous for its advanced doctrine of the Church, far more developed than anything in Paul's other letters, or even elsewhere in the whole of the *NT*. Both its intimate relationship to Christ as his body or his bride and its essential unity are given great prominence, and it is these which are usually thought of as characterising the epistle. It is, however, an error to suggest that teaching about the Church dominates the epistle almost to the exclusion of anything else. The epistle is essentially about Christ, and only about the Church as it fulfils the purposes of Christ; and this Christ is one who first of all renews individual human lives and only then welds them into this new kind of community called the Church. In fact, in chapters 1–3 there is far more about the great privileges which the individual Christian receives from God through Christ than about the corporate life of the Church. The corporate life of the Church may indeed be thought of as one among the privileges granted to those who have faith in Christ. But before the Church becomes possible there is need for the new quality of individual life in Christ which enables the individual—

as the component part of the Church—to rise above such human
prejudices as racial arrogance and antipathy, and natural
impulses to achieve personal aggrandisement and show hostility
to rivals, which all too easily disrupt communities. Only so can
this new community find and maintain that special kind of unity
which can rise above social prejudices and supersede individual
self-seeking.

Basic, therefore, to this new kind of corporate life embodied in
the Church is the renewed life of the individual within the new
community. There is no Church apart from the new kind of
individual whose life has been so changed that he can become
a positive element for peace and harmony within it. It is a mis-
understanding of this epistle to see the Church as a kind of
mystical entity with some kind of ethereal existence apart from
the transformed lives of the individuals who compose it. Membership in the Church is not a substitute for a personal apprehension
of the privileges of the Christian faith, but is the outcome of that
personal faith with its experience of Christ and new life in Christ.
The contents of 1:1-21, as well as much in chapters 2 and 3, make
this emphasis on the individual within the Church very clear, as
it leads up to the emphasis on the Church as co-ordinating all
individuals, in the closing verses of both chapters 1 and 2.

An outline of the contents may be sketched as follows:

PART I

The Privileges of the Christian

1:1-2 Greeting.

1:3-14 Adoring gratitude to God for personal, spiritual privileges
already received through Christ—election, redemption, sonship, insight, the gift of the Holy Spirit, a sense of the purpose
of life.

1:15-23 Prayer for further blessings: for an understanding and
appreciation of all their privileges—their hope for the future,
their inheritance from the past, their awareness of the power
of God at work in their lives (demonstrated by the resurrection
and exaltation of Christ, and his present work through the
Church).

2:1-10 A further reminder of what their Christian privileges are:
their new life in Christ with its deliverance from the 'death' of

an appetite-dominated existence—all as the outcome of God's effective grace in their lives.

2:11-12 Reminder of the shameful past from which they were saved, with its unawareness of Christ and their separation (as Gentiles) from the people of God (Israel), its hopelessness and godlessness.

2:13-22 Reminder of the way Christ has put right these disadvantages by achieving for them reconciliation to God and to God's people, bringing about a new peace and unity, which embraces both Jews and Gentiles, and creates a new corporate life within which and through which God will work within his world.

3:1-13 Emphasis on Paul's part in this great achievement, his understanding of God's purposes, and his effective furtherance of them. It was God's special gift to him which enabled him to bring the gospel to the Gentiles, and to bring them into the community of God's people, the Church.

3:14-19 Intercession for the readers.

3:20-21 Ascription of glory to God.

PART II

The Responsibilities of the Christian

4:1-16 Prayer that the Christian experience of believers may result in appropriate Christian conduct, such as the humility which makes corporate unity possible, and the appreciation of the gifts of others, which excludes jealousy. The aim is total likeness to Christ and the achievement of complete unity within the Christian community.

4:17-5:2 Exhortation to abandon altogether ways of life characteristic of the non-Christian, which belong to the 'old nature'. This means discarding lying, anger, stealing, improper talk, bitterness, and ill-will, and replacing them with kindness and gentleness as seen in God's treatment of us in Christ. They must indeed aim to be like God, since they are children within his family.

5:3-20 Another list is given of wrong attitudes to be discarded: Gentile immorality, shameful talk, drunkenness; and of Christian substitutes to be appropriated: fellowship with other

Christians, singing and thankfulness—all through the gift of the Spirit.

5:21–6:9 Christian counsel to specific groups: wives, husbands (with digression about Christ's love for his Church), children, fathers, slaves, and masters.

6:10 Final exhortation to watchfulness, readiness, and determination in the Christian's struggle with the forces of evil.

6:21–22 Commendation of Tychicus.

6:23–24 Benediction.

THE LETTER
TO THE
EPHESIANS

The conventional opening for a first-century Greek letter was: 'A to B sends greeting.' The sentence which followed was often an expression of gratitude, like 'I am grateful to know (e.g., that you are well)'. Paul in his letters followed this pattern, but he usually amplified it. After both his own name and that of the people addressed, he added further descriptive words. Moreover, he adapted the greeting to make it into one which was specifically Christian. In Ephesians Paul's usual opening formula is followed. Indeed, the greeting here is almost identical with that in Colossians. Here, as at most points, Colossians is of all Paul's letters the one closest to Ephesians.

The writer of the letter is named as **Paul** (and again at 3:1). Some scholars have argued that these personal references to Paul were added later, when what had been originally a spoken address, suited to some liturgical context, was given the form of a letter and then ascribed to Paul. More likely they were inserted by the original compiler who wished to make it clear beyond any doubt that his whole intention in writing Ephesians was to present Paul's understanding of the Christian gospel, probably to provide a convenient summary of Paul's total message for readers of a later generation. Before this Paul's letters had been known only as separate letters to specific churches. It would have been easy to regard them as of little importance except for those to whom they had been in the first place addressed. What was needed was a comprehensive statement of Paul's total Christian outlook, based on the thoughts in his letters, but set free from the merely local and temporary problems of particular areas. It was this that the compiler set himself to produce. It was not his own ideas which he sought to communicate, but only those of his revered master, Paul. Had he lived at a later time he might have preferred to write a pamphlet under the title: *Paul's Message for Today*. But it was more in accord with the conventions of the time to write under Paul's own name, and, since all Paul's writings had been letters, to use the letter-form as his means of communication. He uses Paul's name because he has no other purpose than to let Paul speak to a new generation of Christians. Indeed, he borrows extensively from the actual phrases which Paul had used in his

38

genuine letters. As far as possible it is through Paul's own words
that he writes what he understands to be Paul's message to his own
time, perhaps a generation after Paul's death.

1. Paul is called **an apostle of Christ Jesus.** The word apostle
means one who is sent, a missionary. It was the word applied to those
in the early Church who were held in the highest honour. In the
earliest days it was not restricted to the original twelve disciples,
as it came to be at a later time. Paul could speak of such people as
Andronicus and Junias as apostles (Rom. 16:7). Probably it was
applied to those Christians who had had a very vivid experience
of Christ (cf. 1 C. 9:1), which implanted in them a deep sense of
having been commissioned by Christ to carry his message far and
wide—a commission which other Christians saw to be valid. As
time went on it ceased to be used in a general way for the pioneer
missionary and tended to be reserved for the original disciples of
Jesus, who were regarded as the foundation of the later Church
(see on 2:20), the human embodiment of the truth of the gospel.
Paul had undoubtedly been an apostle in the sense of a pioneer
missionary, but both he and his followers claimed also that he
had the right to the rank of an apostle equally with the original
twelve disciples. His apostolic journeys and his apostolic successes
(1 C. 9:1) entitled him to this status. Yet it is insisted that the
ground of his apostleship lay not in his own achievements: he was
an apostle **by the will of God.** Nothing is clearer in Paul's
writings than his awareness that both his conversion to Christ
(2 C. 5:18) and his commissioning as a missionary (Rom. 1:1;
1 C. 15:10) were 'all God's doing'. It had all happened as a result
of God's initiative. It was not he who had chosen Christ; Christ
had chosen him. He did not assume apostolic duties as his right.
It was Christ who had sent him to fulfil them. This grounding of
Paul's apostleship in God's will is derived directly from Col. 1:1,
but its repetition here in Ephesians has a special appropriateness,
because the opening paragraph of Ephesians (1:3–14) is one continuous affirmation of this central truth that every aspect of the
Christian's experience is to be ascribed to the gracious initiative
of God. Indeed this emphasis is characteristic of the whole epistle.

In Colossians and most other letters Paul associates a colleague
with himself in the opening greeting. But here it is Paul alone who
is named, since it is wholly Paul's message which is being set forth.

To the saints: the word **saints** means 'holy people'. In the Bible the word 'holy' is applied to that which belongs to God in a special way, that which is marked off for the service of God. So the word 'saints' here means 'God's people'. Later the word 'holy' came also to have a moral significance, and 'holy' came to mean 'good'. But the first stage of holiness is 'to belong to God'; it is only as a necessary consequence of this that in the second stage it comes to bear the connotation of goodness, since that which truly belongs to God begins to reflect something of the goodness of God.

The saints are further described as those **who are also faithful in Christ Jesus.** The footnote in *RSV* gives as an alternative translation of the Greek: 'who are at Ephesus and faithful'. The real problem here concerns the phrase 'at Ephesus'. These two words are found in the later MSS, but are omitted from some of the earliest and most reliable ones (e.g., Chester Beatty, Sinaiticus, Vaticanus; Origen also used texts from which these words were missing). Most scholars now agree that in the earliest form of the text these words did not occur. The traditional title of this epistle, which is based on these words 'at Ephesus', may therefore be misleading. They could, however, have been added by someone who knew that this writing had close associations with the church in that city.

Without these two words, however, the sentence does not make very good sense. Many scholars, therefore, have argued that either the name of some other church had originally stood there (before being deleted), or else a blank space had been purposely left so that a name could be inserted later. This has led to a very common belief that the letter was first issued as a circular letter, with a blank space into which the name of any church could be inserted when a copy was being sent to it. Some support of this theory is found in the fact that when Marcion quotes from this letter he refers to it as 'the letter to the Laodiceans'. Perhaps the name of Ephesus came to be accepted in later official copies because of Paul's long association with that city (though this is hardly compatible with 3:2).

If we leave out the words 'at Ephesus' and ignore the awkward gap which their omission leaves we shall have to be content with some such translation as that given by *RSV*. This could be paraphrased: 'To God's own people, who are proving themselves faithful in Christian discipleship'. **in Christ** is a characteristically

Pauline phrase which will be discussed more fully at 1:3. Here it
may be rendered by some such phrase as 'in Christian discipleship'.

2. The greeting is one commonly used by Paul: **Grace to you
and peace from God** (cf. Gal. 1:3; Phil. 1:2). The ordinary
secular word in Greek for 'greeting' is *chairein*. Paul usually
substitutes for this a similar word *charis*, which had come to have
a very special meaning for Christians. It meant **grace,** God's
grace, always available to men and women, but specially so in the
life, death, and continuing presence of Jesus Christ. It is the word
which more than any other expresses God's generous dealings
with his creature man, dealings which are not based on man's
deserving but on the unbelievable goodness of God, as he comes to
rescue man from his distresses, to forgive his sins, and to bring
enabling power for man to achieve what on his own would be
impossible. It is Paul's prayer that awareness of this grace from
God may be the privilege of those to whom he writes.

Just as Greeks used *chairein* as their word of greeting, so Jews
used the word *shalōm*, which is usually translated **peace.** This, too,
is recognised as God's gift to man, the gift which removes the
estrangement between himself and man through the reconciling
power of Christ (2:13-14). The word also signifies that peace
among men which may prevail when goodwill replaces coldness,
suspicion, and hostility (2:16). It means also peace within the
individual human heart as estrangement from God and from one's
fellow-men gives way to reconciliation and friendliness. This
promotes a true sense of well-being. In fact, in Hebrew the word
shalōm includes more than just peace. It means the fullness of well-
being, of which peace is one important constituent part. Almoss
certainly something of this wider meaning of the Hebrew word is
carried over into the Greek word for peace.

God is described as **our Father.** Jesus normally spoke of God
as Father. Indeed he appears to have used an unusually familiar
word for father, which no one previously had presumed to apply
directly to God. It was the word *Abba,* a friendly name for father
within a happy family relationship. It is this word which Jesus used
in Gethsemane as he prayed to his Father (Mk 14:36). He may
well have used it on many other occasions also when the more conventional word Father appears in the Greek text, as for instance
in the Lord's Prayer. But it was not only Jesus himself who was

privileged to think of God in this happy, trusting, affectionate way. It was a privilege which he could communicate to others. In Paul's letters it is clear that Christians, too, could become so sure of the reality of God and of his utter goodwill towards them that they too could speak to him, not only as Father, but even as *Abba*, too (Rom. 8:15; Gal. 4:6; see Jeremias, *The Central Message of the New Testament*, pp. 9–30).

God's grace and peace are described as coming to men from **Jesus Christ,** as well as from God. God is the source of all these good gifts, but it is through Jesus that they are, for Christians at any rate, most commonly brought within their grasp. They may, therefore, be spoken of as coming both from Christ and from God. Christ is their immediate source, God the ultimate source.

Jesus is here given the full title: **the Lord Jesus Christ. Christ** is the Greek equivalent of the Jewish word for Messiah, meaning 'the anointed one'. It was this word that the first Jewish disciples of Jesus used to acclaim their sense of his greatness. The Messiah was one who was expected to come as God's special representative to deliver God's people from their oppressors and to rule over them in the name of God. He was one who would fully represent God in their lives. The Christians declared that this expected deliverer and ruler from God had in fact come in Jesus. He was the long-awaited Christ. This title, however, meant little to those who were not Jews. They continued to use it, since that was how the first missionaries acclaimed the greatness of Jesus, but to Gentiles it was little more than an impressive second name for Jesus. They preferred to affirm his unique significance by means of a word from their own vocabulary. The word that came most readily to their lips and seemed less inadequate than any other was the word **Lord.** It is not true to say that they invented it. Jewish Christians had already confessed Jesus as *Marana*, which means 'our Lord' (see 1 C. 16:22); but this word was one which could be taken over readily by Gentiles, since it was commonly used in Greek in a variety of impressive ways: for the master of slaves, for the Roman emperor himself, for the gods worshipped in various mystery cults, and, in the Greek version of the *OT*, it was a word commonly used for God himself. **the Lord Jesus Christ** was, therefore, the formula in which Jewish and Gentile Christians alike found agreement in their acclamation of their new-found faith in Jesus.

THE OPENING THANKSGIVING I:3–14

This opening passage of the epistle proper is, in the original Greek, one long sentence of twelve verses, which makes it rather ponderous and unwieldy. Modern translators divide it up into several shorter sentences so that its meaning may come over more clearly and pointedly. In *RSV*, for instance, it is split up into six sentences, and in *NEB* into eight. Some commentators, however, complain that this fragmentation, while making for clarity, does in fact rob the passage of some of its essential character. They argue that it is liturgical in character and, therefore, its protracted continuity enhances its impressiveness, whereas the staccato effect of shorter sentences diminishes it.

There are other features also which are claimed to indicate the liturgical nature of the passage. For instance, there is a certain elevation of style which would be rather artificial in a personal letter. This is seen where two words of similar meaning are used in combination, although either by itself would be quite adequate, e.g., **the purpose of his will** (1:5), **will** and **purpose** (1:9), **the counsel of his will** (1:11), **the praise of his glory** (1:6, 12, 14), and **wisdom and insight** (1:9). There is also the repeated use of a verb along with its own cognate noun, e.g., **grace which he freely bestowed** (1:6), which, if translated literally from the Greek, would be 'grace which he graced', **blessed ... with ... blessing** (1:3). Some also note the repeated use of the same words, as some occur again and again, e.g., will, purpose, counsel, praise, glory. In consequence Houlden, for instance, suggests that these verses 'may be a Christian liturgical formula', 'a piece with its own independent life and history'.

There are, however, difficulties in such a view. One is that these characteristics, claimed as indicative of liturgical usage, are found not only in this passage but are sustained throughout the first three chapters. Moreover, it is evident that these twelve verses, just like the rest of the epistle, are built up largely out of phrases taken from the genuinely Pauline letters, with a special degree of dependence on Colossians. This relationship to the Pauline letters, which is characteristic of the letter as a whole, tells heavily against the suggestion that this particular passage originally had 'an independent life' apart from the rest of the epistle.

Kirby has tried to combine the claim that this passage was once a liturgical unit with the fact of its reliance on Pauline language found in the genuinely Pauline letters, but his theory (as was noted in the Introduction, p. 23) requires a far too elaborate process for it to carry conviction.

The basic fact about this passage is the way it reproduces Pauline words and phrases, as found in the other letters. If it has a recognisably liturgical flavour, it is probably because the author found it natural to write in this elevated style, or else because he was aware that what he wrote in this epistle would usually be read aloud for others to hear in the context of a Christian congregation gathered for worship, consultation, and instruction.

Although the passage appears to move on majestically without subdivisions or headings, some have argued for the presence in it of a discernible threefold pattern: (a) 3–6, the greatness of God; (b) 7–12, Jesus Christ; (c) 13–14, the Holy Spirit. Confirmation appears to be provided for this neat progression of thought by the fact that each of the three suggested sections concludes with the phrase: **to the praise of his glory.** It would be a mistake, however, to discern here more than a general development of thought, since throughout (b) as well as (a) God is the subject, and in (a) as well as (b) Christ is the mediator through whom God works. In both (a) and (b) the emphasis is the same: 'from God through Christ'. Indeed, what is most impressive throughout the whole of this passage is its total concentration on the activity of God. It is God who 'chose', 'destined', 'graced' us, and made known his purpose. Christians are referred to only in verbs in the passive voice (with God as the active agent): they have been 'destined', 'appointed', 'sealed'. If active verbs are used they are verbs which imply passive receptiveness: 'receive', 'hear', 'believe'. Nor is Christ ever the subject of a verb. He is everywhere present, precisely mentioned indeed no less than thirteen times, but always as the one through whom or in whom God has acted for the fulfilment of his good purposes for men. It is, however, Christ who defines the nature and character of God, since God is now known particularly as **the Father of our Lord Jesus Christ.**

The whole of this passage is indeed an almost ecstatic declaration of Paul's theology of salvation, as a mere listing of the nouns indicates, as they accumulate throughout the passage: sin, forgiveness, redemption (by Christ's blood and grace), sonship, salvation, Holy Spirit—all these are God's gifts to men through

Christ. The means by which these gifts reach men and women is the gospel, the word of truth. The moment at which this word comes is 'the fullness of time' (i.e., just the right moment) in God's strategy; the controlling hand (*oikonomia*) is God's; and the whole astonishing process is a plan which human intelligence and foresight could never have anticipated. It is God's 'mystery', his secret plan, with Christ, as it were, his secret weapon.

3. Paul's letters usually have a word of thanks to God, following the opening greeting, as he courteously refers to something about his readers on which he can congratulate them. Here, however, the word 'thanks' is not used. Instead, what is substantially the same meaning is expressed in the phrase: **Blessed be ... God.** **Blessed** literally means 'well-spoken-of', but it had become a word in common use to express man's reverence and gratitude before the greatness and goodness of God. **Blessed be ... God** is a phrase continually found in the *OT*. It was also in common use among Jews in the first century, both in their homes (e.g., when they said grace before meals) and in the synagogue where they prayed: 'Blessed be Thou, O Lord our God, King of the Universe, who ...'). Kirby (p. 84) gives several instances of these Jewish prayers, and Vermes (p. 183) gives instances of the phrase in the Qumran literature. These familiar Jewish patterns of prayer may well have been known to the author. In view, however, of his acknowledged dependence on the Pauline letters, he may rather have been remembering the opening exclamation of gratitude in 2 C. 1:3, where the wording corresponds very closely with what we have here: 'Blessed be the God and Father of our Lord Jesus Christ ... who ...' A precisely similar opening is found also at 1 Pet. 1:3, but this is dependent on Ephesians rather than vice versa (see Mitton, *EE*, pp. 176–97).

God is described as **the Father of our Lord Jesus Christ.** This was the way of thinking about God which became distinctive of Christianity. It was characteristic of Jesus that he spoke of God as **Father** (e.g., Mt. 5:16, 45, 48; Lk. 6:36, etc.). Mk 14:36 even records that he used in his personal prayer that very intimate Aramaic word for father, *Abba* (see note on 1:2). These words, Father and *Abba*, serve to declare the Christian's faith that the great power who created, sustains and orders all things is not to be thought of as One remote, formidable, and unknowable, but as one who is near, friendly, and personally lovable, one whose character is known through Jesus. For **Lord Jesus Christ**, see note on 1:2.

God ... has blessed us in Christ with every spiritual blessing in the heavenly places. It is through **Christ** that God has made available to man *all* the richest privileges of the spiritual life **(every spiritual blessing)**, some of which are to be named in the verses which follow: forgiveness, redemption, sonship, salvation, the gift of the Spirit. The main point of emphasis here, however, is not so much on the privileges themselves as the fact that they are to become ours as God's free gift to us, and brought within our grasp by Jesus Christ. The phrase here used to describe Jesus Christ as God's agent in this process is **in Christ**. It is a phrase which occurs very frequently in Paul's letters, where it covers a wide range of meanings, some simple and practical, others deeply spiritual. For instance, in Gal. 1:22, what the *RSV* translates quite fairly as 'the churches of Christ', is literally, in the Greek, 'the churches which are in Christ'. To describe churches as being 'in Christ' is roughly equivalent to calling them 'Christian' (a word not then in common use). Elsewhere the phrase 'in Christ' means 'by means of Christ'—a significance which it very frequently carries in Ephesians. There is, however, in Paul's letters a third sense which has come to be regarded as the one most characteristic of him. In this sense it is used to express identification with Christ, with his death and with his risen life, as though Christ were a kind of corporate personality within which individual Christians and the Christian community as a whole may be included. This way of thinking has sometimes been called 'Paul's mysticism', and it does seek to express something very profound in spiritual experience. Since, however, mysticism often implies that the human spirit is absorbed into the divine Spirit until all distinction between the two is lost, it may be wise to avoid this word in describing Paul's thought, since for him sinful man was always to be distinguished from the pure and holy God. Instances of these profound uses of 'in Christ' may be found in such passages as Rom. 6:11 (as expounded in 6:1–10), 8:1; 2 C. 5:17; Phil. 3:9.

This phrase **in Christ** is very frequently used in Ephesians. There are as many as eleven instances of it in this passage (1:3–14) alone. Predominantly, these appear to fall into the second of the three Pauline meanings mentioned above, and are used to express

'by means of Christ'. Some writers indeed argue that in Ephesians
the phrase is always used in this severely practical sense and never
in its deeper meaning of spiritual identification with Christ. Allan,
for instance, writes (pp. 58–9): 'The formula never seems to carry
the same depth of meaning in this epistle as it does in Paul ...
The writer brings the "in Christ" formula to a level at which we
can appreciate it. He wishes by its use to emphasise that the whole
living purpose of God—all is done through Christ.' It may be,
however, that this over-simplifies the matter, and in fact in
Ephesians there may be echoes of Paul's deeper usage. Indeed,
Abbott believes that one instance of this deeper use is found here
in this context, and he interprets it here as meaning 'by virtue
of our union with Christ', and not 'as if Christ were merely the
instrument'.

us: There is a curious alternation between 'we' and 'you' in
several passages in this epistle. Sometimes there is an obvious
difference between them as at 1:15–16. But at other times there
seems to be no difference of meaning at all between 'us' and 'you'
(see, for instance, the variation in 2:8 and 2:10). It may well be
that part of the explanation is to be found in the fact that the
epistle is pseudonymous, and the author feels himself sometimes
identified with Paul as the writer, sometimes included among
those to whom Paul is now speaking. He is included in both 'us'
and 'you'. In this present context we may assume that all
Christians are gathered up in the word **us,** Paul himself as the one
who writes and all who as Christians will read this epistle or hear
it read.

who has blessed us: In the Greek the tense used for this verb
is aorist, and the function of the aorist is to refer to some definite
action in past time. The reference may be to the experience of
conversion which brought the readers into the Christian life.
Others, however, prefer to see it as a reference to their baptism,
and find in it some confirmation of the argument in favour of the
liturgical origin of this passage. Another possibility is that it refers
back to God's choice of them as his children **before the foundation of the world.** Indeed, if **in the heavenly places** means 'in
God's heavenly counsels' (i.e., before he began to put his plans
into operation upon earth), that would be the most probable
meaning for it.

It is, however, very difficult to define the precise meaning of this phrase. It is never found in Paul's letters, but seems to be a favourite phrase of the writer of Ephesians, for he uses it five times in this epistle (1:3, 20; 2:6; 3:10; 6:12). *RSV* translates it as 'in the heavenly places'. But in the Greek there is no actual word for 'places'. It could equally well mean 'in spiritual things', that is, in spiritual qualities. In some contexts, however, it seems clearly to refer to heaven, thought of as a place, e.g., at 1:20, where Christ sits at God's right hand 'in the heavenly places'.

The order of the words makes it impossible to interpret the phrase as referring to God, who may be thought of as 'in the heavenly places'. It must refer to the privileges (blessings) of the Christian people, which they have received from God. It is a reminder that these privileges are not to be thought of as limited only to this earthly life. Phil. 3:20 speaks of 'our commonwealth' (citizenship) as in heaven, and Phillips translates this passage as: 'He has given us every spiritual benefit . . . as citizens of heaven.' The Christian lives in two dimensions: his life on earth has a counterpart in heaven, God's eternal world; how we live on earth has significance here on earth, but it is also of eternal significance. One is reminded of the words of Jesus in Lk. 10:20: 'Do not rejoice in this, that the spirits are subject to you; but rejoice that your names are written in heaven.' Our obedience to God on earth is, as it were, registered in a relationship with God 'in heaven'. In the twentieth century we do not find it easy to think of heaven as a place. Perhaps its essential meaning can best be represented in some such phrase as 'our relationship with God'.

4. even as is somewhat imprecise. We could represent the meaning by translating 'as is evidenced by the fact that'. Masson translates it simply as 'for'. **he chose us in him before the foundation of the world. he chose us** is a most emphatic way of asserting the belief that God has shaped the lives and destiny of Christians and worked out his purpose in them. Paul similarly was deeply aware that his own conversion and his call to be an apostle were acts of God. God had chosen him. Of that he was sure, though he did not know why. He testified: 'By the grace of God I am what I am' (1 C. 15:10). The conversion of other Christians also he regarded as totally the work of God. Of this 'new creation' in Christ he wrote: 'All this is from God' (2 C. 5:18). So in Jn 15:16 Jesus says: 'You did not choose me, but I

chose you.' In those early days all Christians had the awareness
that for some inexplicable reason God in his mercy had chosen to
come into their lives. Why had he come to them rather than to
others? There was nothing in them to merit such distinction.
Humbly they acknowledged the mystery of God's ways. But they
were sure that it was all God's doing. The writer here goes even
further and declares that this had been God's purpose **before the
foundation of the world.** Their conversion is not a last-minute
idea of God, but part of his age-long strategy. They themselves
were God's chosen agents in the fulfilment of a plan which had
been in God's mind even before the world was created. The fact
that they had come through Christ to know God and obey him
was not just a happy accident, but the achievement of something
which God had set his heart on ages before. Some of the great
men of the *OT* had this deep sense that God's purpose for them
had been built into their lives even before they were born, as, for
instance, Jeremiah to whom God said: 'Before you were born I
consecrated you; I appointed you a prophet to the nations' (Jer.
1:5). What was true of the great prophets of old was now true of
all Christians.

This passage, along with others in the *NT*, has been made the
basis of what has been called the doctrine of election. Its theoretical elaboration, however, has had two unhappy consequences.
Sometimes it has been argued that, if 'all is of God', then not only
the conversion of the Christian man, but the wickedness of the
unconverted man must equally be God's doing. Paul himself
drew dangerously near to asserting something like this in Rom.
9:13–18. But whatever individual texts may seem to say, the
Christian, with Jesus Christ as his guide, cannot believe that God
ever predestines a man to evil. The other unfortunate consequence
is that sometimes those who have found themselves 'converted'
and attribute it all to God's choice of them begin to think that
this must mean that they are God's favourites, and therefore in
some sense superior to other men. Election becomes the ground
of assuming privilege and so an occasion of pride. But God's
choice of a man is not for the purpose of loading him with desir-
able privileges, at least not as we usually reckon privilege. He
chooses men and women in order that they may share in his work
on earth and become the agents of his purpose. Rightly viewed,
indeed, this *is* a great privilege, but it is a privilege which often

brings hardship, rejection, and loss, as it did to Jesus. The Christian is chosen in order to bear his cross for Christ's sake, not to feel disdain for others; to help in winning men from a meaningless life into a life guided by God, not to bask in some imagined superiority of spiritual status.

God chose us **in him.** Christians quickly came to believe that the very life of God had confronted them in Jesus. They also came to realise that this 'Godness' in Jesus had not just started with his birth at Bethlehem. It had been part of God from the very beginning. This 'Godness' in Jesus is sometimes indicated by calling him 'Christ'. Christ had been within the life of God from the very beginning, 'in the form of God' as Paul put it (Phil. 2:6). He had been God's agent at work within the life of the people of Israel (1 C. 10:4). Indeed, it was through the agency of Christ that God had created the physical universe (1 C. 8:6; cf. Heb. 1:2; Jn 1:3). So it was this eternal Christ, later to become known to men through Jesus, who had been God's agent in planning the future salvation and commissioning of those who were now Christians.

The reason why 'we' were chosen was **that we should be holy and blameless before him. holy** is the same word as that translated 'saints' in 1:1. As noted there it primarily means one who belongs to God in a special sense, who is available for God's use, an instrument at God's disposal for the achievement of his purposes. It means, also, people who show the marks appropriate to one who belongs to God, who reflect something of his goodness. This moral aspect of holiness is indicated in the word **blameless,** free from blemish. Moreover, this blamelessness is not just outward, that which passes muster under the scrutiny of other men. They are to be blameless **before him,** the one who reads the heart as well as the open act, and judges men not by merely conventional standards of goodness, but by the searching standards of Jesus.

In the text of *RSV* verse 4 ends at this point, but it is indicated in the footnote that the words 'in love' (from verse 5) can be understood as concluding this verse rather than starting verse 5. If so, then 'in love' adds a strongly positive note to the somewhat negative sound of the word **blameless.** It would mean that God's aim in our lives is not merely to produce blamelessness by eliminating what is evil, but to foster active goodness in its most positive form of 'love'. Love means a deep concern for the true welfare of

another and a practical readiness to do all in our power to secure
that welfare. Its character is movingly described in 1 C. 13.

5. He destined us in love. If the phrase **in love** is to be
linked with this verse rather than the preceding one, then it more
naturally is to be referred to God's love for us, his total concern
for our welfare, than to a spirit of love which characterises **us** as
God's sons. It is his love for us which moved him to destine **us . . .
to be his sons.** The word **destined** re-emphasises the truth
already affirmed in the word 'chose', and indicates the purpose
behind that choice—that we should **be his sons.**

God has already been spoken of as the Father of our Lord
Jesus Christ (in 1:3). We noted there that it was characteristic of
Jesus to speak of God as Father, and that in consequence it came
to be regarded as the great privilege of Christians to find them-
selves also able to think of God in this way (Gal. 4:4–7; Rom.
8:14–17). In Paul's teaching this vivid awareness of God as
Father and of himself as God's child is the special privilege of the
Christian, a privilege into which he is drawn by the gift of the
Holy Spirit—when 'God has sent the Spirit of his Son into their
hearts' (Gal. 4:8), and when they are 'led by the Spirit of God'
(Rom. 8:14). It is to this high privilege that Christians are
destined in God's intention. As with all the other spiritual blessings
this one becomes available to us **through Jesus Christ.** It is
when we receive the 'spirit' of his Son that we can ourselves experience sonship. The spirit of sonship is spoken about also by
Jesus in Mt. 5:45 where he says such a spirit is demonstrated
when we treat others with a generous love beyond anything they
actually deserve, because this is how God treats all men. All this
is **according to the purpose of his will.** Characteristically the
writer adds this phrase, not to say something new, but to underline something already clearly implied in the word 'destined'.

6. to the praise of his glorious grace is another repetitious
phrase. Either 'to his praise' or 'to his glory' would have been
sufficient. But the repetition serves to emphasise the twofold truth
that our attainment to the privilege of sonship is entirely due to
God, and not to ourselves, and that as such it makes us want to
praise God for it. The phrase 'to the praise of his glory' occurs also
at 1:12 and 1:14. This grace, it is again stressed, has been **freely
bestowed on us in the Beloved. the Beloved** clearly means
Jesus. For writer and readers alike it must at this time have been

an accepted name for him. The word is not, however, found in this sense in Paul's letters, where it is used only to describe fellow Christians. A similar word, however, is applied to Jesus in the Gospels—for instance, in all three accounts of the baptism of Jesus (Mt. 3:17; Mk 1:11; Lk. 3:22). On this basis, those who favour a liturgical origin for Ephesians argue that the word **Beloved** here is an echo of the story of the baptism of Jesus, and so has a connotation suitable for a liturgy designed for a baptismal occasion. This, however, is to read into the word more than it can rightly carry, because in the Gospels it is used of Jesus on other occasions as well as at his baptism (for instance, at the transfiguration, and in the context of the parable of the wicked husbandmen).

7–8. The preposition 'in' in the two phrases 'in the Beloved' (1:6) and **in him** (1:7) probably signifies 'by means of'. **In him we have redemption through his blood:** the whole sentence is taken word for word from Col. 1:14. The Greek word here translated **redemption** is *apolytrōsis*, which is closely related to the word for 'ransom' (*lytron*) as used in Mk 10:45. Its main significance is to suggest an entry into a new kind of freedom (instead of captivity or irksome restriction); but also implied in the word is the costliness of the means by which this new freedom is obtained. Here **redemption** is a part of sonship (1:5), as it is at Rom. 8:23, where our 'adoption as sons' is equated with 'the redemption of our bodies'. Paul also associates the two ideas in his memorable phrase: 'the glorious liberty of the children of God' (Rom. 8:21). The captivity from which we are rescued is that caused by the domination of evil of one kind or another in our lives. This causes separation from God, even a sense of being at enmity with God (Rom. 5:10; cf. Col. 1:21: 'estranged and hostile in mind, doing evil deeds'). The word 'redemption' is used again in Ephesians at 4:30, and there it has a future reference as something to be waited for. Here, however, it is part of the present experience of the Christian, a privilege he already 'has', not just a distant hope. Often in the *OT* the word 'redemption' is used in relation to property which a person once possessed but has forfeited. It becomes his own again only when someone 're-deems' (buys it back) for him, so that he is able to repossess it as something which is now his by right. Perhaps something of this thought is present here, since sonship was originally God's inten-

tion for us, but we had lost it and it had to be regained on our
behalf. That which had to be paid in order to redeem what had
been lost is the 'ransom'. This had been provided by Christ: he
is the means by which man can find his new freedom as a son of
God. The cross of Christ, his death, and the shedding of his blood
on the cross in death, which so vividly symbolised the laying down
of his life, are often spoken of in the *NT* as the means by which
men are brought back to God. This utter self-giving of Christ on
behalf of men can be seen in his incarnation, where Christ
'emptied himself' (Phil. 2:7); but Paul saw it even more vividly
in the death of Christ: 'He loved me and gave himself for me'
(Gal. 2:20). It is through his utter self-giving, so clearly seen in
his death on the cross, that we have our redemption—it becomes
ours **through his blood.**

This redemption is further described as **the forgiveness of
our trespasses.** It is strange that this word **forgiveness** does
not occur at all in Paul's letters, except at Col. 1:14. The Greek
word *aphesis* (here translated **forgiveness**) strictly means 'removal'. In its relation to sin it is customary to assume that this
means only the removal of the spiritual consequences of sin, the
guilt; but the phrase actually is 'the removal of sins'. It should
mean that the sins themselves are removed from our lives, not
merely that the consequences of past sins are, as it were, cancelled
out. This is achieved not by human ingenuity or accumulated
goodness, but by God's incredibly generous attitude and action
towards us—by **the riches of his grace which he lavished
upon us** in Christ.

9. *RSV* associates the phrase **in all wisdom and insight** with
the verb in verse 9: **he has made known.** Others prefer to link
them with the word 'lavished' in the preceding verse. *NEB*, for
instance, translates verse 8: '. . . God's free grace lavished upon
us, imparting full wisdom and insight'. This treats **wisdom and
insight** as qualities of human life communicated to men by God's
grace; *RSV* understands them as properties of God as he reveals
his will to men.

It is unlikely that the writer intends to draw any clear distinction between **wisdom** and **insight.** It is characteristic of his style
to prefer to combine two words of similar meaning rather than be
content with one single word.

God **has made known to us . . . the mystery of his will.**

The word **mystery** in the ancient world was readily associated with religion. Indeed, in the first century AD there were several eastern cults, which had established themselves in the west, which were known as 'mystery' religions. The characteristic which they all had in common was the possession of some secret ('mystery') which was made known to initiates, but only under the most solemn pledges of complete secrecy. It could be a secret ritual, or perhaps just a word or a formula. This 'mystery' was held to give the initiate access to high spiritual privileges denied to others with no knowledge of the 'mystery'.

Paul in his letters uses this word 'mystery' several times, but never of a limited privilege available only to a few and to be hidden from all others, as in the mystery religions. Apart from Colossians, he uses it in a very general sense to mean what we might call a 'problem', or else some obscure purpose of God which is wholly or partly hidden. That is, it is used at a fairly practical level, rather than with any deep theological significance. In Colossians, however, where it occurs four times, it has a more profound meaning: there it refers to God's ultimate purpose for mankind, for long ages withheld from human understanding, but now at last disclosed in Jesus Christ. It is a closed secret no longer. All who are willing to open their lives to Jesus Christ and receive the insight he can bring can come to understand it and delight in it, and also offer it to others.

In Ephesians the word occurs six times, and its characteristic use here reveals a further development as compared with Colossians. Here also it refers to God's plan, long unguessed by the human mind, but now at last made known in Christ. The content of that plan, however, is more precisely indicated. It is **to unite all things in him** (Christ), **things in heaven and things on earth.** Later, at 3:3–6, this mystery is further elucidated as God's purpose to bring about through Christ a new, all-involving unity, with special reference to a unity including both Gentiles and Jews: 'the Gentiles are fellow heirs, members of the same body . . . in Christ Jesus through the gospel'. Christ, who has now made known God's mysterious purpose and who is God's agent for the fulfilment of it, is going to break down all man-made barriers, so that men shall be reconciled both to God and also to their fellowmen.

Till now this will and purpose of God had been wrapped in

mystery. But now it has been **set forth in Christ.** This purpose
to achieve a comprehensive unity had not been understood to be
God's intention until Christ had revealed it to men. In his light
men see light. It is when they let Christ shape their thinking that
they begin to be able to sense what God is aiming to bring about
in and through human life; and that aim is now seen to be an
all-embracing unity including all mankind.

10. This is **a plan for the fullness of time.** God is working
out his age-old purpose according to a carefully designed strategy,
in which the coming of Christ to earth was a move of decisive
importance. It was not a last-minute device nor a sudden bold
improvisation to cope with some unexpected emergency. It was
something which God had long intended, something he waited to
implement at that precise moment when Christ's presence on
earth would prove to be most timely and effective (see also on
3:9). He would come when the time was just opportune for him
to make the maximum impact, that is, at **the fullness of time.**
Greek had more than one word for 'time'. The word used here is
one which would not be used for a vague period of time, a merely
uneventful accumulation of minutes, hours and days, but rather
for some 'time' or moment of intense significance. We might
express this sense of **the fullness of time** by translating: 'at just
the right moment' or 'when the time was ripe'. Interestingly
enough, both these words occur at Mk 1:15, where Jesus announced: 'The time is fulfilled', i.e., 'the planned moment has
come'. See also Gal. 4:4.

God's plan is **to unite all things in him** (Christ). In meaning
this corresponds closely to Col. 1:20, but it is worded differently
and the significance is wider. Col. 1:20 speaks of God reconciling
all things to himself through Christ. The estrangement overcome
by Christ is estrangement between God and man. In Ephesians,
however, the reconciliation embraces not only God and man, but
also man and his fellow-man, and indeed everything throughout
the whole universe. **in him** is here probably best understood to
mean 'through the power of Christ'. Others seek to give the
phrase its more profound 'mystical' meaning. *TEV*, for instance,
translates 'in Christ' here with the words: 'with Christ as head'.

The word here translated **unite** means basically to 'add up' in
the sense of adding up individual items to reach a total. It came
also to be used to mean 'sum up', in certain contexts. Paul, for

instance, speaks of the many items of the Jewish Law as 'summed up' in the one sentence: 'Love your neighbour as yourself' (Rom. 13:9). Some commentators prefer to find this metaphorical meaning here. Phillips, for instance, translates: '. . . that all human history should be consummated in Christ, that everything that exists in Heaven or earth should find its perfection and fulfilment in him'. But the word 'sum up' literally means to bring separate items into a single whole (a total), and many commentators agree with *RSV* in preferring here to translate as 'unite'. So does *NEB*: '. . . that the universe . . . might be brought into a unity in Christ'. This emphasis on unity certainly coincides with the dominant note of Ephesians as a whole, that through Christ God is now achieving his original purpose of overcoming among men all rivalries, divisions, and animosities, and in their place establishing unity.

In the teaching of Jesus as recorded in the Gospels there is a strong and repeated emphasis on reconciliation. True worship of God is possible only when the worshipper has done everything in his power to achieve reconciliation with an estranged fellow-man (Mt. 5:23–24). Readiness to forgive those who have wronged us is expected of those who seek God's forgiveness (Mk 11:25; Mt. 18:33; Lk. 17:3–4, etc.). There is also a strong emphasis on non-retaliation and 'overcoming evil with good' (Mt. 5:38: turning the other cheek, and walking the extra mile). This is the spirit of Christ. It is this spirit, when brought into the hearts of men, which dissolves barriers, heals estrangements, and makes reconciliation and unity possible. This reconciliation and unity among men is God's purpose for humanity. This purpose has at last been understood because it has been disclosed and clearly seen in Jesus Christ. God's ultimate purpose is **to unite all things in him.**

The same emphasis on Christian unity is present in Paul. Quarrelling among Christians represents total defeat for Christ (1 C. 6:7), and he bids Christians not only to 'live in harmony with one another' (Rom. 12:16) but to 'live peaceably with all' (Rom. 12:18).

The reconciling power of Christ is to achieve the unity of **all things . . . in heaven and things on earth. all things** (neuter) may be taken literally to mean the whole physical universe as well as personal relationships—the lion and the lamb (as in Isa.

11:7), principalities and powers as well as Jews and Gentiles (as in Col. 1:15–20), and the whole creation now groaning in travail and subjected to futility (Rom. 8:19–22). This, however, leads into the area of speculation. The use of the neuter plural may be merely a very emphatic way of insisting that the reconciling power of Christ is effective in all circumstances, **in heaven** (that is, in reconciling man to God so that men find peace with God) as well as **on earth** (that is, in all the relationships of human life). Although it is true that the phrase **all** *things* is used, the emphasis in Ephesians is certainly on the uniting of all *people*.

11–12. Up to this point 'we' has been used inclusively to mean all Christians, not only Paul (as the supposed writer), but his hearers and readers also. Now, however, (in 1:12) **we** is used in distinction from 'you' (1:13), though both groups are within the Christian community. The **we** is defined as those **who first hoped in Christ**: this could mean the first generation of Christians as opposed to 'you', those of a later generation. It could also mean Christians of Jewish race, like Peter and Paul, as opposed to those of Gentile race, who became Christians at a later time. Since most first-generation Christians were Jews, some contrast between Christians of Jewish and those of Gentile origin may well be implied.

Once again there is emphasis on the fact that it is God who first chose and later claimed them as Christians. It was **according to the purpose of him who accomplishes all things** (or, as *NEB* puts it: '. . . whose purpose is everywhere at work). The point is further laboured in the following phrase: **according to the counsel of his will,** in the repetitious style characteristic of this writer.

The word **hoped** reminds us of the future dimension of the Christian faith. Up to now the emphasis has been on God's choice of the Christian in the past and the privilege of his present experience of forgiveness and sonship. But the total privilege of the Christian includes the future also, as something to look forward to, something which will complete and crown all the anticipations of it already experienced. We have been **destined and appointed.** Here again the emphasis is on God. He intended it all from the first, assigning us a privileged place in his total plan. His choice of us, however, is not for our own satisfaction or advancement. We are chosen in order **to live** and work and witness **for the praise of his glory.** This concluding phrase has already occurred at 1:6 and will come again at 1:14.

13. In him you also: you must here mean second-generation Christians, almost all of whom were Gentiles by birth. It was not only those who had known the human life of Jesus who were able to claim the privileges associated with faith in him, but those who had only heard of him from others and who even belonged to a different race. This at first seemed quite extraordinary to the first Christians. 1 Pet. 1:8 expresses this surprise: 'Without having seen him you love him.' Particularly they found it hard to believe that Gentiles could enjoy all the privileges of Christian believers without first needing to conform to the basic requirements of the Jewish way of life, which the first Christians accepted because they had been brought up within them. Many indeed argued that this was totally impossible and must not be tolerated. Paul's missionary work was opposed and hindered by Jews and Jewish Christians who believed that all Christians should conform to the Jewish way of life. Part of the theme of Ephesians is that this impossible thing has actually happened, and within the Christian family Jews and Gentiles (who previously had no friendly dealings with each other) take full and equal share in the same great privileges and in the life of the same community. **you also** here means people of a later time (than Paul) and of a different race. They first **heard the word of truth,** and then **believed in him.** Hearing precedes faith. They **heard the word,** through preaching or witnessing, and became believers. The link of hearing with believing is constant in the *NT*: 'How are they to believe in him of whom they have never heard?' (Rom. 10:14); 'Faith comes from what is heard, and what is heard comes by the preaching of Christ' (Rom. 10:17). The positive content of this preaching or this witnessing is described as **the word of truth,** and further explained as the **gospel of your salvation** (cf. Col. 1:5). This 'true word' about God and his dealings with man is the **gospel** (good news) which when accepted in faith brings salvation to the believer. This good news has in it the power to transform human life, changing it from something totally unsatisfactory and unsatisfying into something about which men felt 'this is what life was meant to be'. That so high a quality of life was available was indeed 'good news'; that it changed life so wonderfully was the reason they called it **salvation.** It set men free from meaningless-

ness and emptiness in life, from the tyranny of what was evil and
degrading, and instead awakened a sense of the purpose of life and
of joy in fulfilling it. Moreover, it brought them as individuals
into a company of people all of whom in various degrees had
experienced a similar deliverance. This personal transformation
of their own lives was confirmed and enlarged by the fellowship
experienced within the Christian community. This personal and
corporate experience is what was meant by **salvation.** It is true
that the word **salvation** in Paul can sometimes carry a large
degree of future significance, in that the fullness of salvation includes the victory over death. Paul can write: 'Now is your
salvation nearer than when you first believed.' But in this context
in Ephesians **salvation** means mainly the present privileges open
to the Christian, as the following words about the Holy Spirit
make quite clear, though the future dimension is also recognised
at the end of verse 14 in the word 'inheritance'.

believed in him. Hearing, though important, does not of itself
lead to salvation, unless it awakens faith. The exposition of the
parable of the sower in Mk 4:15–20 contains warnings against
those who hear, but do not take the further step of belief. *RSV*
represents this as belief **in him** (Christ). The Greek could equally
well mean belief 'in it' (that is, the gospel). To believe the good
news means that one not only hears it, but allows it to begin to
rule one's life. Paul speaks of the kind of belief which leads to
salvation as 'believing with the heart' (Rom. 10:9). Hearing
leads to faith, and true faith leads to salvation. This salvation is a
privilege they have already begun to enjoy. It was made securely
theirs when they **were sealed with the promised Holy Spirit.**

This linking of believing with the gift of **the promised Holy
Spirit** is a true representation of Paul's teaching. Writing to the
Galatians, for instance, he asks: 'Did you receive the Holy Spirit
by works of the law or by hearing with faith?' (Gal. 3:2). It was
a rhetorical question to which both Paul and his readers knew the
correct answer. They had received the Holy Spirit; that was an
undoubted fact; and it was through their faith that the Holy
Spirit had been given to them. Paul felt that he could assume that
anyone who was a believing Christian had received the Holy
Spirit. It was the privilege granted to *all* believers, not to only a
few. When men and women believed in Christ and committed
themselves to the Christian truth they had heard proclaimed, they

received the Holy Spirit. It is a mistake to suggest that the gift was
bestowed only when faith was given open expression in baptism.
In Ac. 10:44–48 Cornelius and his friends receive the Holy Spirit
directly in response to their faith, and baptism follows as a consequence. The episode also in Ac. 19:1–7 (about the twelve men
of Ephesus) reveals this characteristic assumption on the part of
Paul that every true Christian (one who believes 'with the heart')
receives the Holy Spirit, and the baptism not accompanied by
this true faith does not provide this gift.

If we ask what the gift of the Spirit meant for the early Christians, the answer is that it was the element in their Christian
experience which was manifestly the mark of God's present
activity in their lives—something which in no way could be
derived from themselves. It was God's gift. Sometimes even the
faith which received the gift could also be thought of as God's
gift (Ac. 18:27), but usually there was also an element of
human response to God's offer in the act of faith, even if it was
God who awakened that faith. The gift of the Holy Spirit, however, was that in their Christian experience which came clearly
from beyond themselves. The Christian experience had two
elements in it: a definite step of commitment to God in obedience
to him (cf. Rom. 1:5, 'the obedience of faith'), and an experience
of inward renewal which came from God; life was lifted to a new
level of possibility, totally beyond man's power to achieve. It was
marked by a new sense of freedom, peace, and joy, an awareness
of a power for goodness that brought the possibility of victory over
evil, and of new love towards all men. This was manifestly something which God himself had brought about in response to their
faith. They spoke of it as God's Spirit breathed into their lives,
and it was God's free gift, for all they themselves had done was to
accept the message of the gospel and let the Christ of the gospel
take control of their lives.

This sequence in Ephesians, therefore, of hearing, believing,
and receiving the Holy Spirit, is a true representation of the
teaching of Paul.

The clause: **you . . . were sealed,** has often been interpreted
as a reference to baptism, as also at Eph. 4:30. So, too, at 2 C.
1:22, which is very similar to this verse in Ephesians, where we
read: '(God) has put his seal upon us and given us his Spirit . . .
as a guarantee.' A seal was a mark of ownership. Cattle and slaves

were branded with the owner's seal. It is also used in Rom. 4:11
of the significance of circumcision for the Jews: it was the mark
that they belonged to God and accepted God's rule in their life.
It is probably true that, for Christians, baptism came to have
something of the same meaning that circumcision had for the Jew.
Originally, among Christians, baptism was the outward sign that
a man had committed himself in faith to Christ, and in that
commitment, whether at the moment of conversion or in its
public expression in baptism, the Holy Spirit was bestowed. For
the early Christian, faith, the gift of the Spirit, and baptism were
three aspects of one and the same step by which he became a
Christian and identified himself with the Christian community,
accepting his responsibilities in it and enjoying the privileges it
conferred. Baptism may, therefore, be thought of as putting the
seal on faith, since it proclaimed in outward act the inner significance of faith: 'I belong to God.'

Although it is customary to understand sealing as a reference
to baptism by water, and certainly at a later date the word seal
was applied to such baptism, this interpretation does not go
unchallenged. J. D. G. Dunn, in his careful and persuasive book,
Baptism in the Holy Spirit, argues strongly that sealing here and
elsewhere in the *NT* does not refer to water baptism, but to the
coming of the Holy Spirit into the life of an individual, which is
sometimes referred to as baptism by the Spirit (see pp. 131, 133,
158). We have noted that for Paul this coming of the Spirit produced in the person concerned something that was recognisable,
and its absence in a Christian was noticeable (Ac. 10:47, 19:2).
It was this difference in the character of the person which was the
seal of the Spirit—the marks in human life produced by the
coming of the Spirit. There is much to be said for this interpretation. Abbott also rejects any reference here to water baptism:
'There is no reason to suppose such a reference here, which would
be too obscure' (ICC, p. 22).

There is reference to sealing also in Revelation: 'who have not
the seal of God upon their foreheads' (9:4); cf. 22:4: 'his name
shall be on their foreheads'. It is not clear whether this refers to
baptism by water or to the marks of the presence of the Holy
Spirit.

The Holy Spirit is described as **promised.** Peter in Ac. 2:17
speaks of this promise in the *OT*: 'In the last days it shall be, God

declares, that I will pour out my Spirit upon all flesh.' In Lk.
42:49 the risen Christ re-affirms the promise: 'Behold, I send the
promise of my Father upon you . . . power from on high.' Paul,
too, in Gal. 3:14, speaks of 'the promise of the Spirit'. John the
Baptist is reported as promising that Jesus would baptise with the
Holy Spirit, in contrast to his own baptism of repentance.

14. The coming of the Holy Spirit into the life of the individual
believer is called **the guarantee of our inheritance.** The word
inheritance is used in the *NT* for the privilege of the Christian,
partly appropriated already, and yet to some degree awaiting
completion in the future. An inheritance is something which is
marked out for us, not because we have done anything to deserve
it, but because we are a member of a family. Perhaps something
of this corporate significance is present in the writer's mind here.
It is the individual's privilege because of his place in the family.
Here, however, it is the future aspect of the word **inheritance**
which is to the fore. The gift of the Holy Spirit is that part of our
inheritance which we may enjoy here and now in this mortal life,
and this gift already received is here spoken of as the **guarantee**
of that other part of our inheritance which awaits us when this
mortal life is ended.

The word translated **guarantee** could perhaps be more
adequately rendered by a combination of the two words: 'foretaste and guarantee'. The actual word used is *arrabōn*, originally
a Semitic word which the Greeks took over into their language.
In the *OT* it is used of a token (such as a signet ring) given in
guarantee that a proper payment will be made later. The word
passed into Greek, probably through the Phoenician traders, to
signify a down-payment of a proportion of the agreed price in
some commercial transaction which at the same time guaranteed
the full payment at a later specified date. In modern Greek the
word has come to mean an engagement ring.

Ephesians derives its use of *arrabōn* from 2 Corinthians where it
occurs twice, at 1:22 and 5:5. At 1:22 Paul writes that God 'has
given us his Spirit in our hearts as an *arrabōn*'; but it is at 5:5 that
he makes clear what this *arrabōn* guarantees. He has been writing
of the life-beyond-death and the Christian's hope that what in
him is mortal will be 'swallowed up in life', and that he will find
provided for him in that future 'a house not made with human
hands, eternal in the heavens'. The present experience of the

Spirit in our hearts is the *arrabōn*, the guarantee of the reality and
certainty of heaven. In Ephesians this heavenly life is called the
inheritance which is being held in reserve for us, and the Holy
Spirit is the *arrabōn* of it.

How does the Holy Spirit in the heart of the Christian become
to him the guarantee of the life of heaven? For Paul the gift of the
Spirit was a foretaste of the life of heaven because both represented
the God-controlled and God-filled life. In both God is the actual
ruler. It was because it was a foretaste of the life to come that the
gift of the Spirit was an assurance (guarantee) of the reality to
follow. The original significance of the *arrabōn* probably goes back
to a time before coin was in common use as a trading exchange.
A dealer who brought bales of cloth for sale at a Palestinian port
and wanted in return some tons of wheat would have to arrange
the sale by barter—so many sacks of wheat for so many bales of
cloth. The merchant, however, would not be able to transport
with him all the wheat he had for sale. He would bring a few sacks
to serve as a sample of the quality of the whole consignment.
When the deal was complete he would leave his sample sacks with
the cloth merchant as the *arrabōn*. They were in commercial usage
a guarantee that the full delivery would follow in the agreed time,
and that it would be of the same quality as the sample already
deposited.

So for the Christian the Holy Spirit as known 'in his heart' is a
sample or foretaste of the life of heaven, the life where God is
fully present and in full control. An anticipation of heaven has
been provided, and as such it is a guarantee of the reality and the
nature of heaven, of which it is the foretaste.

> That, that is the fullness,
> But this is the taste.

Paul uses a similar metaphor, borrowed from agriculture, in
Rom. 8:23, where he describes the gift of the Spirit as 'the first-
fruits' (that is, a representative sample) of the life of heaven.

The Spirit may also be regarded as good seed sown in the life
of the Christian, which, given appropriate soil and good hus-
bandry, produces a splendid harvest of Christlike qualities, such
as love, joy, peace, etc., the 'fruit of the Spirit' (Gal. 5:22). These
qualities characterise the life where God is in complete control.
They will only be seen in perfection in the life of heaven where

God's rule is undisputed. But it is the Christian's privilege to have some foretaste of them here also, when his life is guided by the Spirit. The full **inheritance,** however, is not yet his. There is a period of waiting **until we acquire possession of it.** But in the meantime we have the *arrabōn*, or first-fruits, of it; this is already ours, and is sufficient to sustain hope, courage, and perseverance, while we wait for the fulfilment. All these benefits which are ours —God's choice of us in the first place, his claiming of us when the time was ripe, his gift to us of his Holy Spirit now, and the sure hope of heaven later (of which the Spirit is the foretaste and guarantee)—are **to the praise of his glory** (the same phrase as at 1:6 and 11). The manner of their coming to us makes men exclaim: 'This is the Lord's doing; it is marvellous in our eyes' (Ps. 118:23).

PRAYER FOR GOD'S GIFTS I:15-23

This passage carries forward the thought of 1:3-14. There the prevailing emphasis was on the good things which the readers had already proved within their own experience. In this passage two further dimensions of the Christian faith begin to emerge. First, there is a glance into the future. The apostle prays that their faith may be enlarged with wisdom and insight, so that they may be able to grasp what is meant by Christian hope, that which can look into the unknown future with a sense of eager expectation. Secondly, they are reminded of the objective realities of their faith, in addition to the glad certainty of inward experience. These comprise a reminder about the inheritance which any one Christian shares with all others, the firm reality of Jesus Christ himself, risen from the dead and exalted to God's right hand, and the fact of the Church, whose life is controlled by Christ and the means by which Christ continues to be effective here on earth.

This is one of the three passages in Ephesians which contain personal references to Paul as the author of the epistle. The other two are 3:1-13 and 6:19-21. In each of them the word 'I' is introduced with a special emphasis.

Some scholars regard these personal passages as additions, inserted later into what was originally a liturgical composition, in order to give it the appearance of a personal letter from Paul. J. C. Kirby, for instance, argues (p. 132) that it is a later insertion

on the ground that it interrupts the sequence of thought between
1:14 and 2:1, and also because **for this reason** in 1:15 has no
clear link with the preceding paragraph, but is merely a link-word
to introduce a later insertion. Houlden comments: 'There is much
to be said for this view.'

There are, however, arguments which in our opinion are
decisive against it. In the first place, we find in the paragraph
those features which are characterised as 'liturgical' when they
appear elsewhere in the epistle. But even more conclusive is the
fact that it reveals a close interdependence with Colossians of
precisely the same kind as that in the preceding and following
paragraphs. It is hardly credible that a later interpolator would
here be able to build up his material from components derived
from Colossians (largely Col. 1) in a similar way and with a
similar proportion of borrowed material to that in the supposedly
original document. Even if he had the skill to do it, he would not
have been likely to find words and phrases from the opening
verses of Colossians which the original writer had conveniently
passed by—which is what the writer of 1:15-23 has done.

The similarity of this continuing dependence on Colossians in
these different passages can be briefly indicated. If we regard a
minimum of two identical words used in close propinquity to each
other both in Ephesians and in Colossians as an indication of
interdependence, the following instances occur:

Eph. 1:3-14 (*from the supposedly original liturgical document*)
Eph. 1:4 :: Col. 1:22   holy and blameless before him
Eph. 1:7 :: Col. 1:13   in him we have redemption ... for-
                        giveness
Eph. 1:9 :: Col. 1:9   in all wisdom
Eph. 1:9 :: Col. 1:27   made known the mystery
Eph. 1:10 :: Col. 1:16 all things in heaven and things on
     (Col. 1:20)   earth

Eph. 1:15-23 (*from the supposedly epistolary later insertion*)
Eph. 1:15-16 :: Col. 1:9   for this reason ... I do not cease
Eph. 1:15 :: Col. 1:4   because I have heard of your faith
                           in Jesus and your love toward all
                           the saints
Eph. 1:16-17 :: Col. 1:3   give thanks for you ... praying

Eph. 1:17 :: Col. 1:3   the God of our Lord Jesus Christ . . .
                              Father
Eph. 1:18 :: Col. 1:27   hope . . . what are the riches of his
                              glory
Eph. 1:19 :: Col. 1:29   power . . . according to the working
Eph. 1:21 :: Col. 1:16   rule, authority, . . . and dominion.
Eph. 1:22–23 :: Col. 1:24 Church, which is his body

It would be most improbable that a later interpolator could
produce in Eph. 1:15–23 the same curious interdependence
between Ephesians and Colossians which is evident in Eph.
1:3–14, and at the same time use material from Col. 1 which had
not already been used in the earlier passage.

Whatever evidence there may be for liturgical influences in
Ephesians, it is not at all probable that Ephesians was first a
liturgical form of service, into which, at a later stage, passages
were inserted to give it the appearance of being a Pauline letter.
The Pauline passages were part of the original form of the writing
and any explanation of the epistle's origin must take account of
that fact. Eph. 1:15–23 has been built up by the same procedures
as were used in the compilation of Eph. 1:3–14.

15. For this reason must refer to the facts mentioned in
1:13–14—that those addressed have heard the gospel and believed it, and have received the gift of the Holy Spirit. This is
sufficient to lead the writer to say that he has **heard of** their
faith, and this makes him want to thank God for them in his
prayers. This faith is described as **faith in the Lord Jesus,**
which corresponds to what was said in 1:13: 'You have believed
in him.' The fact that the writer says that he has *heard* of their
faith is often noted as a reason against Pauline authorship, since
Paul had spent some years at Ephesus, and, therefore, knew well
the Christians at Ephesus through personal acquaintance, and
did not need to 'hear' about them. The writer also mentions their
love toward all the saints. Some MSS, among them such important ones as Vaticanus and Sinaiticus, omit the word **love.**
This would mean that their **faith** was being described as not only
faith in Jesus Christ but also faith 'toward all the saints'. There is
no *NT* parallel for 'faith' being 'towards other people', and most
commentators assume that **love** belongs to the original text and
must inexplicably have been omitted from these MSS. A true under-

standing of Paul could have led to the association of love with
true faith, since for Paul faith 'works through love' (Gal. 5:6).
Moreover, 1:13 speaks so confidently of the fact that the readers
had received the Holy Spirit that it could be assumed that love,
the first element in the 'fruit of the Spirit', has appeared in them
(Gal. 5:22). But 1:15 is, in fact, almost word for word a repro-
duction of Col. 1:4, where faith and love are associated in an
identical way. Love, it should be noted, in the *NT* use of the word,
is not just a warm feeling of affection, but rather a deliberate
attitude of practical concern for the true welfare of another. It
came to be known as the chief mark of relationships between
Christian people. It was also an attitude shown equally to strangers and even to enemies. Because it was an attitude of will, and
not a feeling, it could be commanded as a Christian duty. **all
the saints** means all one's fellow Christians (see 1:1).

16–17. The presence of this twofold mark of true discipleship
in his readers, faith in Christ and love towards one's fellows,
warms the writer's heart with gratitude as he recalls it: **I do not
cease to give thanks for you, remembering you in my
prayers.** But the prayer is more than one of thanksgiving for
what already is; it becomes also a petition for still better things
yet to come. God is referred to again by the same phrase already
used at 1:3: **the God of our Lord Jesus Christ,** to which is
added a further descriptive phrase: **the Father of glory** (*NEB*
translates: 'the all-glorious Father'). The prayer asks that God
will raise their faith to higher levels of maturity to include **a
spirit of wisdom.** The word **wisdom** was used earlier at 1:9,
but there it was God's wisdom. Here it is the wisdom of the true
believer. In 1 C. 2:7 it is called 'wisdom from God', as distinct
from merely human wisdom, and in 1 C. 1:24 this true wisdom
is identified with Christ himself. Here this true wisdom is said to
consist in knowledge of him, a wisdom which in 1 C. 2:10 is said
to be revealed to us by God through the Spirit. Wisdom, as a
quality which man may come to possess, is usually distinguished
from cleverness and erudition. It is at one and the same time a
humble knowledge of God (rather than just information about
him) and a sense of 'how to live'. Wisdom is here bracketed with
revelation, that is, 'insight' into the ways and purposes of God.
In the *OT* an oft-repeated phrase insists that the beginning of
wisdom is found in the fear of the Lord. The *fullness* of wisdom,

however, is seen in Christ (1 C. 1:22), and obedience to him produces wisdom in the human life. In Christ we see more clearly than at any other point the two aspects of wisdom—insight into the purposes of God and also into the quality of life which is real life, life as it was meant to be. The apostle prays that **God . . . may give** them all these good things. They come to man as God's gift. This emphasis on God's giving is, as we have seen, characteristic of this writer.

18. The prayer continues by asking that **the eyes of your hearts may be enlightened.** In the Bible the heart is the seat of understanding and intention even more than of feeling. This is a prayer, therefore, for spiritual understanding. As the light of day enables our physical eyes to see things hidden by the darkness, so the light which shines from Christ enables us to grasp the truth in what earlier seemed puzzling and obscure. In particular, light will be shed on some of the obscurities of the future, enough at any rate to bring into our lives the quality of **hope.** In these four verses (15–18), therefore, we meet the great *NT* triad of faith, hope, and love. **hope** for the Christian is not to be thought of as an uncertain feeling of mingled longing and misgiving, as when we say that we hope it will be a fine day tomorrow, knowing that it may well be nothing of the kind. Christian hope is a glad confidence in good things to come. It is sure, not tentative. The certainty of its fulfilment is not in doubt; the only matter of doubt is the length of the interval before it is fulfilled. But the hope itself is sure and, because of it, we can bravely face all the hazards and hardships that intervene. Its meaning is conveyed better by our phrase 'look forward to' than by the degree of uncertainty often involved in our word 'hope'. In some parts of the *NT* this Christian hope is associated with a second coming of Christ in victory and the end of this present dispensation. The second coming, however, has no place in Ephesians, and so this hope refers rather to the certainty of life with Christ in heaven which awaits the Christian beyond death. This hope is one **to which he has called you;** it is part of the Christian's calling, part of his equipment as one who has been brought by God (**called**) into the Christian life. The object of their hope is **the riches of his glorious inheritance in the saints.** For **inheritance** see 1:14. The word gathers up all the privileges and responsibilities which become ours as we take our place within the continuing Christian community (among **the saints**). As sharers in such an **inheritance** we receive richly from the 	lth of the past, rejoice in the privileges of the present, and acce	responsibility for the future.

19. Once again in this verse the writer pauses to emphasise his own deep awareness of God's achievements on our behalf through Christ. The effectiveness of God's enabling strength is here described as **the immeasurable greatness of his power.** But this is qualified by the added phrase: **in us who believe.** This tallies with the emphasis of Jesus: 'All things are possible to him who believes' (Mk 9:23). God's gifts become ours 'according to our faith' (Mt. 9:29). Mark tells us that on one occasion Jesus 'could do no mighty work there because of their unbelief' (Mk 6:5–6). Human faith in some curious way enables God's power to become fully effective. One should add that for Jesus faith did not mean believing statements about God or himself, but simply turning to him in the conviction that God through him could do the good thing being asked of him. The use of the word **believe** in this verse carries a similar significance.

The writer wishes to emphasise his confidence that nothing is too great for God to do. He does this in his own characteristic way by an accumulation of four different words, all with much the same meaning: **power, working, might, strength** (the words translated by *RSV* as **great might** are literally 'his might and his strength'.

20. The clearest evidence of this strength is in what God **accomplished in Christ when he raised him from the dead.** The people of Israel, when they wished to point to the most outstanding evidence of God's power, recalled their ancestors' deliverance from slavery in Egypt. Similarly, the Christians remembered the resurrection of Jesus from the dead. In the *NT* this is commonly spoken of as something God did: **he raised him.** The reality of this resurrection of Jesus fills the *NT*. Every book in it either specifically affirms it or assumes it. It is the fundamental conviction in all Christian faith. The *NT* writers do not precisely explain what they mean by the resurrection of Jesus, but for all of them it included the undoubted certainty that Jesus Christ, in spite of his death on the cross, is effectively present in the personal lives of his followers. He is alive in their midst, and still very much one of their company. They never think of him as one who is dead, or as one who belongs to the past. They speak

of him always as one who is present with them. It was this astonishing truth which was the transforming factor in all Christian
experience. The impossible had come true; and it was all God's
doing, the act of one who 'gives life to the dead and calls into
existence the things that do not exist' (Rom. 4:17). If God could
do that, then clearly there was nothing he could not do.

In the same sentence the writer affirms that God not only
raised Christ, but also **made him sit at his right hand in the
heavenly places.** The early Church held two apparently con-
flicting convictions about Jesus following his crucifixion: one was
that he was very much alive in their midst, their unfailing com-
panion; the other was that this same Jesus was with God in
heaven, directing the course of history and controlling human
destiny, and this they expressed by saying that God had exalted
him to his right hand. The inconsistency is, of course, only apparent. Christ is with us and with God, just as God himself is both
immanent and transcendent. The difficulty comes from our
human way of trying to speak of spiritual truths in spatial terms.

Some scholars have argued that in the early days of Christian
thinking the resurrection of Jesus and his exaltation to God's
right hand were two ways of expressing the same truth of his
victory over death, rather than two distinguishable truths. Luke
in his Gospel and in Acts distinguishes them and even specifies an
interval of forty days between the two events. John (20:17) also
speaks of the ascension as subsequent to the resurrection. Luke's
chronology has become the accepted view of the Church and has
been built into the Christian year. The one advantage of this is
that it assigns proper emphasis to each aspect of the truth. But
other NT writers seem to regard the resurrection and ascension
as different ways of affirming the same basic truth (cf. Rom. 8:34;
Col. 3:1; Phil. 2:9; 1 Tim. 3:16; and even Ac. 2:32–33). It is
possible that Eph. 1:20 also belongs to this point of view.

That the truth of the exaltation of Christ to share in God's
sovereignty should be described as his being made to **sit at God's
right hand** sounds strange to modern ears. It is a very anthropomorphic way of speaking about God, as if he were an eastern
potentate with his chief executive at his right hand, available to
share his consultations and carry out his judgments. The metaphor
seems to have been taken from Ps. 110:1: 'The LORD says to my
lord: "Sit at my right hand, till I make your enemies your foot-

stool." ' This text was soon vested with Messianic implications and is quoted at many places in the *NT*, e.g., Mk 12:36; Ac. 2:34; Heb. 1:13, and the phrase 'at the right hand of God' is applied to Jesus in several other places also, e.g., Mk 16:19; Rom. 8:34; Col. 3:1; Heb. 10:12; 1 Pet. 3:22. Indeed the psalm as a whole, and not just its first verse, exercised a wide influence on *NT* thought. It is for instance from verse 4 of the psalm that the writer to the Hebrews derived the phrase, so influential on his mode of thinking: 'a priest after the order of Melchizedek'.

In spite of the oddity of the phrase **sit at the right hand of God,** most modern translators are content to retain it. J. B.) Phillips, however, allows himself an interpretative paraphrase: 'God gave him the place of highest honour in Heaven.' Perhaps, however, the emphasis is on Jesus as God's executive power rather than to a merely honorific status.

For **in the heavenly places,** see on 1:3.

21. The writer is at pains to emphasise the total supremacy of Christ. Not only is all human life under his authority, but also every other power in the universe. In the ancient world there was a widespread belief in spiritual powers other than God himself, and the early Christians shared this belief. Some of these were good powers working under God's direction, and these were usually known as good angels. Others were in rebellion against God and as such were enemies both of God and of the human race. They are described in different ways, in terms taken from the thought-forms of that time. In the Gospels we read of Satan as the chief of the powers of evil, and of demons and evil spirits as his servants. Indeed, it appears to be assumed that the world at this time had fallen under the power of Satan and needed to be rescued (Lk. 4:6–7, 10:18, 13:16; Jn 1:31, where Satan is called 'the ruler of this world'). Paul, whose vocabulary is taken from the Hellenistic world rather than the merely Palestinian, usually avoids the word 'demons'. He does, however, recognise the reality of evil influences, which try to separate the Christian from the love of God, and at Rom. 8:38 speaks of them as angels, principalities (*archai*), and powers (*dynameis*). Similarly in 1 C. 15:24 rebellious powers which will be subdued by Christ at his second coming are called rulers (*archai*), authorities (*exousiai*), and powers (*dynameis*). In Col. 2:15 principalities (*archai*) and powers (*exousiai*) are mastered by Jesus. In Ephesians some of

this Pauline terminology is retained. It is true that the word
'Satan' does not occur, being replaced by 'devil' (4:27, 6:11),
but at Eph. 6:12 the spiritual powers hostile to man include
principalities (*archai*) and powers (*exousiai*), and here at 1:21 they
are listed as **rule** (*archai*), **authority** (*exousiai*), **power** (*dynameis*)
and **dominion** (*kyriotēs*). These correspond very closely to those
named in Col. 1:16—dominion, principalities, authorities, and
thrones—although in that context they are not specifically
characterised as evil.

All these are somewhat imprecise terms and it is futile to try to
draw any sharp distinction between them. Indeed the *RSV* varies
its translation of the words, *exousiai* being sometimes 'authority'
and sometimes 'power', and *archai* being sometimes 'principalities' and sometimes 'rule'. They must all be accepted as
names for indeterminate powers hostile to man's best interests. In
the pagan world they were often associated with the heavenly
bodies which were thought to exercise some control over the lives
of men. Whatever they were, ancient man without Christ lived in
fear of them as powers able to dominate and injure his life, and
was always trying to devise means to placate them and avert their
hostility against him. In union with Christ the Christian believed
himself to be allied with one who had proved his power to defeat
them and to protect from their malice all who entrusted themselves to him.

Those who seek to demythologise these terms from the ancient
world and to interpret them in concepts appropriate to the
changed conditions of our modern world suggest that for 'principalities and powers' we substitute such evil powers in our contemporary world as racism, nationalism, hate, fear, uncurbed
sexual desire, drug-addiction, alcoholism, etc. As with 'principalities and powers', before these the individual feels helpless,
even though he recognises their power to destroy the best things
in human life. The writer of Ephesians, however, is concerned not
to explain what these destructive powers are so much as to give
the assurance that Christ is one who is their master and who can
deliver those who trust in him from their power.

  and above every name that is named. Probably this means
those names in the ancient world which were thought to possess
divine powers—ancient deities of the Greek pantheon (e.g.,
Diana of the Ephesians), the so-called gods and goddesses who

gave their names to the various mystery religions (Isis and Osiris, etc.), and such concepts as Fate and Luck which were venerated as powerful deities. These words from Ephesians are a clear echo of Phil. 2:9 ('God bestowed on him the name which is above every name'). **not only in this age but also in that which is to come:** that is, Christ's power is supreme, on earth and beyond the earth, in the present and also in the future. Christians, perhaps taking over a manner of speech from Jewish apocalyptic, tended to speak of time as divided into two ages, the present evil-dominated age and the coming age when God would rule supreme. Christians believed that the first coming of Jesus to earth had inaugurated the new age, but it would not be completely established until the time of the second coming of Christ. The period between the first coming and the second coming was thought of as a kind of overlap between the two ages, during which the evil age still persisted side by side with the new age which had begun (cf. 1 C. 10:11, where Christians are those 'upon whom the ends of the ages have met'). The writer of Ephesians, however, is not concerned with this overlap between the ages, but only with the two ages as representing the present and the future. It is curious that he writes in this way, because in this epistle he shows no interest in the concept of the second coming. It is even possible that he is merely using conventional language for the present and the future, when his own way of thinking, influenced by Greek modes of thought, was in fact different. He usually seems to have thought 'vertically' (rather than horizontally), as though this present evil age were 'below' and the spiritual, eternal world 'above'. But whether he thought horizontally or vertically (or perhaps an unco-ordinated amalgam of the two), his words here proclaim his faith in the total authority of Christ both in the present and in the future.

22. The supremacy of Christ is further emphasised: God **has put all things under his feet.** These same words appear also at 1 C. 15:25, and represent a paraphrase of Ps. 110:1 '... till I make your enemies your footstool'. This psalm was quoted in Eph. 1:20. He **has made him the head over all things: head** is used in the sense of 'chief', as we speak of a headmaster or a head of government. The writer of Ephesians proclaims this as if it were a present fact. More realistically, the writer to the Hebrews sees it as a coming certainty not yet fully implemented: 'We do not yet see everything in subjection to him. But we see Jesus . . . crowned with glory and honour' (Heb. 2:8–9). Sometimes the certainty of the future is so spoken of as to make it sound like a reality in the present (see Rev. 11:15). In the meantime Christ's headship is not acknowledged in the world. The old age has not been finally replaced by the new. But even in this present evil age there are those who have stepped into the new age. For them Christ is even now supreme, acknowledged as such and obeyed as such. These are God's people, the Christians, the Church. For them Christ is now what he will in due time be for all men; that future hope for mankind is the present reality **for the church.** For the Church Christ is even now head over all things. Perhaps there is also the implication that the Church has in Christ one who is greater than all the powers of evil ranged against it.

The word **church** (*ekklēsia*) occurs in the Gospels only twice (Mt. 16:18; 18:17), but it is very frequent in the Pauline epistles, in Acts, and Revelation. In the LXX the Greek word is used to translate the Hebrew word *qâhâl*, which basically means a gathering of people, and may refer to the whole community of Israel. In the NT it primarily means a Christian congregation, sometimes one which meets in a particular house (Rom. 16:5), or in a particular town (1 C. 1:2). In the plural it can be used of the Christian congregations in a certain area, e.g., Galatia (Gal. 1:2) or Macedonia (2 C. 8:1). Sometimes these congregations throughout the world can be associated together as a single unit and called 'the churches of Christ' (Rom. 16:16). The phrase 'church of God' is also used, as at Gal. 1:13. Since the word *ekklēsia* can be used in a purely secular context for a company of people, it may be misleading to see any significance in the word's derivation, which in secular use seems to be ignored. But in origin the Greek word means that which is 'called out'. Since, however, the company of Christian people are sometimes called the 'elect' (*eklektoi*), those who have been selected, it may be that one of the reasons why *ekklēsia* came to be used regularly for their gatherings was the awareness that by derivation the word sounded like an equivalent of *eklektoi*.

It is commonly said that in the genuinely Pauline letters the word *ekklēsia* means only a local congregation, never the Church universal, and that it is only in Ephesians that this universal

connotation of the word appears. There are, however, indications
that Paul could think of the word in its universal sense. Some have
argued, for instance, that when he speaks of 'the church which is
at Corinth', he means, not just the local congregation, but the
universal Church in the form it takes at Corinth. Still nearer to
the universal usage is its meaning in 1 C. 15:9 where Paul says:
'I persecuted the church of Christ' (cf. also Gal. 1:13, Phil. 3:6).
Also when in 1 C. 12:28 Paul writes: 'God has appointed in the
church first apostles, second prophets, etc. . . .', the implication is
that the Church is something wider than a single congregation.
The word is used twice in Colossians, also in the universal sense,
but not all scholars treat Colossians as one of the genuinely
Pauline epistles. Col. 1:18 and 24 identify the Church with the
body of Christ. This universal sense of the word is its characteristic use in Ephesians. Indeed, in all the nine instances of the word
in this epistle (1:22; 3:10, 21; 5:23, 24, 25, 27, 29, 32) there is
not a single case where it means a local congregation. This is one
of the features of Ephesians which distinguishes it from the Pauline
letters. Here **the church** always means the universal Church
within which are included all individual churches, and which is
at the same time something more than the aggregation of the
parts.

23. The brief parenthesis **which is his body** seems to be
slipped in here without adding anything very significant to the
meaning of the whole passage. We have seen that Ephesians is
greatly dependent on Colossians, and in each of the two instances
where *ekklēsia* is used in Colossians to mean the universal Church
it is also identified as 'the body of Christ': Col. 1:18: 'He is the
head of the body, the church'; Col. 1:24: 'for the sake of his body,
that is, the church'. Eph. 1:23 has every appearance of being
derived from these, especially as the significant word *plērōma*
(**fullness**) also appears in Col. 1:18–19 as well as in Eph. 1:23.

Some scholars, however, argue that the relationship between
Ephesians and Colossians at this point is more complicated than
this. They suggest that in these two sentences in Colossians the
word 'church' did not originally occur at all, and that the word
'body' there meant the whole universe, not the church. Houlden,
for instance (p. 171), argues that at Col. 1:18 the presence of the
word 'church' spoils 'the parallelism of the lines of the hymn and
the universal scale of the vision which it otherwise presents'.

Masson also (p. 155) treats 'church' in Col. 1:18 and 1:24 as a later insertion and believes that it was transferred back into Colossians from Ephesians.

The actual phrase 'the body of Christ' occurs also in genuinely Pauline letters, though not precisely in association with the word 'church'. At Rom. 12:5 we read: 'We, though many, are one body in Christ,' and at 1 C. 12:12: 'As the body is one and has many members . . . so it is with Christ.' And at 1 C. 12:27: 'You are the body of Christ and individually members of it.' These references speak of Christ as being himself the totality of the body with individual Christians as members of it. Christ is the unifying vitality within the whole, and the Christian people the means by which the vitality expresses itself. In Ephesians, however, this concept has been modified, and perhaps not improved. Christ is no longer the totality of the body, but the head which directs the body. It is true that a homiletic use can be made of this metaphor by emphasising that if the body become separated from the head it dies. But less happily, of course, the same is true of the head separated from the body. It is, therefore, a misleading metaphor if anyone presses it beyond its immediate usefulness. The point being made in Ephesians by the metaphor of the body is not that of Romans and 1 Corinthians. There the main emphasis is on the unity and mutual inter-dependence of all the different members of the body. In Ephesians, however, the main emphasis is on the supremacy of Christ as head over his Church and the total dependence of that Church on Christ, and the need for that Church to offer total obedience to Christ. Allan aptly comments (pp. 110–11) that, for the writer of Ephesians, his concern for the Church is at the practical and spiritual level. In his devotion to the Church he surrounds it 'with a lovely halo of mystery and emotion'. 'His statements concerning the body do not help to formulate theological definitions but do deepen love and affection for the Church and inspire us to play our full part in the corporate life.'

the fullness of him who fills all in all are very difficult words to interpret. This is unfortunate because one feels that the writer intends to say something very important, but precisely what that is cannot be determined with any degree of certainty. This is because there are three items in the verse, each of which could with equal probability bear two quite different meanings.

To appreciate the full complexity of the problem a knowledge of Greek is needed. Here the best that can be done is to indicate where the difficulties lie, what the possible translations are, and to suggest a personal preference.

All commentaries give considerable space to this problematic verse, and apart from the commentaries, there are other detailed examinations of it. One important study is found in Appendix IV (pp. 167–9) in C. F. D. Moule's *Colossians and Philemon*, and a second is an article by R. Yates on 'The Re-examination of Eph. 1:23' in *ExpT* 83 (1971–2), pp. 146ff.

The three ambiguities in the verse are:

(1) The word translated **fullness** (*plērōma*) may have (*a*) an active sense and mean 'that which fills or fulfils', as, for instance, cargo in a ship or a patch on a worn garment (Mk 2:21). Or (*b*) it may have a passive significance and mean 'that which is filled', in the sense of 'its totality' (e.g., the ship plus its cargo), as it has at Col. 2:9, where, we read, that in Christ the whole 'fullness' of deity dwells bodily.

(2) The Greek word *plēroumenou* can be treated (*a*) as a participle in the middle voice, which may be translated, as in *RSV*, as **who fills**; or (*b*) it may equally be a passive form, and in that case would have to be translated as 'who is filled'.

(3) The word **fullness** (*plērōma*) in the Greek is grammatically in apposition to one of the words earlier in the sentence, a word which must be in the same case and as near as possible to it. (*a*) Almost universally it has been regarded as an apposition to the word **body**. (*b*) It can, however, be argued that the brief sentence, **which is his body,** is an aside, and not really part of the basic structure of the sentence. The word **fullness** cannot, however, be regarded as standing in apposition to the word **church,** which precedes the parenthesis, because this word is in a different case (in the Greek). The remaining alternative, therefore, is that it is in apposition to **him,** that is, Christ; so that it is Christ, and not the body (i.e., the Church) who is **the fullness of him who fills all in all.**

Competent translators by selecting different alternatives from these three ambiguities reach, in the main, four possible translations:

(i) *TEV* (similar to *RSV*) has: 'The church is Christ's body, the completion of him who himself completes all things everywhere.'

(ii) Phillips: 'The Church is his body, and in that body lives fully the One who fills the whole wide universe.'

(iii) *NEB:* '. . . his body and as such holds within it the fullness of him who himself receives the entire fullness of God.'

(iv) *NEB* footnote: '(body) and as such holds within it the fullness of him who fills the universe in all its parts.'

All these translations take **fullness** as in apposition to **body** (= Church). There is, however, the other possibility that it refers back to **him** (Christ)—the parenthesis **which is his body** being treated as an aside with no integral position in the main sentence. Although this is rarely approved, it has some points in its favour. It gives *plērōma* the same reference (i.e., to Christ) and the same meaning as that which it carries in the two parallel passages in Colossians. This cannot be regarded as decisive, since it is one of the curious facts about Ephesians that it uses important words, apparently borrowed from Colossians, with surprising changes of meaning. If, however, this way of interpreting the verse is followed, it means that it could be translated like this: 'God has made Christ head over all things (supreme head) for the Church. Christ is filled by God (as at Col. 2:9), who himself fills the whole universe. And the Church is his body (his effective instrument on earth).'

St Teresa's prayer makes an apt comment on the Church as Christ's body:

You have no body on earth but ours,
No hands but ours, no feet but ours,
Ours are the eyes showing your compassion to the world;
Ours are the feet with which you go about doing good;
Ours are the hands with which you are to bless us now.

The *RSV* translation **the fullness of him** is ambiguous, because the word **fullness** is ambiguous. If, however, it means 'that which completes', it implies that Christ is incomplete until the Church provides something which is lacking. Some expositors shrink from suggesting such an explanation, but perhaps unnecessarily. It is an incontrovertible fact that a sub-Christian

Church thwarts the work of Christ, whereas a truly Christian
community makes Christ effective, i.e., fulfils him. Paul indeed
applied the same thought to his own sufferings endured for the
cause of Christ. He dared to speak of them as 'completing'
(*antanapleroō*) what is lacking in the afflictions of Christ for the
sake of his body, that is, the Church (Col. 1:24).

It must be frankly confessed that the meaning of these concluding words in verse 23 is quite uncertain and, therefore, they
cannot legitimately be used to support any item of doctrine about
Christ or his Church.

TRANSFORMED LIVES 2:1-10

So far the epistle has been recording the great privileges of those
who are believers in Christ. In 1:3-14 they are reminded that
they have been chosen by God and by him given their purpose in
life (destined); they have come to know the meaning of God's
grace in that they have received from him redemption, forgiveness,
understanding, salvation, and the crowning gift of the Holy Spirit.
In 1:15-23 these privileges are extended to include faith, love,
hope, wisdom, and insight, a secure place in the community of
those who are to receive God's inheritance, a knowledge of Jesus
Christ risen from the dead and ruling at God's right hand, and
membership in the Church which is his body on earth.

Because the Church figures more prominently in Ephesians
than in any other epistle in the Pauline corpus (and indeed any
other book in the *NT*), and because the word here carries the
impressive meaning of the 'Church universal' rather than a local
congregation, there is a tendency to think of Ephesians as totally
absorbed in the subject of the Church. This would be a serious
error. The writer introduces the first reference to the Church
only after twenty-two verses, in which he has emphasised joyously
and confidently the great privileges of the individual Christian
who has come to know Christ and his gifts. It appears only after
this emphatic declaration of what Christian experience may mean
for the individual. The Church for this writer is effectively the
Church only when its individual, component parts are themselves
vitally alive in the Christian faith. Only then can the community
to which they belong be totally obedient to the will of God,
and happily united in mutual dependence on one another and

responsibility for one another, and fully committed to serve the purpose of Christ in the world.

The writer has introduced the subject of the Church, but is still not ready to develop it. In 2:1–10 he turns back again to the individual, to insist on the sad plight of human life lived without Christ, and the healing powers of the salvation which Christ brings. Lest his full statement in chapter 1 has left anything unsaid which ought to be said, he states again what salvation is, the way it comes to the believer (and the way it does *not* come), and what it leads to. He is proceeding to the point where he can again take up the subject of the Church and enlarge on what is meant by it; but, almost as though he fears that there may be some who think that membership in the Church is the be-all and end-all of the Christian life, he pauses to make further emphatic statements about what is meant by individual salvation. It is as though he were affirming that the only way to become a member of the Church is first of all to become a Christian. One becomes part of the Church by first becoming a believer; one does not become a Christian by joining the Church.

These ten verses are a splendid summary of Paul's teaching about what it means in one's own personal life to be a Christian. Nowhere, not even in the genuine letters, is Pauline thought more succinctly and emphatically stated. The passage contains a large number of Pauline phrases borrowed from the earlier letters, but there are instances also where Paul's thought is pungently expressed, but in words other than those used by Paul.

The first three verses emphasise the dire predicament of human life when Christ is totally absent from it, and the remaining seven verses describe the difference which the coming of Christ achieves.

1. The writer begins by reminding his readers that, though they are now Christians rejoicing in the full privilege of the Christian life, they had not always been so. He recalls what life felt like before they became Christians. Looking back they now describe that old life as a kind of death: they had been **dead through ... trespasses and sins** (a phrase taken from Col. 2:13). It is probable that in the phrase **trespasses and sins** we have another instance of the writer's love of a repetition of synonyms. Abbott-Smith describes these two words as synonyms, and in Rom. 5:12–21 they seem to be used interchangeably. By

derivation, however, the words have different origins, and some
commentators see the words as together combining two different
thoughts of sin. **trespasses** (*paraptōma*), the same word as in 1:7,
can be used to indicate a deliberate transgression of a known law.
At Rom. 5:20, for instance, it is used precisely in connexion with
the word 'law'. **sin** (*hamartia*) on the other hand means basically
to 'miss the mark'. It can be argued that the writer by **trespasses**
means doing those things which we ought not to have done, and
by **sins** leaving undone those things which we ought to have done.
But this may be reading into the words more than the writer
intended.

The consequences of sin in a human life lead to something
which can be called 'death'. This is how Paul thought: 'The
wages of sin is death' (Rom. 6:23); 'Sin came into the world
through one man and death through sin' (Rom. 5:12). This is a
reference to Adam's disobedience to a known command of God,
and in the story of Gen. 3, the word 'death' may mean actual
physical death: it was Adam's disobedience which brought death
to human beings, who otherwise would have been immortal. But
more commonly in Paul the word 'death' is used metaphorically
of spiritual and moral corruption. When he writes in Rom. 7:13,
'Sin worked death in me', he clearly means death in a spiritual
sense. This metaphorical meaning of the word is similarly found
in the words of Jesus: 'Leave the dead to bury their dead' (Mt.
8:22; cf. Lk. 15:24 and 32).

'Death' is an apt description of the results of sin: constant
repetition of evil does produce callousness (deadness) towards
others whom the sin hurts and insensitivity towards the deterioration in one's own character which follows; one's conscience becomes hardened towards actions of which it was once ashamed.
This moral degeneration is a kind of 'death': it robs men of the
sense of God's nearness and love, which is the very essence of fullness of life (Jn 17:3). The Christians for whom this epistle is
written can look back on a time in their lives when all this was
true of them. All the deterioration which accompanies careless,
wilful sinning had begun to be apparent in their lives.

The transformation which Christ produced in their lives was
the complete contrast to all this. Previously they had been 'dead'
because of sin, but now they were alive: **you he made alive.** As
'death' was a fitting description of 'then', so 'life' is the right word

D

for 'now'. Life means a new awareness of what is meant by goodness and its claim upon us, a new sense of God's nearness to us
and the peace which reconciliation with God brings, a sense that
life has now begun to be something near to what God meant it to
be: authentic, abundant life. Jesus, too, uses 'life' in this sense.
He speaks of a narrow gate which leads to life and of the need to
lose 'life' if we are to gain 'life'. In the fourth Gospel life and
eternal life are the commonest ways of describing what Christ
came to bring to men. Paul uses it constantly: to be spiritually
minded is life (Rom. 8:6); the Spirit gives life (2 C. 3:6); Christ
is our life (Col. 3:4). So in 1 Jn 5:12: he who has the Son has
life.

2. The trespasses and sins are described as those **in which you
once walked.** That is, they actually took part in them. It was
not merely that they lived among people who behaved like this.
'Walk' in the Bible indicates a way of life, a mode of conduct.

A little later the writer will indicate that one of the causes of
sinfulness lies in our own passions and desires. But here he mentions first two pressures from outside ourselves which increase the
probability of sin. His readers had followed **the course of this
world.** The outward pressures of the society within which they
lived predisposed them to evil living and demanded that they
conform to sub-Christian standards of behaviour. Abbott suggests
that 'the spirit of the age' would be a good translation for **course
of this world.** In the *NT*, **world** can mean the whole of creation
as God made it and as he loves it (Jn 3:16). Or it can mean the
world as it has become, alienated from God, hostile to him, and
poisoned with evil. In this sense of the word the Christian is called
upon to be on his guard lest he become 'conformed to the world'
(Rom. 12:2). Our own inward tendencies to evil are in themselves difficult enough to resist, but when these are reinforced by
the pressures of the evil world about us the difficulties are im-
measurably increased. For instance, some degree of racial prejudice affects all of us, but it is much harder to master if the whole
of the society in which we life approves and encourages that
prejudice. It is never easy to be scrupulously honest, but it is in-
finitely harder in a situation where honesty is laughed at and
even regarded as disloyalty to the group where it is practised by
common consent. Sexual purity is not easy to maintain, but it is
harder than ever if you have to live in a community where

chastity is sneered at as a sign of weakness or timidity or un-
friendliness.

The word here translated **course** is the Greek *aiōn*. Some argue
that this word, literally-meaning 'age' or 'period', had come in
some contemporary forms of religion to represent a deity: the
Aion of the world. If so, the next phrase would be in apposition
to it. This Aion would be further described as **the prince of the
power of the air.** It is improbable that the writer intended this.

The Christian's struggle against evil, however, is not here
thought of as a straight-forward conflict between man's own
moral strength and the pressures of the evil world about him. The
writers of the *NT* without exception are aware of another dimension of evil. Reference has already been made to supernatural
forces of evil actively hostile to man's true welfare and to God's
purpose for him. In 1:21 they are called 'rule, authority, power,
and dominion'. They re-appear in 6:11–12 as 'principalities and
powers', where their leader, the symbol of their total strength, is
named as the devil. Elsewhere this master of evil is called Satan,
and in the Gospels he is the active cause of both sickness and evil,
the one who stirs men up with enmity against Jesus and perverts
even the closest friends of Jesus (Lk. 22:3; Mk 8:33). In Ephesians
also man is beset by 'the wiles of the devil' (6:12). Here he is
called **the prince of the power of the air** (cf. Jn 12:31: 'the
prince of this world'). The word **prince** sounds a bit archaic, but
the Greek word simply means 'ruler', and not necessarily a royal
personage. The word **air** is used to indicate the area between the
earth, where man disobeyed and sinned, and the highest heaven,
where God ruled with unquestioned authority. In the ancient
world this intermediate area was thought of as the home of all
kinds of spirits, many of which were evil. Indeed in Eph. 6:12
these evil spirits operate even as high as 'the heavenly places'
themselves. All these evil forces have suffered a decisive defeat at
the hands of Christ (Eph. 1:21–22; Col. 2:15), and those who
have learned to put their trust in him do not need any longer to
fear these powers. But those who do not know Christ and his
power are at their mercy, as the readers of this epistle well remember. This power of evil is further described as **the spirit that
is now at work in the sons of disobedience. sons of disobedience** is a Hebrew mode of expression meaning those who
are disobedient to God. Similar phrases are everywhere in the *NT*,

e.g., 'sons of this world' and 'sons of light' in Lk. 16:8. *NEB*
translates the phrase as 'God's rebel subjects'.

3. Among these we all once lived. As in other places in this
epistle there is an unexplained switch from 'you' (2:1–2) to **we.**
A similar change was noted in 1:11–23. The explanation seems
to be that the writer, although he writes in the name of Paul, is
aware that in many ways he is also totally identified with those to
whom he writes. What was true of them in pre-Christian days was
true also of him. He feels himself as included both in 'we' and 'you'.
It is not likely here that 'you' means Gentiles and 'we' means
Jews, though that may be true in some passages. What is said in
the words following is not more applicable to Jews than to
Gentiles—rather the reverse. Nor can the change of pronoun
within verse 5 be so explained. For this interchanging between
'you' and 'we' in pseudonymous letters, see Mitton (*EE*, pp.
225–7) and compare Heb. 13:20–21. The addition of the word
all gives particular emphasis to the identification of writer and
readers. **Among these** has more than local significance. It does
not mean merely that they all lived in the same neighbourhood,
but that they all shared this same kind of life. So *NEB*: 'We too
were of their number.' What characterised them all was that they
lived in the passions of the **flesh.** In 2:2 the writer has named
two forces which pressurised their pre-Christian lives towards evil:
one was the constant demand that they should conform to the
environment in which they lived, and the other was the spiritual
powers of evil against which, in their pre-Christian days, they had
had no means of defence. But both these external forces of evil
exercise their power largely because there are within the human
personality other forces on whose support they can rely. These
form, as it were, a kind of 'fifth column' on the inside, a traitor
within the gates, who will open to the invaders. This element is
described in true Pauline fashion as coming from **the flesh.** By
passions of our flesh is meant feelings, appetites, and desires
which arise from 'the flesh'.

Sometimes in the *NT*, and indeed in Paul's writings, the word
flesh is used in a neutral way to mean the physical aspect of
human nature: e.g., 'Flesh and blood cannot inherit the kingdom
of God' (1 C. 15:50); 'The Word became flesh' (Jn 1:14). But
very commonly in Paul's writings it is used to describe those
elements within human nature which most readily resist God's

rule and ally themselves with evil. It is often linked with 'desires' or 'passions' as here (cf. Rom. 7:5, 13:14). In conventional usage **passions of the flesh** tend to be identified with what are called 'physical appetites', such as an undue preoccupation with food, drink, and sex, leading to gluttony, drunkenness, and fornication. But when Paul speaks of the sins of the flesh he means a much wider range of evil than that. Among the 'works of the flesh' in Gal. 5:19–20 the gratification of these physical appetites is certainly included; they lead to 'fornication, impurity, indecency, drinking bouts and orgies' (as *NEB* translates). But also included as 'works of the flesh' are various feelings and attitudes which arise from the human impulse to self-aggrandisement, and from the rivalries and hostilities which result when this is thwarted: selfish ambition, envy, jealousy, fits of rage, a contentious temper, and also those community ills to which these things lead, such as quarrels, dissensions, and party intrigues. The list also includes idolatry and sorcery, devices for inducing the forces of the universe to forward one's own interests.

Here the writer clearly wishes to emphasise that 'sins of the flesh' include more than merely excessive physical appetites by adding a phrase which amplifies what has already been said: **following the desires of body and mind.** The introduction of the word **mind** indicates this. Henry Drummond used to distinguish between 'sins of the body' and 'sins of the disposition' (and to insist that the latter were every bit as evil, even if more respectable). By sins of the disposition (or the **mind**) are meant those sins which we listed in the second group, i.e., those springing from a desire for self-aggrandisement. For Paul, however, as for this writer, they are all sins of 'the flesh'.

The description of the writer and his readers in their pre-Christian days is summed up in the words: **and so we were by nature children of wrath.** The word **wrath** is left without any further definition. It is not precisely called 'the wrath of God'. By doing this the writer follows Paul's usage. In Romans the 'wrath' is mentioned eleven times, but only once (at 1:18) is it called 'the wrath of God' (although the *RSV* misleadingly translates 'the wrath of God' at Rom. 5:9, 12:19 and 13:5, though in the Greek the words 'of God' do not occur). Dodd noted this in his commentary on Romans, and associated with it the fact that Paul never 'uses the verb "to be angry" with God as subject'. He argued from these two facts that 'wrath' for Paul was largely the law of retribution built into the very fabric of the universe. It is not so much a surge of anger on God's part against some particular human sin, but rather his age-long persistent opposition to sin, represented by his making a universal law that sin always produces evil consequences. Dodd described it as 'an inevitable process of cause and effect in a moral universe'. That is, 'we reap what we sow'. Usually in Paul it describes a process continuously at work at the present time, so that one can see its consequences in progressive moral deterioration (Rom. 1:18–32); sometimes, however, it can be 'the wrath to come' (as in 1 Th. 1:10), where it means the final punishment of sinners at the last judgment. The 'wrath of God' is therefore the counterpart, the dark shadow, of the truth that all God's commands are 'for our good' (as in Dt. 10:13; cf. Jer. 32:38, where the prophet speaks of those who 'fear God' as acting 'for their own good and the good of their children after them'). To disobey God's commands is to miss this good and instead to choose the very evil which the commands are there to guard us against. 'The fear of the Lord' is therefore the recognition of the fact of this wrath, and of the truth that to disobey God inevitably brings evil consequences upon man. (At Eph. 5:6 the full phrase 'wrath of God' is used, borrowed from Col. 3:6. There too it is used in association with the word 'disobedience', as here.)

Whether 'wrath' is taken as a personal attitude of God towards the sinner, or as a process of retribution which God has built into the structure of the universe, it still has its source in God. The phrase 'wrath of God' has become a standardised phrase, but in fact the word **wrath** here is simply a translation of the Greek word *orgē*, which in other contexts is translated as 'anger', e.g., Mk 3:5; Jas 1:19–20. **wrath,** though just another word for 'anger', is no longer used in modern English, and has come to be reserved almost entirely for this archaic phrase 'the wrath of God'. Modern translators of the *NT* find difficulty in deciding what word to use for it. The ordinary translation of the Greek *orgē*, anger, seems almost out of place when applied to God. In human life anger is so commonly an evil thing that it seems improper to ascribe it to God. *The Jerusalem Bible*, however, frankly translates *orgē* here as 'God's anger'. Knox prefers 'God's displeasure', and *NEB* paraphrases as 'the dreadful judgment of God'. Understandably, however, Phillips, *TEV*, and *RSV* keep the familiar word 'wrath', in spite of its archaic sound.

children of wrath is another instance of the Hebraic idiom like 'sons of disobedience' in 2:1. 'Sons of disobedience' means people whose lives are marked by disobedience. So **children of wrath** means people in whose lives you can see the effect of **wrath,** that is, the punishment that follows sin, the evil consequences of sin. Some commentators, however, prefer a variant translation: 'people worthy of God's wrath', that is, living in such a way that, if they get their dues, God's punishment will in due time fall upon them. This is a possible meaning, because parallel phrases can be quoted from the *OT*. For instance, the phrase 'sons of stripes', a literal translation of the Hebrew words in Dt. 25:2, is rendered in the Greek Septuagint as 'those worthy of stripes'.

by nature has been claimed as a text which gives support to the doctrine of original sin. It is improbable, however, that the writer had this thought in mind. He is rather making the factual statement that before these Christians were converted, their actions, when they did just what they felt like doing, 'doing what comes naturally', were sinful. It is a sad fact of human life that if we were left to ourselves to do whatever we felt like doing (that is, acting 'by nature') we should continually do evil things. As Paul put it in Rom. 8:7, 'the mind that is set on the flesh is hostile to God'. Gentiles, unlike Jews, did not have the benefit of the restraining influence of the law. These Gentile Christians remember the time when they followed unchecked their own 'natural' appetites and impulses and in this careless way of life were **like the rest of mankind.**

Verses 1–3, therefore, describe the plight of those who lived in the Gentile world before Christ began to claim and shape their lives. In 4–10 the writer goes on to describe the change which Christ has made in these Christians—the remedy he has provided, how it has been applied to their need, and the consequent change in the quality of their lives.

In verses 1–3 the writer has been describing the plight of those whose lives are dominated by evil forces they cannot withstand, a condition which both he and his readers remember as their own experience before they became Christians. Now he describes the change which God through Christ has brought about. Those who interpret Ephesians as a baptismal liturgy suggest that these verses (4–10) served as the response of the candidate for baptism.

4. As in the whole of the opening section of the epistle, God is acknowledged as the sole author of this transformation, and the motive which prompted his action was not a wish to reward goodness and honest endeavour, but because he is **rich in mercy.** **mercy** is one of several words used by this writer to describe the outgoing love of God to those who in no way deserve it. Grace has already been used (1:6–7), and **love** appears in this same sentence. The Christian can see no explanation of this unbelievably wonderful thing which has happened to him except that God has generously given it to him, in spite of the plain fact that there has been nothing in him to merit it. There can be no other cause of it than the sheer goodness of God—**the great love with which he loved us.** The word **love** has already been ascribed to God at 1:5. It is the word used in the *NT* to describe the essential nature of God, which is most clearly seen in what he did for the good of mankind in Jesus (1 Jn 4:10).

5, 6. God, **even when we were dead through our trespasses, made us alive:** These words are repeated from 2:1, though the 'you' of verse 1 now somewhat oddly becomes the **we** of verse 5. The translation 'God made us alive' at 2:1 inadequately represents the Greek verb, whose full meaning is brought out in verse 5: God **made us alive together with Christ.** What has happened to **us** is seen as in some degree a participation in the resurrection of Christ.

Paul in his writings used many compound verbs beginning with the Greek preposition *syn-* (together with) to indicate the Christian's association or identification with Christ. The Christian dies *with* Christ (Rom. 6:8; Phil. 3:10), is crucified *with* Christ (Gal. 2:20; Rom. 6:6), is buried *with* Christ (Rom. 6:4; Col. 2:12), is raised *with* Christ (Col. 2:12), and lives *with* Christ (Rom. 6:8). The writer of Ephesians takes over some of these, e.g., **God ... made us alive together with Christ, raised us up with him, and made us sit with him in heavenly places.** Here he does not speak of 'dying' with Christ, perhaps because he has just used the word 'dead' in a different sense, to describe the effect of sin upon us. Nor does he seem to intend any distinction between the verb he **made us alive** (used also at Col. 2:13) and he **raised us up with** Christ (2:6; used also at Col. 3:1). Sometimes the 'resurrection' which the Christian shares with Christ consists of his triumph over physical death (1 C. 15:22), but here it is a symbolic resurrection (as at Rom. 6:8; Col. 2:12, 3:1) from the spiritual 'death' brought about by sin into a new quality of life shared with Christ. It describes a spiritual transformation available to the Christian *now* in this life. This privilege of the Christian is further described: God **made us sit with him in the heavenly places in Christ Jesus.** The verb 'made to sit' is the same as that used in 1:20 to describe Christ's own exaltation to God's right hand, except that there it is not compounded with *syn-* (together with). Here, however, the compound verb is used, because the Christian is given this privilege, not in his own right, but because of his identification with Christ. It is not said, however, that the Christian is made to sit 'at God's right hand'. That is Christ's unique place of privilege. The Christian 'sits with Christ'.

It is difficult to assess what the writer meant by this expression, largely because the tense of the verb is in the past (*made* **us sit**) and therefore refers to something which has already happened. In the Gospels there are similar phrases with reference to the future: 'In my kingdom you will sit on thrones judging the twelve tribes of Israel' (Lk. 22:30; Mt. 19:28). James and John asked to 'sit' at Christ's right and left hand in his glory and were reminded that only God could give that privilege (Mk 10:37-40). Men will come from the ends of the earth and 'sit at table in the kingdom of God' (Lk. 13:29). But all those are promises for the future, apparently beyond this earthly dispensation. Here the tense refers to what has already happened. Some scholars are so sure that this phrase (about being made to sit in heavenly places) could not refer to anything which has already happened, that they devise means of giving it a future reference (in spite of the past tense of the verb). They argue that it means that their places in heaven have been already assigned to them, and their future is, therefore, so secure that it can be spoken of as something which has already taken place. 'He made us sit' is taken to mean 'he has assigned for us places' in heaven. In order to be consistent those who take this point of view also argue the same about 'he raised us up'. The resurrection, though it still lies in the future, is referred to in a past tense because the future resurrection has already been guaranteed to us and so is sure (so Masson, p. 16).

But we have already seen that the resurrection here refers to the
spiritual experience into which the readers have already entered,
and since 'he made us sit' seems to be entirely parallel to 'he raised
us up', it is reasonable to assume that they refer to the same
period of time. If so, we are compelled to understand the phrase
as a vivid pictorial way of describing nearness to God now and
enjoyment of God's presence, which is, as it were, an anticipation
of the life of heaven. The word **sit** perhaps applies to the sharing
of a common meal rather than occupying a throne (as in Lk.
13:29). As such it suggests that the Christian finds himself, as it
were, an honoured guest, or an adopted member of the family,
in God's household, not just one who waits at table. This interpretation is open to the accusation of being very like what
Christian Gnostics claimed for themselves—that they fully
possessed here and now what other Christians hoped for in the
future. But that does not mean that it has to be rejected. The
writer may be daringly appropriating Gnostic phrases at this
point, because they represent a real aspect of the truth. He does
not need to fear the charge of undue sympathy towards Gnosticism, because in his later emphasis on the Church and the importance of Christian conduct he will reveal an understanding of
the Christian faith sharply at variance with that professed by the
Gnostics. **in the heavenly places** is a phrase already used at
1:13 and 20. Here we understand it as a vivid phrase to mean
'in God's presence'.

The sentence has already affirmed the Christian's very close
relationship to Christ: he is alive with him, raised with him, and
made to sit with him. There is further emphasis on this in the
closing phrase of the sentence: **in Christ Jesus.** This may mean,
as in Paul's usage, 'all this has come about because of your total
identification and union with Christ'. Or it may, more practically,
be just a means of asserting once again that the agent of all this is
Christ, as if it affirmed: All this has come about only through
Christ.

We have so far ignored the parenthesis slipped in at the end of
2:5: **by grace you have been saved.** At that point it seemed to
interrupt the flow of the sentence, and it is reaffirmed and amplified in verse 8, where it is the central affirmation of a very important sentence. A full consideration of it, therefore, will be left
till verse 8. Here it is sufficient to say that by slipping the words in

here, in a kind of anticipatory way, the writer is reminding
readers of two points already well emphasised: (*a*) All the privileges listed in chapter 1 and the new life affirmed in 2 : 1–5 are
ours only by the grace of God; but (*b*) they are already securely
ours now, not just promises for the future. The word 'save' is here
in the perfect passive tense, and in Greek this emphasises two
things: that something has happened and that what has happened
continues to be true. 'You have entered into salvation' would
indicate both these meanings. Perhaps a third point is worth
noting—that this new life may be described as 'salvation'.

7. the coming ages is open to different interpretations.
Usually in the *NT* there is a contrast between this present age and
the coming age (as at Mk 10:30), and the coming age is that
which will follow the end of this present dispensation (see Eph.
1:21). Some scholars insist that in this context also **the coming
ages** (even though **ages** is plural) must mean either that which
lies beyond human death, or that which begins when this present
age ends with the second coming of Christ. This assigning of an
other-worldly meaning to **the coming ages** is often associated
with the view that the tenses in verses 5 and 6, though past, must
be given a future reference. There are difficulties in this interpretation, however. It is a considerable *tour de force* to claim a
future significance for these past tenses; and also in Ephesians
there does not appear to be any anticipation of a second coming
which will end this present era; moreover, the phrase **coming
ages** is plural, and when it is applied to the age beyond death it is
usually in the singular, meaning the coming age in contrast to
the present age. It is, therefore, simpler to interpret the phrase to
mean 'the coming generations' of Christians. So Phillips translates
'for all time', and *TEV* 'for all time to come'. God has accomplished for these first generations of Christians what, in consequence, all future generations will be able to make their own.
This interpretation would not fit easily into Paul's way of thinking.
For him the second coming of Christ was soon to usher in a new
age. But it is quite appropriate to the writer of Ephesians. He
sees the Church facing a continuing task on earth; the second
coming and the end of this present era are no longer the imminent
certainty that once they seemed to be. It is part of this writer's
importance that he not only re-presents the essence of Paul's
teaching, but where the form of it is no longer applicable to

changed times, he re-interprets it. Here he tells his readers that
what God has done for them is not only for themselves, but in
them God has demonstrated what he is ready to do for every
subsequent generation of men. God has done all this for them in
order **that in the coming ages he might show the immeasurable riches of his grace in kindness towards us in
Christ Jesus.** The word translated **kindness** is another term,
like grace, mercy, and love, which emphasises God's utter goodness to man. If one presses the precise meaning of this word, it
indicates an attitude towards others of sympathetic consideration
for their welfare and a willingness to adapt one's own behaviour
to their individual needs.

8–10. These three verses are an inspired summary of Paul's
evangelical theology. Allan aptly describes them as 'Paul's
gospel in a nutshell'. It is, however, the whole of these three verses,
not just the opening few words in verse 8, which merits this description. In them are brought together the main features of what
is meant by salvation: God's part in it and man's part; the right
and wrong ways of trying to secure it; its practical outcome in
daily conduct.

The word **grace** (already used five times in this epistle, and to
be used six times more) finds its classic expression here. It is a
word which Paul made peculiarly his own (though other writers
in the *NT* do occasionally use it also). The present writer has discussed it in *The Interpreter's Dictionary of the Bible.* Before Christian
times it had been an ordinary word meaning pleasantness, favour,
gratitude. Paul seized upon it and endowed it with such special
Christian content that he could use it to express the very heart of
the Gospel. He used it to describe God's action towards man, first
of all in his gift of Jesus Christ to the unworthy race of men, and
then in his offer to them of salvation through Christ. Grace
is utter generosity, unselfish, spontaneous, recklessly prodigal
generosity, which acts wholly out of loving concern for the other's
need, even if he is completely unworthy of the love and help thus
offered to him. This grace is primarily found in God, but it may
equally well be spoken of as 'the grace of our Lord Jesus Christ'.
God is its source; Jesus Christ is the means by which it is con-
veyed to man. In a sense, of course, there is no such thing as
grace in the abstract, but only God acting graciously. It was
God's grace which led to his gracious act in bringing Christ to

live among men; it is God's grace mediated to man through Christ which brings life and salvation to undeserving man. Because through grace there come to man blessings which he usually tries to achieve by his own endeavours, but with no success, we find that in Paul's letters it is often contrasted with words which imply man's self-directed effort, such as obedience to the law, or 'works of the law'. It is the very essence of Paul's gospel that man is justified by God's grace, and not by his own meticulous fulfilment of religious rules and regulations.

Grace, however, is not just an attitude of indulgent kindness on God's part towards sinful man, a forgiving disregard of his sins. It does bring forgiveness, but with it comes also a vigorous enabling power by which evil in man is overcome and weakness in man can be reinforced. It was God's grace which called and equipped Paul for his work (1 C. 15:9–10) and which enabled him to overcome personal difficulties which threatened to overwhelm and crush him (2 C. 12:9). So powerful is God's grace in its action upon man that it has sometimes been represented that when God acts man cannot do other than submit. This, however, is not as Paul understood it. God's grace does not override man's freedom of decision and action. Man can defy God's grace (Gal. 2:21), defeat it (2 C. 6:1), and fall from it (Gal. 5:4). Indeed it is only as man responds to God's grace in faith that God's grace can be fully effective in his life.

It is **by grace you have been saved through faith.** The writer deliberately places grace prominently at the front in order to give it special emphasis. The order of the words would almost entitle one to translate it as: 'It is entirely by grace that you have been saved.' Grace is God's initiative. Faith is man's response. This stress on God as the sole source of man's salvation suggests that the writer may well have found himself having to oppose and correct in his fellow Christians a tendency to adopt a moralistic attitude towards God. He writes to bring them back to an appreciation of the gospel as utterly the free gift of God to man.

8. It is by the gracious action of God that **you have been saved.** The preceding part of the epistle makes clear what the writer means by salvation. It is a comprehensive word to include all such aspects of Christian experience as redemption, forgiveness, the gift of the Holy Spirit, knowledge of God, new life through Christ, and hope. These are all qualities of life into which the readers have already entered. There is, of course, a future dimension in salvation, but here the writer is stressing those aspects of salvation which have already been given to them; the reality of salvation is very present with them. That is why the writer chooses to use this unexpected tense of the verb 'to save'. It is the perfect passive tense and in the Greek means: 'You have entered into salvation and are still in present enjoyment of it.' The tense clearly indicates two things: the reality of a definite starting point in the past and the continuing validity in the present of what then happened.

It can be argued that this is quite unlike Paul's way of speaking about salvation. Certainly he does not use the word 'save' in this particular tense. Paul nearly always used it in the future tense (thirteen times, in fact); three times he uses a present tense ('you are being saved') and only once an aorist passive, meaning 'you were saved' (referring to some precise moment in the past). This aorist passive could refer either to the moment of conversion or possibly to the death of Christ, when the means of salvation was made available. In the main, however, Paul's use of the word 'save' is related to the future, and usually to a future beyond death or beyond the end of the world. This tallies with some uses of the noun 'salvation', as at Rom. 13:11 where the apostle says: 'Salvation is nearer to us than when we first believed.' It is, however, very difficult to deny something of a present meaning in such contexts as Rom. 10:10 and 2 C. 6:2.

Here, however, in Ephesians salvation is an inclusive word embracing all that Paul meant by such expressions as justification, reconciliation, adoption, etc. These can definitely be spoken of by Paul in the past tense as having already happened (Rom. 5:1; 2 C. 5:18; Rom. 8:15), though this does not exclude a large element of 'more to come'. For instance, at Rom. 8:23 'adoption' is something to 'wait for' although at Rom. 8:15–16 it is a present privilege. So with salvation it has begun, is now continuing, and is to be completed in the future. But it is the first two of these aspects that the writer wishes to emphasise here: the fact that salvation is something they have entered upon and now are aware of. So he uses this unusual tense to make sure that both these aspects are unmistakably underlined. This emphatic way of stating his conviction leaves the impression that in the community to which he writes there are those who are questioning the reality of

the present dimension of salvation and thinking of it merely as a
hope for the future.

It is perhaps worth noting that this writer is not the only one
in the *NT* to use the word 'save' in the perfect tense. It is found
also in the Synoptic Gospels, usually of physical healing, as at
Mk 5:34, 10:52, and Lk. 17:19, but also of spiritual health in
Lk. 7:50 ('your faith has saved you').

It is to be noted, however, that when Paul uses the word 'save',
it is not in any instance associated with 'grace' or 'faith'. It is the
word 'justify' which pre-eminently has these associations. 'Justify'
and 'justification' are words which Paul uses much more frequently than 'save' and 'salvation', although in fact their use is
restricted to the three letters, Romans, 1 Corinthians, and Galatians. He writes in Romans: 'they are justified *by his grace* as a gift
(3:24); 'a man is justified *by faith*' (3:28); and in 3:22 'the
righteousness of God' (i.e., justification) is '*through faith*'—a combination of 'grace' and 'faith' very similar to that in Eph. 2:8. So
what Paul said about justification in Rom. 3 serves as the pattern
for what this writer says about salvation: **by grace you have
been saved** (justified) **through faith.** 'Justification' has a
Hebrew background and would not readily be understood by
Gentiles, whereas the word 'save' was part of the common religious vocabulary of that time. For this writer 'salvation' includes
what Paul meant by 'justification', which is roughly equivalent
to what in Eph. 1:7 is called 'redemption through his blood' and
'the forgiveness of trespasses according to the riches of his grace'.
It is part of this writer's skill as an interpreter that he can convey
the meaning of a Pauline doctrine so that the readers will understand what Paul intended, even though Paul's actual words may
have to be modified.

This salvation, made ours by the generous action of God in
Jesus Christ, is appropriated **through faith. faith,** like grace, is
a word to which Paul gave his own special significance, and this
writer of Ephesians fully grasped the inner meaning of it. Sometimes in the *NT* the word is used at a level lower than its full
significance for Paul, for instance, to mean intellectual assent to a
proposition, or loyalty to a person; sometimes 'the faith' stands
for 'Christianity', and Christians are those who have faith (believers). But its most characteristic use in Paul is to indicate an
attitude of complete openness to God so that God may do with

us what he will, whether it be rebuking, commanding, healing, or enabling. It implies a total abandonment of self to God, 'handing oneself over to Jesus Christ', or 'a complete surrender to him' (two phrases borrowed from Bonsirven). It implies (i) a willingness to receive the benefits God wants to give us; and (ii) a readiness to obey whatever God commands. Sometimes it is the former of these two elements which is prominent, sometimes the latter.

There is a sense in which even faith itself is a gift from God. Paul writes in Phil. 1:29: 'It has been granted to you that . . . you should . . . believe.' Certainly not only Paul but all Christians who have come into the faith by an experience of conversion have a deep sense that the change which has come to them is not at all their own doing. Even their power to accept what is offered seems to be given them from outside rather than worked up from within. It is all God's doing, God's **gift** from beginning to end. Our part has been simply to stop resisting God and let him have his way, and even this power to abandon resistance has been made possible by God. There is a certain passivity in faith. Brunner describes faith as 'the readiness to allow oneself to be given salvation by God' (*Commentary on Romans*, p. 89).

There is, however, another element in faith, an active element, something which man must offer, something too which he can withhold. There is that in man which can frustrate the grace of God. Faith implies at any rate the readiness not 'to nullify God's grace'. It includes a willingness not only to receive the gift but also to follow where God's grace leads, that is, obedience. Brunner indeed almost seems to contradict his earlier definition of faith when he seeks to do justice to this element: 'Faith is obedience, nothing else—literally nothing else than obedience.' However, would it not be nearer the truth to say that faith is, not so much obedience, as the willingness to be made obedient?

In this verse it is (i), the first of these two component parts of faith, which is emphasised, when the writer insists: **this is not your own doing, it is the gift of God. faith** is the willingness to receive that gift. Some commentators have argued that here the word **gift** is meant to describe 'faith' rather than 'salvation'. *The Living Bible*, for instance, translates 'even trusting is . . . a gift of God'. But the form of the Greek makes it difficult to place this interpretation upon it. What the Greek indicates is that the whole process of salvation (**by grace . . . through faith**) is something which we do not do for ourselves; God does it for us. But he acts through man's faith. It is as though faith were the channel through which God's grace is poured into our lives. Lest, however, any believer should begin to think that his faith is the central factor, achieving his own salvation, the writer states explicitly: **this is not your own doing.** Paul did not use this precise wording in his letters. Often those to whom he wrote had a Jewish background and themselves made their points in Jewish turns of phrase. In that context Paul could insist that a man is not justified 'from works of the law', i.e., from what he does in keeping the rules of morality. But this writer knows that his Gentile readers would not understand such a phrase as 'works of the law', and so he wisely finds the nearest equivalent to it in Greek terminology. So he writes: **this is not your own doing, it is the gift of God.** Grace, mercy, love, kindness, have all been used already in verses 4–7 to describe the generous act of God. Here the word **gift** is added, a word which Paul was glad to use on many occasions in a similar context (see Rom. 5:15–17; 2 C. 9:15). The writer then makes the same point in different words: It is **not because of works** (*NEB* has: 'not a reward for work done', which gives the meaning well). Again the writer avoids Paul's standard phrase 'the works of the law', retaining only **works** without any reference to law. 'Works' by itself to the Gentile reader means 'what we do', and he would understand that salvation is the gift of God and not achieved by 'what we do'. If salvation could be achieved by man by what he did, by obedience to a code of rules or exceptional holiness of life, then its achievement might become a ground for some measure of self-congratulation and pride—the sin of the Pharisee (cf. Lk. 18:11). But pride in the presence of God is a most objectionable sin. If salvation could be achieved in that way, it would create sin rather than release men from it. So in God's good providence it is wholly the gift of God and not dependent on what man may do, **lest any man should boast. boast** is not a wholly satisfactory translation, since in English the word usually refers to boastful *words*. It really describes the attitude of mind—self-congratulation and pride—which may lie behind boastful words. The word occurs so often in Paul's writings that one is aware that he recognises in it his own besetting sin, against which, even as a Christian, he must constantly be on the alert. As a *Pharisee*, he had longed not only for salvation, but that kind of salvation in which he could feel that he himself had taken a major role. He wanted salvation; but he wanted also to be able to feel he had gained it on merit. As a *Christian*, he had to acknowledge, at first with humiliation, later with gratitude, that he himself had contributed nothing to his salvation, except to accept as a gift the salvation God offered.

For we are his workmanship. *NEB* renders this in more modern idiom: 'We are God's handiwork.' In the Greek, however, it is the word 'his' (i.e., 'God's') which stands first and carries the emphasis, as though it meant: It is God (not we ourselves) who has made us Christians (cf. Paul's 'By the grace of God I am what I am' in 1 C. 15:10). **We are ... created in Christ Jesus.** The reference is not to our natural birth, but to re-birth, or re-creation, as implied in the new life of 2:5. There is a recollection here of 2 C. 5:17–18: 'If any one is in Christ, he is a new creation.' Again, the phrase 'in Christ' could mean either 'through our inward unity with Christ' or 'by the power of Christ'.

The writer has repeatedly emphasised that everything about this salvation is ours only as the gift of God. He now turns to the second element in salvation—our willingness to be commanded, directed, and shaped by God, as well as healed and restored by him, the willingness to obey what we know to be God's will for us as we have seen it in Christ. Some evangelical movements have allowed this stern moral element in salvation to be underrated and in consequence have evaporated into sentimentalism. It is not easy to keep in proper balance these two elements in faith: receptiveness before God and active obedience to God. Usually one aspect is stressed at the expense of the other. Luther, whose tendency was always to give special prominence to the givenness of salvation (since this was the aspect of truth largely neglected in the average Christianity of his day), nevertheless knew how indispensable is this second element. He wrote: 'Faith is a living restless thing: it cannot be inoperative; we are not saved by works, but if there are no works, there must be something amiss with faith.' T. W. Manson summed it up well by saying that works are a requisite of faith, though not a pre-requisite. We are not saved by works, but we are saved **for good works.** Faith is not true faith unless it 'works through love' (Gal. 5:6). God does not intend that the saved Christian should luxuriate in his inward experiences, but, in the strength of his new-found health, offer himself in total and glad obedience to the will of God. Jesus put it very plainly: 'Not everyone who says to me, "Lord, Lord," shall enter the kingdom of heaven, but he who does the will of my Father' (Mt. 7:21).

This same insistence on 'doing God's will' is here in 2:10. We were given this new life, the writer insists, that it may be used **for good works. good works** is not a characteristic Pauline phrase, though he does speak, with approval, of a 'good work' (in the singular). 'Works' in the plural are in Paul's writings self-directed endeavours to keep rules in order to gain personal merit, and as such are suspect. 'Good works', however, frequently appear in post-Pauline writings (such as the Pastoral epistles, where the phrase is found eight times; cf. also Mt. 5:16), where it means 'acts of love' (rather than mere rule-keeping). In fact, at Heb. 10:24 the author urges the readers to 'stir up one another to love and good works', as though 'love' and 'good works' were virtually synonymous. It is 'works' in this sense which for James were inseparable from true justification. It means 'showing mercy' as in the parable of the good Samaritan, or offering friendship and practical help to the hungry and thirsty, the outsider and convicted criminal, those who are ill and inadequately clothed (as in the parable of the sheep and the goats, Mt. 25:44).

These **good works** are then described as the actions **which God prepared beforehand, that we should walk in them.** It would be treating the words too literally to say that this means that God has prepared each good work in advance so that we may practise it. Rather, it means that God's intention from the very beginning (in bringing salvation into the world in Christ) was that people should be enabled to rise above love of self and give themselves in love for others and in practical concern for their welfare. *NEB* represents this well: '. . . good deeds, for which God has designed us'. The final phrase about our 'walking in them' reminds us that fine phrases or eloquent sermons about love are not what is required, but the actions, costly actions, which express in practical conduct the love which God's saving power has created in our hearts.

Although these verses, 2:8–10, so admirably express in summary the essence of Paul's gospel, several expressions are used in them which are not characteristic of Paul. These are:

(1) The use of 'salvation' in place of 'justification', and its close association with 'grace' and 'faith'; and the use of the perfect passive tense to mean 'you have been saved'.

(2) The phrase 'not from yourselves' as an interpretation of 'not from works'.

(3) The use of the phrase 'good works' to mean deeds of love and mercy (not just keeping rules) which is characteristic of the post-Pauline writings.

We have interpreted these features as indicative of an author, other than Paul, who brilliantly presents Paul's essential teaching, and at the same time the more effectively conveys the apostle's meaning to a new generation of readers by his readiness to vary the form of words which Paul had used many years before when writing to readers of a very different kind.

UNITY IN CHRIST 2:11–22

In chapter 1 the writer has enumerated the many personal privileges of the believer. He writes in the name of Paul, and when at 1:12 he writes 'we who first hoped in Christ', the 'we' seems to refer to Jewish Christians, among whom was Paul. In verses 1:13, 18, etc., the readers are addressed as 'you', but there is nothing to suggest that they are Gentile Christians, as opposed to Jewish, until 2:1. Even then it is not explicit until 2:11, when they are spoken of as **you Gentiles in the flesh.** This is a deliberate reference to the fact that within the Christian community are included people of both Jewish and non-Jewish origin. Jews and Gentiles were usually totally incompatible, incapable of being fused into a single corporate life. Here, therefore, is the recognition of a problem which is social as well as individual. From this point the whole emphasis of the epistle moves away from the privileges of the Christian as an individual to the privileges of the community which is made up of Christians of different racial origin. This awareness of the corporate nature of the Christian faith now becomes prominent. But it is the fact that all as individuals, whatever their background, now share a common experience of Jesus Christ which forms the uniting bond amid all the

other differences. Moreover, this sense of belonging together and
sharing something very precious is a dimension of their new faith
hardly less important than their individual relationship to God
through Christ.

This new community, whose common uniting bond is a shared
knowledge of Jesus Christ and total commitment to him, is one in
which this common tie takes precedence over all former attach-
ments. Jew and Gentile find themselves united by their common
love of Christ in a union far stronger than their former separateness on racial grounds. Perhaps there was no clearer mark of the
power of Christ to transform human nature than that such old
enemies as Jew and Gentile should be able to lay aside old
prejudices and learn to enjoy one another's company, discovering
that what now united them was stronger than what had divided
them. The author writes as though all the old struggles in the
Church over the relationships of Jew and Gentile within the
Church (so clearly reflected in Galatians) were now over, and
this may be largely true. But the fact that he gives prominence to
this issue suggests that there are still those in the Church who are
uneasy about it. It is not usual to emphasise what no one questions.
It may be that the old tension is now taking on a different form.
In Paul's day Jewish Christians wished to compel Gentile Christians to be circumcised and to observe Jewish diet-laws. The
difficulty now may be rather that the Gentiles, by this time in a
great majority, are questioning the value of trying to maintain
the earlier link with the Jewish past of the Church. Whatever
may be the occasion of the restlessness within the Church, the
fact that the writer feels he must stress so emphatically the reality
of their unity suggests that there is still some degree of uneasiness
to be settled.

11. The passage begins with **Therefore.** The argument for
corporate unity is based on the reality of the good things they have
already experienced as individual Christians (as outlined in 1:3
to 2:10). The Christians here addressed (**you**) are reminded that
they are **Gentiles in the flesh.** Spiritually, now that they are
Christians, they belong to the new people of God. But **in the flesh,**
that is, either by their birth or by their outward physical condition, they are non-Jews. Jews, who regarded only themselves as
the people of God, excluded Gentiles from that privilege. In
their natural condition Gentiles had not belonged to the people of

God. The distinguishing mark of the Jew was **circumcision,** and Gentiles were uncircumcised, and as such were branded as inferiors with no place among the people of God. They were **called the uncircumcision** by Jews, a term of abuse and contempt (cf. 1 Sam. 17:26, 36). By contrast, the Jews are **what is called the circumcision**—the so-called circumcision. The writer (by using 'so-called') quietly hints at his disapproval of this arrogant attitude of the Jews. The writer adds, in criticism of the Jewish claim, that circumcision is **in the flesh** (a purely physical mark), something **made by** (human) **hands.** In this it is very different from the special privilege of *all* Christians, which is something of a deeply spiritual nature and something which God has brought about. Circumcision had at first been intended as 'an outward sign of an inward and spiritual grace'; it was intended to be a visible sign that a man belonged to God. But Paul in Rom. 2:28 had had to insist that true circumcision was not something external and physical, but 'inwardly' and 'of the heart'. The outward mark had come to be not so much a sign that God ruled the man's heart, but all too often a substitute for it. So in Phil. 3:3 Paul wrote to those who had become Christians, whether Jew or Gentile: 'We are the true circumcision, who worship God in spirit, and glory in Christ Jesus, and put no confidence in the flesh' (i.e., in the merely physical mark of circumcision).

12. The Gentile Christians are told to **remember** the past, marked as it was by separateness and hostility in their relationship to the Jews, in order to stir up their joy in the present, in which these hateful divisions have been reconciled. In 2:1–3 the writer had reminded them of the moral evil of their earlier lives, which separated them from God; now they are reminded of those things in the past which separated them from God's people, the people of **Israel.** In a similar way in earlier days, the people of Israel themselves had been urged to remember their degraded past, that they had been slaves in Egypt (Dt. 15:15, 16:12) in order that they might be humble before God and grateful to him.

It is a little surprising, when the writer appears to be recalling their former estrangement from the people of Israel, that he begins: **you were at that time separated from Christ,** because this seems to refer to their lack of specifically Christian privileges. It may be that the writer mentions this first because it was their major deprivation, before going on to their alienation from Israel. This is the way the sentence is usually explained. In that case it will need to be subordinated to the other elements in the paragraph: **you were at that time** (when you were separated from Christ, i.e., before you became Christians) alienated from the commonwealth of Israel. That is, the whole of verse 12 is a description of what was true when they were **separated from Christ,** just as all the contents of verse 13 describe those who are 'in Christ'. Since, however, this reference to their being 'separated from Christ' falls within the passsage dealing with their former relationship to Israel, it is possible that **Christ** is here used in the general sense of 'Messiah'. They did not share any of the Jews' Messianic hopes for the future. Two factors favour this view: (i) In verse 13 the words 'Christ Jesus' are both used, Jesus being added, perhaps to make clear that now the Christian Messiah is meant, not the Jewish one. (ii) In Rom. 9:4–5, where Paul lists the privileges of the Jew, he includes, along with such things as the covenants, the law, the promise, etc., 'the Christ according to the flesh'. So here Christ could mean 'the Messiah of Jewish hopes'.

alienated from the commonwealth of Israel. As Gentiles they were deprived by the fact of their birth of full participation in the national life of the people of Israel, and thus excluded from all their privileges (see Rom. 9:4–5). That meant that they were **strangers to the covenants of promise.** The covenant represented the very heart of Israel's relationship with God. The people had pledged their obedience, and God had pledged his protecting care. So the covenant was not only a solemn responsibility accepted by the Jewish people; it was also God's promise to them of continuing help. Hence they are **covenants of promise.** It is surprising to find the word **covenants** in the plural (as also at Rom. 9:4). Usually the covenant is thought of as that negotiated through Moses; but there were other covenants with Adam, Noah, and Abraham, and these also must be in the writer's mind.

The Gentiles, prior to their Christian conversion, are described as **having no hope.** The same phrase is used at 1 Th. 4:13, where hope means hope for life beyond the grave. Death for them was the end of all, an attitude to life which often leads to either despair or recklessness (cf. 1 C. 15:32). Here too in Ephesians it is probable that **hope** refers to hope for an after-life. They were also **without God in the world.** Other nations beside the Jews had belief in gods, many gods. Some philosophers in the pagan world had indeed reached a belief in one true god. But no nation as a whole unambiguously proclaimed their faith in the one God as Israel did. As a pagan a man had no clear sense of one single over-ruling divine power in charge of the world's affairs. The phrase **in the world** probably applies both to **hope** and to **God**. It means they had to live their daily life here on earth without any hope beyond death to inspire them and without a present faith in God to sustain them. In our own time Bertrand Russell spoke of himself similarly as without hope and without God, and it was in recog-nition of this that he wrote: 'Only on the firm foundation of unyielding despair can the soul's habitation henceforth be safely built.' Some may be able to produce such stoic courage, but all too often human life begins to go to pieces in so bleak a world.

13. This verse begins to describe the change which has come to these Gentiles. **But now** (as opposed to 'at one time' in 2:11) **in Christ Jesus** (as opposed to 'separated from Christ') their desperate need has been fully met. The inclusion of **Jesus** leaves no doubt that here by **Christ** the writer does not mean the Jewish Messianic hope, but the Messiah as Christians had found him in the risen Jesus. In Jesus all God's promises to the people of Israel had been fulfilled, and in him made available to all men. Gentiles are no longer shut out in the cold, but welcomed into the warmth of a loving family. The writer expresses this by recalling words from Isa. 57:19: 'Peace, peace, to the far and to the near, says the Lord.' He writes: **you who once were far off have been brought near.** (The word 'peace', though not used here, appears in the next verse.) They have been **brought** into the family of God, and, reconciled to God, have discovered that as a conse-quence they are reconciled to all others who shared the same reconciliation.

This, of course, does not mean that converted Gentiles are reconciled to Jewish people as a whole. It is rather that those Jews who have accepted Jesus as Christ, and who thereby are the 'true Israel', the real people of God, and Gentiles who through Christ have also become members of the people of God, are now all members of that same divine community. Within this new com-munity they find that their mutual faith binds them together in a loving unity which overcomes all their former separateness and alienation. Jews and Gentiles within the Christian community are reconciled and made friends. This actually happened. It was not merely an ideal. Paul saw it taking place (Gal. 3:28; Col. 3:11; cf. also Ac. 10:34ff., etc.). But human sinfulness was always there—and still is—ready to disrupt this peace which God had created.

The agent of this new reconciliation is **the blood of Christ.** Vincent Taylor (*Atonement in the New Testament,* p. 179) suggests that by **blood** is meant 'life freely surrendered'. The word has already been used at 1:7, and at 2:16 there is reference to the cross. At Col. 1:20 the two words are brought together in the phrase: 'the blood of the cross'. Paul, and other *NT* writers as well, saw in the death of Christ on the cross and the giving of his life there, i.e., in the shedding of his blood, the effective means of reconciliation to God. It was this shared reconciliation with God which also reconciled to one another those who previously had no dealings with each other.

14. he is our peace. This is a strong way of declaring that **our peace,** peace with God and peace with our fellow Christians of whatever race, has its source in him. In the Greek there is more emphasis on the word **he** than appears in the English translation. It could almost be translated as: 'He and he alone' is our peace, that is, 'he and no other'. He can be called **our peace,** because **he has made us both one.** Again, this may be slightly misleading, because in the Greek the words **both** and **one** are in the neuter gender, which gives the statement a more general sense than a precise reference to **us.** It means that he has made two separate entities into a single unity. He **has broken down the dividing wall of hostility.** The **dividing wall** literally means a wall erected through the middle of an area to keep apart those on either side of it—like the wall in Berlin isolating east from west. Here, however, it is used metaphorically of an attitude of mind, and is interpreted as **hostility,** which holds apart whole communities of people in suspicion and hatred of one another. Such a barrier did separate Jews from Gentiles, especially in anything which had to do with religion. It was this hostility, firmly implanted in human hearts, which Christ had melted away, so that Christians, whether Jewish or Gentile, found themselves knit together in a new and unbelievable friendship. Besides this emotional hostility, however, there was also a real wall in Jerusalem which symbolised this hostility and the feelings of contempt and superiority which Jews had towards Gentiles. This was the partition between the outer and inner courts of the Temple. The outer court, known as the court of the Gentiles, was the only area of the Temple which Gentiles were allowed to enter. The inner court was reserved for those of Jewish race. At the gateway in this partition, leading from the outer court into the inner courts, there were prominent notices in different languages stating that death was the penalty for any non-Jew who dared to pass the partition. In 1871 one of these threatening notices carved in stone was recovered from the ruins of Jeruslam, where presumably it had lain since the destruction of the Temple in AD 70. Our suggested date for Ephesians is later than AD 70, and many find a deeper significance in these words of verse 14 if they were written after the destruction of this physical barrier. Some have found a parallel to this affirmation of the demolition of the dividing wall in the story in the Gospels about the veil or partition in the Temple being split from top to bottom at the time of the crucifixion. In the cross of Jesus Christians believed that all God's privileges were made available to all God's children of all races. Barriers of privilege were down.

15. Christ in his death had dissolved this racial enmity in the hearts of those who had become Christians **by abolishing in his flesh the law of commandments and ordinances.** This accumulation of three words of similar meaning may be just one more instance of the writer's mannerism of using several synonyms together in order to gain effect. But a significant meaning may be found here by taking the words in their distinctive senses. A literal translation of the words would be: '**the law** consisting **of commandments** which are expressed in rigid rules (**ordinances**)'. The whole Mosaic law consisted of broad commandments (like the Ten Commandments), and these were then elaborated in numerous precise regulations (the oral tradition of the Pharisees).

The enmity between Jew and Gentile is here seen as embodied in the law of the Jews. This consisted partly of high moral commandments, which the best among the Gentiles approved, and partly of ritual regulations. These latter prescribed circumcision, a strict diet, methods of slaughter of animals, sabbath behaviour, etc. Anyone who did not keep these rules was excluded from social intercourse with those who did. To the Gentile, however sympathetic he might be to the moral standards of the Jews, these ritual rules often seemed petty and pointless. No rational explanation could be given for them. They must be obeyed because God had commanded them. It was wrong to ask why. The Gospels represent Jesus as challenging these rules in respect of diet and sabbath observance. To him they did not represent the will of God. They made it appear that God required of man both purposeless and inhuman actions. It was these aspects of the law which proved to be obstacles to Gentiles who were drawn to other aspects of the Jewish faith. The early Christians believed and proclaimed that Jesus had brought to an end this old Mosaic law, replacing it with something nearer to the will of God. He had come to 'fulfil' the law. In this sense he may be said to have 'abolished' the old law as it was. It was also clear that slavish obedience to this old law did not provide the means by which a man could find acceptance with God, as many Pharisees appear to have believed. Jesus, however, had provided such a means—in his life, death, and resurrection—and in this sense had shown the old law to be inadequate and had provided a substitute for it. He had 'abolished' the law.

This did not, of course, mean that Christians abandoned the moral standards required by God in the law. These standards, however, they no longer found written in the law of the Jews, but in the person of Jesus, as he in his life and teaching had 'fulfilled' them, that is, refined them so that they truly represented God's will. Paul could say that Christ had abolished the law (e.g., Gal. 3:13, 24); but he could also say that he himself was now 'under the law of Christ', which means that Christ had become for him the controlling force which represented and interpreted for him what God's will was. This new Christian form of the law Gentiles could accept as well as Jews.

The Jewish law is said to have been abolished **in his flesh.** This may be simply a variation of words to mean the same as 'in his blood', or on his cross, by means of his self-giving in death. There could, however, be some special interest in this phrase if it could be taken to refer to the actual ministry of Jesus, and the way he defied the Jewish law at points where he saw it mis-represented the will of God, and carried his defiance to the extent of dying rather than agreeing to conform to it. In that case it might be possible to translate **in his flesh** as 'by what he said and did'.

The word **that** in 2:15 expresses purpose and this needs special emphasis. It might be well to start a new sentence here and say: His purpose in doing this was to **create in himself one new man in place of the two.** In 2:10 the writer has already described Christians as men 'created in Christ Jesus'. In Paul's words any man who is in Christ is a 'new creation' (2 C. 5:17). This new creation is here called a **new man.** Instead of being Jew and Gentile, two different kinds of 'men', there is now **one new man,** the Christian. Many Christians felt just this—that what had happened to them was so new and decisive that they had ceased to be nationals of any one country and were now simply 'Christians'. Some early Christians when required in law courts to declare their race insisted on saying only: 'I am a Christian.' When differences of race and class had been deprived of their power to provoke rivalry, hate, and hostility, then the result was **peace,** the social harmony which emerges when causes of discord have been removed and one overruling loyalty inspires the corporate life.

16. The Jewish law and its requirements had created the barrier that separated Jew and Gentile. Christ had replaced this and become for all Christians, both Jews and Gentiles, the true standard of behaviour and the open way to God. The person who is thus reconciled to God and controlled by Christ as Lord is a new type of humanity, the new man. Thus Christ's purpose can be described as reconciling **both to God in one body.** The whole community, as well as individuals in it, knows itself at peace with God and is ready to be used as his agent in the world. The phrase **in one body** emphasises their corporate obedience to God and their sense of oneness with one another in God's purpose. Thus Christ **through the cross,** by which their individual reconciliation to God had been achieved, has brought the hostility to an end. The hostility between people of different race is ended because both are reconciled to God through Christ, and in turn their reconciliation to one another adds a new dimension to their sense of peace with God (Mt. 5:24; cf. 1 Jn 4:20–21).

This reconciliation is **through the cross.** In Paul's writings reconciliation is closely associated with the cross (Rom. 5:6–11; 2 C. 5:17–21; Col. 1:21–22). The **cross** can make a man aware of those evil things in himself which hurt God, till he becomes ashamed of them and eager to be free from them. The cross also brings the assurance of God's forgiving love when man turns to

him in penitence. Theories of the atonement seek to explain why
the cross has these undoubted powers. Whether we feel that one
theory or another can give the explanation, the fact of the cross
and its power remains a reality of Christian experience.

One can sense the joy of Christian achievement in verses 14–16.
The most stubborn and bitter of estrangements, that between Jew
and Gentile, has been healed within the Christian community.
But there are other continuing estrangements which Christ has
not been allowed to heal, even within his own community. In
some churches black and white people may not mix freely as
members of one single community; in others Christians of one
denomination will not share their full communion at the Lord's
table with Christians of a different denomination, thus inflicting
hurt and humiliation on their brothers in Christ. This is an
apartheid no less offensive to the true spirit of Christ than the
early separation of Jew and Gentile within the Church. In each
case strong theological reasons can be found for the disunity; but
in each case the Spirit of Christ will not rest till he has broken
down these dividing walls.

**17. he came and preached peace to you who were far off
and peace to those who were near** (cf. 2:13–14 and Isa.
57:19). In the commentaries there is discussion about the meaning of Christ's coming and preaching. Most scholars find in the
phrase either a reference to his resurrection appearances, or to
his preaching, either to departed spirits in Hades or to angelic
powers at his ascension, or to the spread of Christianity into non-
Jewish lands through the Christian mission. Most commentators
decline to refer it to the earthly ministry of Jesus. Yet the word
came fits this interpretation better than the others, and 'preaching' is one of the constant activities of Jesus in the Gospels. It is
true that if **you . . . far off** means the Gentiles, there is not much
in the Gospels about Jesus preaching to Gentiles (though even
here there were conversations with the Syrophoenician woman, the
Roman centurion, the Samaritan leper, the Samaritan woman,
and the centurion at the cross). But one of the undoubtedly
historical items in the Gospel record of Jesus is his insistence on
taking his message and friendship to those who were regarded as
'beyond the pale', usually lumped together under the phrase
'tax collectors and sinners'. These could well be understood as
being **far off,** and as roughly equivalent to the Gentiles in the

later stage of the Christian mission. At Lk. 4:17ff. Jesus is represented as quoting Isa. 61:1–2 to describe his own mission. It
includes 'preaching good news' to the poor. The Greek word for
'preach good news' is the same as that translated **preached** in
this verse. It was this feature of the work of Jesus which the
apostles carried out into the world. If, however, the preaching
here does not refer to the ministry of Jesus, it would then refer to
the mission of the disciples, as though Christ preached through
them (see 2 C. 5:20).

18. Christ has become the means of reconciling both Jew and
Gentile to God and to one another. The result of reconciliation is
that those who were once estranged can now approach each other
in a friendly spirit and worship together. Thus it is **through him**
that **we both have access in one Spirit to the Father.** (For
access see Rom. 5:2). Since the community is now one body
(2:16), it is activated by **one Spirit.** They have become a fellowship of the Holy Spirit. The marks of the Spirit's presence are love,
joy, peace, etc. These are the marks of this newly formed community. But another mark of the Spirit's presence is a glad dis-
covery that they can approach God as a loved child does its father
(cf. Gal. 4:6: 'God has sent the Spirit of his Son into our hearts,
crying "Abba! Father!" '). So it is that **in one Spirit** they **have
access** to God whom they now know as **Father.**

19. When the people of God consisted only of the people of
Israel, Gentiles were excluded from their number. They were
strangers, i.e., foreigners, totally outside the community. Even
if they had come to live in Jewish territory they were not allowed
to be integrated in the society, but remained as **sojourners,** i.e.,
resident aliens, permitted to reside, but with no rights as citizens,
and liable to be expelled without right of appeal. Now, however,
that the people of God are the new Christian community, Gentile
Christians are welcomed and accorded full rights as citizens with
all others. They are **fellow citizens with the saints,** that is,
with all God's people (see 1:1). They are **members of the household of God,** members of the family of which God is Father,
and in which Jesus Christ is the eldest brother (Rom. 8:29),
and they the younger children. The Christian is both citizen
of the new kingdom and a member of God's new family, as
though God is thought of as both King and Father. The same
combination of metaphors is found in the Lord's Prayer, where

we address God as Father, but also pray for the coming of his
kingdom.

20. We have noted some places where the writer has boldly
interpreted the Christian experience in a way which the Gnostics
would have applauded. He speaks, for instance, of some spiritual
privileges as already present in their lives, which earlier Christians
would have spoken of as still an object of hope in the future. For
instance, Christians have already entered upon the resurrection
life and begun their heavenly status (2:6). Even though Gnostic
thought was suspect, this writer does not shrink from speaking as
Gnostics did when their words expressed a genuinely Christian
truth, because on other more fundamental issues he dissociates
himself emphatically from the Gnostic point of view. One such
difference is his stress on the importance of a Christian's membership of a community (over and above his own personal experience), and a community firmly based on a historical event and
linked with it by a historical continuity. This community does not
float uneasily on an unstable swell of spiritual excitement; it is
built upon the foundation of the apostles and prophets.
apostles and prophets are clearly thought of here as the leaders
of the early Christian community, who provided a sure link
between Jesus himself and later generations of Christians.

This wording seems to imply a considerable distance in time
between the earliest Christians and the readers of this epistle.
Even cautious commentators feel bound to recognise that this is a
feature which favours post-Pauline authorship (see Percy, p. 334).
It also seems inconsistent with Paul's own emphatic declaration
that there can be no other foundation for the Church than Jesus
Christ himself (I C. 3:11). This writer clearly sees in Jesus the one
from whom it all began, but he also sees in the apostles and
prophets the ones who began to build the post-resurrection
Church. If he thought of Christ as the builder, it was not unnatural for him to refer to the apostles and prophets as the
foundation which Christ the builder had laid. It was they who
provided stability to the early Church. The writer insists that it is
in loyal conformity to them that the Church must be built. It
must avoid being swept away by novel developments which are
not a true expression of the founder's original intention.

apostles and prophets are associated again at 4:11, where
they stand first in the list of those whose work enriches the Church.

At 1 C. 12:28 also they stand together at the head of the Pauline list of Church leaders. The meaning of 'apostle' was discussed at 1:1. In Ephesians Paul is clearly thought of as an apostle (1:1), and it is probable that in that term the original twelve disciples are also included. Riessenfeld and Gerhardsson have argued that Jesus, following the customary methods of rabbis, had insisted on his disciples memorising parts of his teaching. If so, they would be well equipped to remember it and pass it on. These scholars suggest that this was the reason why apostolic authority was felt to be a basic qualification of any book accepted into the canon, since such authority assured a genuine link with the teaching and purpose of Jesus. Certainly this writer seems to regard the apostles in this light, as providing a firm link with the founder of the faith, and themselves as it were, 'founding fathers' of the Church.

prophets must here refer to the other group of leading figures prominent in the early Church (though some scholars have argued that the word here means the *OT* prophets). The prophets of Israel were men who were inspired to speak God's word to their own day. They did not hark back to what earlier authorities had said, but declared: 'Thus says the Lord.' So in the early Church the prophets were those who were inspired to speak the 'mind of Christ' to their day. If so, the **apostles** may have represented in the Church the active memory of what Jesus had said and done, and the **prophets** the understanding of the earliest community of what Jesus, the now risen and ascended Christ, was calling for in the developing circumstances of the Christian mission. Paul describes his understanding of the function of a prophet in 1 C. 14:3. The writer of Revelation speaks of his book as 'the words of this prophecy', as though he himself were a prophet. In this capacity he heard Jesus speaking from heaven, and proclaimed as his such words as are recorded at Rev. 1:17–18, etc. His identification as a prophet is even more specific at Rev. 22:9. J. V. Taylor writes (p. 69): 'What turned a man into a prophet was not eloquence, but vision; not getting the message across, but getting the message.' The characteristic ability of the prophet was not the power to foretell the future, but to interpret the mind of Christ for his own time.

This new **household of God** is built on the foundation represented by the apostles and prophets, **Christ Jesus himself being the cornerstone.** The meaning of the Greek word (*akrogōniaios*), here translated **cornerstone**, has been the subject of considerable debate. The word occurs only once in the LXX (at Isa. 28:16), and there, as the context makes clear, it is applied to a stone which has some important place in the foundation. Apart from this single instance, however, and passages derived from it, it is claimed that in every other known case the word means (not part of the foundation but) 'the stone which crowns the building' (so Jeremias in *TDNT* i, p. 792). Similarly, in the *Patristic Greek Lexicon* (ed. G. W. H. Lampe) its meaning is given as the stone at the 'topmost angle or point of pyramid, obelisk, etc., which being cut before being set in position and being the last laid, would not fit if the construction were not true'. Jeremias gives the German equivalent as *Schlussstein*, the keystone, the stone at the summit of an arch locking the whole structure together. Houlden (p. 293) accepts this as the meaning here in Ephesians. But it is very difficult to make sense of this interpretation. Several reasons may be given:

(1) It is sharply at variance with Paul's affirmation that Jesus is the foundation of the Church, that on which the whole building rests and stands firm, not the stone which is put in only when all else has been completed.

(2) This building in Ephesians is not yet completed; it is still 'growing' (2:21). This means that Christ, if he is the 'stone which crowns the building', is given no place in its present stage of development, but waits to be incorporated only when all else is complete.

(3) It is difficult to see how Christ can be assigned any position which is not obviously prior to that of apostles and prophets.

(4) The whole development of the argument in 2:19–22 points to the conclusion that as the apostles and prophets are the foundation, Jesus is the keystone around which the foundation itself has been built.

(5) In Isa. 28:16 the cornerstone is clearly understood as part of the foundation. It reads:

> Behold I am laying in Zion for a foundation
> a stone, a tested stone,
> a precious cornerstone, of a sure foundation.

The meaning of the Hebrew is difficult to assess precisely,

E

but *NEB* gives the same meaning as *RSV*: 'a precious cornerstone for a firm foundation'.

It is clearly the meaning of the word in Isa. 28:16 which determines its meaning in Ephesians. It may be that the translator of the LXX used *akrogōniaios* in a sense different from that which was customary in current Greek, but there can be little doubt that he intended it to mean what Isaiah's Hebrew had meant. In Isaiah and, therefore, in all passages derived from Isaiah, the word clearly meant the cornerstone in a foundation, not 'the head of an arch', i.e., the final stone which completes the building.

We take it, therefore, that **cornerstone** here means a very important stone in the foundation. Masson (p. 170) accepts this interpretation and describes the stone as 'the most important stone of a building, placed first at the junction where two walls meet'. But what exactly is this **cornerstone** of a foundation? One remembers many years ago watching a single builder starting to build a small brick shelter. The earth had been dug away to a depth of three or four feet, and the ground levelled and prepared for the foundation. The first act of the builder was to choose the brick, a specially strong and well-shaped one, with which he would begin. One was impressed, almost amused, at the laborious care he took to get this placed exactly right, testing it with the spirit-level at each of the four sides, testing it also to make sure it was perfectly upright at each of the four edges, tapping it to ensure that the two sides making the angle were in perfectly true line with the intended form of the building. He took the utmost pains to make sure that every line, left and right and upwards, and every level, was scrupulously accurate. This was because every line of the building was to be calculated from this keystone of the foundation. Only when this was well and truly laid could other bricks be added to it and set in their own place by aligning them to the brick at the corner. The first stone at the corner, the one to which all others will be aligned, this is the cornerstone of the foundation, as important to the foundation as the foundation is to the whole building.

apostles and prophets can be spoken of as the bricks which form the **foundation,** but the **cornerstone** to which they are laid is **Christ Jesus.** The Church of Jesus Christ is strong and enduring, able to withstand the ravages of time, if it is built in lines which are true to the cornerstone of its foundation.

21. Since Jesus is the cornerstone of the foundation, by which every line and upright of the future building will be gauged, it can be said: **in him the whole structure is joined together.** The word **structure** is the same as that translated 'building' in 1 C. 3:9: 'You are God's building.'

the whole structure: It is very doubtful if this can be regarded as a fair translation of the Greek words, although *NEB* ('the whole building') follows the same line as *RSV*. *NEB*, however, in a footnote indicates that an alternative rendering would be 'every structure'. Masson describes this alternative as 'the only translation grammatically possible', and other translators adopt it: *The Jerusalem Bible* has 'every structure is aligned on him', and Phillips gives 'every separate piece of building'. Dibelius agrees that this is what the Greek means grammatically, but thinks the writer has made a careless mistake in his writing and intended to write 'the whole structure', even though the words he wrote mean 'every structure'. This is a somewhat desperate decision. Others argue that he has allowed a Semitic idiom to affect adversely the accuracy of his use of Greek words. Basically, this decision seems to be due, partly to an attempt to justify a translation which is felt to be preferable in the context, even though it is grammatically wrong, and partly to an inability to make good sense of the strictly grammatical translation. The first question to ask is, what sense can be made of it if the phrase is translated accurately as 'every structure'? It must mean, when understood literally in relation to the building of bricks and mortar, 'every separate part of the building', 'every room'. Metaphorically, it must mean every separate local congregation within the universal Church, and which is nevertheless an integral part of the one Church. This is probably the right interpretation. It is similar to the thought of 3:15: 'from whom every family ... on earth is named', where 'every family' may refer to the local congregations as opposed to the one Church which incorporates them all in its unity.

The Church, therefore, composed of many local congregations, all based on the truth mediated through apostles and prophets, and aligned in all they do and stand for to Jesus Christ who was the starting point from whom it all began, is constantly growing. Its goal is to become **a holy temple in the Lord.** For the Jew the Temple was the place where God was uniquely present (Ps. 11:4), where men might become aware of him in his greatness and worship him in his holiness; it was there that provision was made to meet all the deepest spiritual needs of human nature, especially that of forgiveness and atonement with God. For the Christian, however, it is in the Church, the community of Christian people (not a building), that all these benefits can most surely be found. For the Christian, therefore, the community of Christians has replaced the Temple. Even the outsider would sometimes be compelled to acknowledge: 'God is really among you' (1 C. 14:25), and the believers themselves knew this to be wonderfully true. It was in this community of love and faith that they themselves received forgiveness of sins and deliverance from guilt and fear; it was here they could most readily offer worship and praise to God and find their awareness of his presence renewed.

Jesus had been accused at his trial of speaking words against the Temple at Jerusalem, and was denounced as a blasphemer, because to be critical of the Temple was equivalent to blaspheming God whose holy presence was there. The charge is reported in all four Gospels and in Acts, and there must be some historical substance in it, though the precise form of what Jesus said has probably been distorted by the accusers. It seems likely that Jesus had spoken of the coming doom of the Temple (Mk 14:59; Mt. 26:61; Jn 2:19), but declared that nevertheless God's presence and availability, his forgiving mercy and healing power would not thereby be removed from mankind, that a living community would come into being where all these things would be found. It is this hope which the writer here takes up and sees fulfilled—or partly fulfilled—in the Christian Church. It was mediated to him by Paul's own description of the Christian community as God's **temple** (1 C. 3:16; 2 C. 6:16).

in the Lord: This means either that their holiness as God's temple is due to their belonging to God and indwelling by God, or else that all that is happening—the extension and increasing unity of the Church—is God's doing.

22. The Christian community is being compared to a building, with its foundation and its different rooms, the whole structure becoming a temple of God. But all this is a metaphor and cannot be pressed any further, because in fact this building is constructed out of people not stones (cf. 'living stones', 1 Pet. 2:5). Ephesians keeps the metaphor of the physical building as far as 2:21 and then instead of speaking further of stones or rooms the writer says 'you':

you also are built into it (this new temple). Either this means that each individual becomes an integral part of this structure, or else each separate congregation is an intrinsic element in the Church as a whole. Wherever this spiritual temple is to be found, there is **a dwelling place of God;** there God may be found (cf. 1 C. 14:20) in his love, forgiveness, and renewing power. God's presence is there **in the Spirit.** That is how men knew God's presence in their own lives and in the experience of the Church. The Holy Spirit is God with us (1 C. 3:16). Here also the word **Spirit** may indicate something of the unrestricted freedom of God's presence in his Church as compared with the localisation of God in the Temple at Jerusalem. God in his Spirit knows no limitation of space (Ps. 139:7-12). Others, however, make the phrase **in the Spirit** adjectival to the idea of **a dwelling place of God,** meaning 'a spiritual house', a house in a spiritual sense, a household, as it is understood at 1 Pet. 2:5.

PAUL'S MINISTRY 3:1-13

The paragraph 3:1-13, along with 1:15ff. and 6:21f., is the most personal in the whole epistle. At no point is it more precisely asserted that Paul is the author. Those who understand the epistle as post-Pauline see this as a device, common in ancient times, by which the actual writer disclaims all credit for what he writes and ascribes it to the one he seeks to represent. This writer feels that he is merely reproducing what he has learnt from Paul. His intention is to convey Paul's teaching to men of his own day, as if Paul himself were writing to them from prison, as he had done to the Colossians. Therefore, he writes in the name of Paul. A similar approach is seen in 2 Pet. 1:1, 3:1, 3:15, where the anonymous writer seeks to indicate that the letter is to be regarded as Peter's. Those who regard Ephesians as predominantly a liturgical document feel themselves compelled to treat these three highly personal passages as later insertions, introduced into the original document at the time when it was being revised to make it appear as a Pauline epistle. It is, however, impossible to treat this paragraph as a later insertion, or as the work of someone other than the author of the main body of the epistle. As at 1:15ff., the decisive argument here is that we find in these passages precisely the same kind of dependence on Colossians which characterises the

other parts of Ephesians. At 1:15ff. we drew up tables to indicate
this basic similarity. We give a similar table for this passage, which
can be seen to exhibit just the same features:

Ephesians 3:1	=	Colossians 1:23
3:2		1:25
3:3		1:27
3:4		2:2
3:6		1:23
3:8		1:27
3:9		1:26 (and 1:16)
3:10		1:26
3:13		1:24

It seems to us most unlikely, if not actually impossible, that a different writer at a later date would reproduce this same pattern of
close yet flexible dependence on material in Colossians as we find
also in the non-biographical sections.

1. For this reason translates two Greek words (not found in
Paul's genuine letters) which are repeated at 3:14, when the
writer resumes his train of thought, after being interrupted at the
end of 3:1 by a long parenthesis. This parenthesis, verses 2–13,
consists of one long sentence in the Greek, just as 1:3–14, 1:15–23,
and 2:15–23, are similarly long, single sentences. The parenthesis
here is introduced to emphasise the outstanding part played by
Paul in God's master-plan for mankind and his unique suitability for the role.

Although the words **For this reason** seem to stress a direct
connexion between what precedes and what follows, it is not easy
to establish any clear sequence of thought. In so far as there is a
logical link, it is easier to find it with the whole of the earlier parts
of the letter than with the verses immediately preceding. **For this
reason** refers to all that God has done for the individual Christian
and for the whole Christian community. Even then the link is not
precise, and some commentators see it as little more than a convenient device for moving on to another point. Houlden, for
instance, describes it as 'the loosest of connexions with what has
gone before'.

I, Paul. These words occur in Col. 1:23, a chapter in Colossians frequently quoted in the opening parts of Ephesians. They
are also found in 2 C. 10:1 and Gal. 5:2. **a prisoner for Jesus**

Christ. The Greek actually has: the prisoner *of* Jesus Christ.
RSV gives only part of its meaning by indicating that Paul's
imprisonment is part of his service for Christ, but misses something
the writer may also have intended to include—the fact that Paul
is a prisoner in the grip of Christ, as well as in the power of Jews
or Romans. This precise phrase occurs twice also in Philemon (1
and 9) and it is probably intended that readers should think of
Ephesians as written from the same period of imprisonment which
produced Colossians and Philemon. These two letters are in fact
themselves very closely associated with each other (see, e.g.,
Col. 4:9), and it is not surprising to find a writer who so clearly
reflects an intimate knowledge of Colossians echoing also words
from Philemon. Traditionally, this imprisonment which produced
Colossians and Philemon was thought to have been in Rome, but
strong arguments have been produced to identify it rather with
an imprisonment in Ephesus. The word **prisoner** serves to remind
the readers of what Paul has suffered **on behalf of you Gentiles.**
In Acts it is clearly indicated that Paul's troubles, even with the
Roman authorities, arose mainly from the hostility of Jews. This
hostility was caused, not so much by the claims he made for Jesus
(the original twelve disciples made similar claims, but were
apparently largely exempt from persecution by the Jews; see,
e.g., Ac. 8:1), as by his determined insistence that through Jesus
God had made available to Gentiles privileges which the Jews
regarded as their own prerogative. Acts makes this clear, emphasising both Paul's resolute concern that the Gentiles should
receive the gospel (13:46, 14:27, 15:3 and 7, 18:6), and the
opposition from Jews which resulted (14:2, 21:19–22, 22:21–22).
Both these points are borne out also in Paul's letters: Gal. 1:16,
2:2; 1 Th. 2:16. In spite of the danger and actual suffering
involved, Paul pressed on with the assignment, which was his
within the strategy of God, to proclaim the gospel, which he saw
to be God's means of uniting Jews and Gentiles within one new
community. Paul is identified as the one who, more than any
other of the Christian leaders, saw what God was seeking to do
(his secret purpose, his 'mystery')—and set himself to carry that
purpose forward no matter what the opposition or what the cost
to him personally.

2. Various attempts have been made to make 3:1 into a complete sentence, but without success. The writer simply breaks off

in the middle of something he had intended to write. Then, what might have been merely a passing reference to Paul's part in God's purpose, lengthens out into a long appreciation of Paul, and the original sentence is left unfinished. **assuming that you have heard:** Those who hold to the belief that Paul was the actual writer of Ephesians are compelled by this phrase to acknowledge that he could not have written it for Christians at Ephesus, since he had spent a ministry of many months among them and his prowess and Christian discernment was well known to them. Paul would hardly have written to them: **assuming that you have** *heard.* Those who treat the letter as post-Pauline see this phrase as one of the indications in the letter that Paul cannot have been the actual writer.

Paul makes reference to **the stewardship of God's grace.** God's **grace,** that is his astonishing generosity to undeserving men, brought to its sharpest focus in Jesus, has been the dominant theme of the opening chapters. The word 'steward' is a common one in the *NT.* Literally, it means one entrusted with the management of a household. The owner gave him instructions and left him with the responsibility of carrying them out. So Paul is 'a steward of the mysteries of God' (1 C. 4:1–2). As such he has been told what God's strategy is and given the responsibility of carrying it out, using what tactics may be required in each situation. Here, in Eph. 3:3, this purpose is referred to as 'the mystery', because no one in advance had been able to anticipate what it would be. In Col. 1:25 it is the stewardship which is bestowed on Paul; here, however, what is given to Paul is not the stewardship but the grace of God (although this is not clear in *RSV*). This may be merely a verbal change without significance. But the word 'stewardship' is used elsewhere in Ephesians with a meaning noticeably different from that which it carries in Colossians and in Paul's other letters. For instance, *RSV* translates it at 3:9 as 'plan'. It may be that this non-Pauline use of the word is to be found here also. It is, however, perhaps easiest on the whole to treat this as an instance of the normal Pauline usage similar to that in Col. 1:25, but the question will be raised again at 3:9.

God's grace that was given to me for you. 'Grace given to me' is a recurring phrase in Paul's letters (e.g., Rom. 12:3, 6; 15:15; 1 C. 1:4; Gal. 2:9, 3:10). Here it is given to him **for you.** Sometimes **God's grace** was given to Paul to meet his own need

(2 C. 12:9), but even then it was to meet his need in order that he might be the better equipped to do God's work for others.

3. how the mystery was made known to me by revelation. The **mystery** is God's purpose for mankind which no one has known until now. In 1:9-10 we were told 'God has made known to us the mystery of his will to unite all things in Christ'. Here it is explicitly stated that it was to Paul that this knowledge was revealed. The content of this 'mystery' has been partly unfolded in 2:13-22, and in 3:6 is even more explicitly stated, viz., that in Christ Jesus the Gentiles are fellow-heirs with Jews in God's promises. This deep insight into God's hidden purposes came to Paul **by revelation.** He had not found it through the study of the *OT* Scriptures, nor worked it out on theological principles, nor learned it from human teachers. The truth had come to him, as it were, from beyond himself and his counsellors. It came as something unexpected and unpredictable, yet carrying its own compelling authority with it. It came, he believed, from God. This meaning of **revelation** is made very clear in Gal. 1:12: 'I did not receive it from man, nor was I taught it, but it came through a revelation of Jesus Christ'; and in Gal. 1:16: 'God was pleased to reveal his Son to me, in order that I might preach him among the Gentiles.'

as I have written briefly: This could refer to the brief references to the mystery in 1:9-10, or to the occasional uses of the word 'mystery' in Paul's own letters, where its meaning is not developed and there is no hint of the deeper meaning given to it here in Ephesians.

4, 5. When you read this: For those who have no personal knowledge of Paul, the reading in Ephesians of this summary of his teaching and reminder of his achievements will enable them to perceive his **insight into the mystery of Christ** (cf. Col. 4:2), that is, his understanding of the hidden purposes which God was fulfilling in Christ. For the Jews, the Christ (or Messiah) was closely associated with the fulfilment of national hopes and prestige, and not infrequently with the humiliation of the Gentiles. God's purpose to include the Gentiles in his promises and to unite Jews and Gentiles in one community through his Messiah (Jesus) had not been **made known to the sons of men** (an Hebraic type of phrase for 'mankind') **in other** (i.e., previous) **generations.** It is true that some prophets had dreamed of the coming day when

Gentiles, too, would know God (e.g., Isa. 11:10, 60:3; Jer. 16:19; Mic. 4:2; Zech. 2:11, etc.), but there had been no vision of a united community embracing both Jews and Gentiles on an equal footing. Paul had certainly played a major role in perceiving that this was God's purpose, and proclaiming it, and making it effective in the Christian mission. For those who take Ephesians as a genuinely Pauline letter, this complacent reminder of Paul's special part in the Christian mission is something of an embarrassment. It is one of the features which fits more easily into the post-Pauline interpretation.

as it has now been revealed to his holy apostles and prophets by the Spirit. On **apostles and prophets,** see 2:20. It was not only Paul who sensed God's purposes in Christ, though he may well have had to play the part of pioneer. The other leaders in the earliest Christian community came to accept Paul's insights, though Acts reports that some, even Peter and James, grasped the truth more slowly and less clearly than Paul had done, and there were others in the Church who bitterly opposed any integration of Jew and Gentile. Ephesians, however, here represents Paul's position in the matter as the one universally accepted by the leaders of the early Church (**apostles and prophets**). Col. 1:26 speaks of the mystery as 'now made manifest to his saints' (that is, to all Christians). In Ephesians, however, the emphasis is on the revelation to the leadership of the early community rather than to all its members. Moreover, these leaders are called **holy.** In Paul, and elsewhere in Ephesians, all God's people are 'the holy ones', the saints, because they are set apart for God. Here the apostles and prophets are called 'holy'. They, of course, would be set apart for God equally with other Christians. Here, however, the word **holy** seems to suggest a special degree of holiness in their case. Does it suggest a reverence for official leadership which some characterise as a mark of 'early catholicism'? **by the Spirit:** the **Spirit** is God active in the lives of men. One of the functions of the Spirit is to enable men to see truths to which they have hitherto been blind (1 C. 2:10–13).

6. The word **mystery** has been mentioned twice already. At 1:9–10 its meaning was clearly stated: it had long been God's unguessed intention to unite all things in Christ. At 3:3 it was claimed that the 'mystery' was made known to Paul by revelation. Here in verse 6 its meaning is clearly spelt out: that **the**

Gentiles are fellow-heirs, members of the same body, and partakers of the promise. If God's ultimate purpose is 'to unite all things in Christ', one of the first (and hardest) steps in this process is to unite Jew and Gentile in one Christian community. We have already noted the fondness of this writer for Greek words compounded with the preposition *syn-*, meaning 'together with'. Sometimes they are used to emphasise the Christian's identification with Christ (e.g., 'raised together with Christ', 2:6). Elsewhere they are used to emphasise the unity of the Gentile converts with the rest of the Christian community (as in the three compounds with *syn-* in 2:19-22): they are citizens *together with* them, joined *together with* them, built *together with* them. Here in 3:6 three adjectives compounded with *syn-* emphasise this unity of Gentile with Jew within the Church: Gentiles are 'fellow-heirs *with*', 'one body *with*', and 'joint partakers *with*', those of Jewish birth; the unity is complete once they are all incorporated within the people of God. An heir is one who by his membership of the family is entitled to his share in what the family possesses. The Christian Church is the new Israel, the new people of God. God's promises to his people (once the people of Israel) have now been transferred to his new people. In that community Gentiles are equally a part with Jews, and so are **fellow heirs** of all the promises made to God's people. All Christians are equally **members of the same body,** the Church (see 1:23). The Church does not consist of isolated groups of Christians only loosely related to each other. Every Christian is a member of the world-wide community of Christians. He is an integral part of this body, whether he be of Gentile or Jewish origin. As members of the new people of God, Gentiles are joint **partakers** with Jews of God's promises to his people. These promises included forgiveness of sin, enabling-power for all the tasks of the present, and hope for the future. All these privileges had come to the Gentiles because of **Christ Jesus** and **the gospel.** This breaking down of barriers had been the work of Jesus, in his life and teaching and death (2:14-16). What Jesus had set on foot, the early preachers and Christians leaders carried forward, as they proclaimed Jesus Christ and his gospel. For the meaning of **gospel** see 1:13. The gospel is the proclamation of all the privileges which Christ has made available to men, and also the offer here and now of these privileges to those who respond in true faith.

7. Of this gospel I was made a minister (cf. Col. 1:23). Paul speaks of himself elsewhere as a **minister** (servant) of God (cf. 2 C. 6:4) and a servant of Christ (2 C. 11:23). Here he is the servant of the gospel, the good news initiated by God and put into effect by Christ. Paul fulfils this task **according to the gift of God's grace which was given** him. Once again we meet the recurring emphasis that everything Paul has become and achieved in the Christian life and mission is not his own doing, but the result of **God's grace**—God's choice of him, God's call to him, God's enabling power (cf. 1:6–7).

by the working of his power reminds us of the truth that God's grace not only brings forgiveness and new life, but the strength to enable the Christian to fulfil whatever his calling involves.

8. this grace that sets each man to his task **was given** to Paul to enable him **to preach to the Gentiles.** The word **preach** really means 'proclaim the good news'. It was used at 2:17 to describe the purpose of Jesus. Here it is part of Paul's purpose. He regarded preaching as the very essence of his ministry. Christ had sent him **to preach** (1 C. 1:17) and to preach among **the Gentiles** (Gal. 1:16); it was his ambition to preach the gospel especially where Christ had not yet been named (Rom. 15:20); to refrain from preaching, through fear or discouragement, was shame and dishonour (1 C. 9:16).

The gospel he was commissioned to preach was **the unsearchable riches of Christ.** Material **riches** are regarded in the *NT* as a danger and a hindrance to full Christian living (Mk 10:25, 8:36; Lk 6:24). But the word can be used metaphorically of spiritual riches. A man can be 'rich toward God' (Lk. 12:21) and can possess 'true riches' (Lk. 16:11). While summoned to renounce earthly treasure, he is invited to set his heart on treasure in heaven (Mk 10:21). These true riches, or heavenly treasure, are always available to the Christian, because there is an inexhaustible supply in Christ on which he can draw. Here in Ephesians it is spoken of as **unsearchable** riches. **unsearchable** suggests the picture of a reservoir so deep that soundings cannot reach the bottom of it. No limit can, therefore, be put to its resources. *NEB* suggests 'unfathomable'.

The task of preaching God's inexhaustible grace, as offered through Christ to all men (Gentiles included), has been laid on

Paul. It is a mark of the measure of God's grace that so unworthy a person as Paul had been chosen—one who is described as **the very least of all the saints** (i.e., the most unsatisfactory Christian there ever was). This sounds a little like false modesty. In 1 C. 15:9 Paul recalls how the risen Christ came to claim him for his service as an apostle. With deep shame Paul adds: 'I am the least of the apostles, unfit to be called as apostle, because I persecuted the church of God.' This is a cry of genuine remorse. The memory of his fierce hostility to the Church was an unceasing cause of bitter remorse to him. It is often felt, however, that the words of Eph. 3:8 lack something of this genuine feeling. They sound artificial and exaggerated, like the similar over-statement in 1 Tim. 1:15 where Paul describes himself as 'chief of sinners'— the worst of all bad men. The words are more easily understood as those of the later disciple who wished to make his master appear as excelling in penitence and humility as well as insight. For **saints,** see 1:1.

9. Paul's commission as an apostle was to preach the gospel (e.g., 1 C. 9:16), but also to proclaim it in such a way that its implications were unmistakably clear, so as **to make all men see** God's unfolding plan. To accept the gospel meant a glad participation in all that the gospel was meant to achieve, and this includes the creation of a community in which a shared gratitude to God and mutual love welded all the different participants into a strong unity. This was God's intention, **the plan of the mystery hidden for ages in God.** The word translated **plan** (*oikonomia*) is the same word as that used in 1:10 ('a plan for the fullness of time'). In both instances the word means 'a plan of campaign'. This plan had long been in God's mind, but unguessed by men. It was now at last, however, disclosed and in process of being worked out as a practical operation.

At 3:2 the same Greek word was used—apparently in a different sense. It was there translated as a 'stewardship' (an 'assignment'), and was understood as a particular commission which God had given to Paul. In this sense it corresponds to the meaning of the word in the genuine epistles (as at Col. 1:25, 1 C. 9:17). The meaning of the word in Eph. 1:10 and 3:9 is, however, quite different. It signifies not an assignment to Paul but a plan of campaign within God's own mind. There is no parallel to this meaning of the word in Paul's letters, and many scholars have seen this unusual use of the word as evidence that someone other than Paul is writing this letter. In the light of this it may be opportune to look back at its use in 3:2. There it seemed to correspond to Paul's normal use of the word, as it is found for instance in Col. 1:25, and we felt it right to allow its use in the parallel verse in Colossians to determine its meaning at that point in Ephesians. But we did note one variation from the phrase in Colossians which seemed significant. Col. 1:25 writes of 'the divine office (= stewardship, *oikonomia*) which was given to me for you'. Eph. 3:2 largely repeats this, but with a variation. It writes of the 'stewardship (*oikonomia*) of God's grace, the grace which was given to me for you'. The difference is that in Eph. 3:2 it is not the *oikonomia* which is given to Paul, but the *grace*. This is clear in the Greek, though not in the English translation. It can be argued that the writer of Ephesians makes this change because for him the word *oikonomia* means God's master-plan (as in 1:10 and 3:9), and so could not be used of an assignment which God entrusts to Paul. In that case one would translate 3:2 in some such way as this: 'assuming that you have heard of the master-plan of God's grace—that grace which was given to me for you'.

mystery: see 1:9 and 3:3. **hidden for ages:** see 3:5. **in God who created all things:** This plan, though not understood by men, had been in the mind of God, the creator of the universe, for untold ages. He who had called the created universe into being and given life to man on earth had planned the introduction of this healing power of reconciliation as something which would finally overcome the forces that make for division in the world of men.

10. This reconciling power was to become known and to be exercised **through the church** (see 1:22). In **the church,** through the reconciling powers of Christ, all former divisions were to be healed. This master plan of God, for bringing unity and peace in place of hostility and estrangement, had been put into effect in Christ, and his Church was to be the continuing centre of this reconciling spirit. The establishment of the Church, within which all divisive forces can be neutralised and where an all-inclusive fellowship has been established, is proof of **the manifold wisdom of God.**

Rather surprisingly, those who through the Church are to become aware of the wisdom of God are **the principalities** (*archai*) **and powers** (*exousiai*) **in the heavenly places.** Previously in this epistle the phrase **heavenly places** has been used only in relation to God and God's agents (1:3, 1:20, 2:6). But these same **principalities and powers** are named again in Eph. 6:12 (see also note on 1:21), and there they are associated with 'the spiritual hosts of wickedness in heavenly places'. So the heavenly places are apparently a sphere where evil as well as good forces are found at work.

There appears to be a discernible sequence in the stages by which God's master-plan has been revealed. It was made known first to Paul (3:3), then to the apostles and prophets (3:5), then to **all men** (3:9). Only then, as God's reconciling power in Christ became effective in his Church and produced a united fellowship out of elements which in the world had seemed irreconcilable, did the powers of evil realise what God was achieving. Their purpose had been to foster strife and division among men. Now they saw at work a force powerful enough to neutralise their evil intentions and bring peace. It is not easy for us in the twentieth century to know what these **principalities and powers** meant for the readers of this epistle. Allan suggests that their introduction here is largely a form of impressive rhetoric rather than a precise concept: 'Except as a rhetorical flourish, this may have meant little more to the writer than it can mean to us.' We need, however, to remind ourselves that unseen powers of evil were much more real in the first century—though even in this century men face to face with Nazism and anti-Semitism, racial hatred, violence, the destructive power of drug addiction, and witchcraft, have felt the threat of an evil which seems to have larger than human dimensions.

God's plan, first revealed in Christ, and then actualised in the Church, is evidence of **the manifold wisdom of God.** The essence of **wisdom** is that it enables someone to set a course and make decisions which, though they may seem to others at the time to be foolish and ill-conceived, are in the end proved right by the good results they achieve. So Jesus on his cross is acclaimed as the wisdom of God (1 C. 1:23–24), although to bystanders at the time it all seemed a terrible folly. God's strategy, though human wisdom cannot see how it can succeed, is proved 'wise' by its results. The Greek word translated **manifold** deserves something more picturesque, if a suitable word can be found. It means 'richly diversified'. *The Jerusalem Bible* seeks to suggest something of this in 'comprehensive', and Phillips in 'complex'. *NEB* has 'wisdom in all its varied forms'. One is tempted to borrow Francis Thompson's more adventurous phrase, 'many-splendoured'.

11, 12. All **this was according to the eternal purpose** of God, a purpose formulated 'before the foundation of the world' and reaching forward as far as the human mind can reach. But it is now more than just a purpose in the mind of God; **he has realised** it **in Christ Jesus our Lord.** He has put it into effect through what he has done in Christ. For **Christ** and **Lord,** see 1:2.

From the various spiritual endowments with which Christ enriches the hearts of those who put their faith in him, two are chosen here for special mention: **boldness and confidence of access.** The word translated **boldness** literally means 'boldness of speech', and in Acts it is commonly ascribed to one who bears fearless witness to his faith, especially in the presence of those with power to inflict punishment for it. But the word can also mean courage and confidence in a more general sense. Here it is linked with **confidence of access** to God, and so must mean boldness in our approach to God. Christ has removed those things which would make a man timid and unsure in the presence of God. God is no longer feared as one who is unpredictable or ruthless, because Christ has revealed him to us as he is. Nor need we shrink before him as our judge in remembrance of our guilt. Christ has brought assurance of God's forgiveness. It is in Christ that men have found this new serenity and composure, even in the presence of God. He has made it possible for us to think of God without fear, even to speak of him as Father, *Abba* (see 2:18, where this same word 'access' is used again). All this is ours **in Christ;** but this is now amplified by the phrase **through our faith in him.** It is not just an automatic or one-sided process, but the result of a truly personal relationship in which our lives are opened to Christ in faith, both to receive the gifts he waits to bestow and the commands by which he guides and shapes men's lives. Literally **our faith in him** in the Greek is 'through the faith *of* him'. Most translators interpret this as *RSV* does, but G. Howard has argued persuasively that where this phrase occurs in the *NT*, it really means 'Christ's faith'—the quality of faith Jesus himself had (*ExpT* 85 (1973–4), p. 212).

13. The writer has introduced this paragraph (3:1–12) to make clear that his words are to be understood as Paul's own message. He writes, as in Colossians, as if Paul were in prison (Eph. 3:1). At Phil. 1:12 Paul insists that his sufferings have in fact 'served to advance the gospel' so that 'most of the brethren have been made confident in the Lord because of my imprisonment, and are much more bold to speak the word of God without fear'. But it must sometimes have worked the other way and awakened fear among his fellow Christians. This writer represents Paul as saying: **I ask you not to lose heart over what I am suffering for you. Lose heart** means to act in a cowardly way, to give up when difficulty and danger threaten. As in Col. 1:24, Paul's suffering is described as **for you.** His concern to bring the message of Christ to the Gentiles was the cause of his various punishments.

RSV notes that another translation of the Greek words is possible: 'I ask that *I* may not lose heart' (as though Paul himself were in danger of giving up the struggle and had to pray hard to be enabled to remain true). This, though possible in the Greek, does not sound like Paul, nor is it the way a disciple would wish to represent him. Not only *RSV*, but most other modern translators also, reject it. **which is your glory:** This must refer to the thought of the whole preceding sentence. For the readers to find courage rather than discouragement from the thought of Paul's ordeals, courage to be willing to share them, if need be, rather than timidity to find some way of avoiding them at any cost: this is their **glory.** The fact that Paul's example stimulates them to emulate his faithfulness is something of which they can be truly proud.

THE LOVE OF CHRIST 3:14–21

This short paragraph is one of the gems of the *NT*.

Those who believe that Ephesians is primarily a liturgical document, used in connexion with a baptismal occasion, suggest that these verses were used as a prayer that those newly baptised shall bring forth the fruits of their Christian profession.

14, 15. It begins by the writer picking up the phrase with which verse 3:1 began. That sentence was left unfinished, because the writer allowed himself to be led off on to a long digression about Paul himself. Now that the digression is ended, the writer picks up the thread of what he intended to write by repeating the same three words: **For this reason.** The **reason** referred to consists of the contents of all the earlier part of the epistle, not to any single item in it. **I bow my knees before the Father.** It is sometimes pointed out that the bended knee was the posture of homage (cf. Phil. 2:12; Rom. 14:11) rather than of prayer, and that for the Jews it was customary to stand rather than kneel for prayer. But there are instances where kneeling was used in prayer, e.g., Stephen's prayer in Ac. 7:59–60 and Daniel's in Dan. 6:10. Here in Eph. 3:14 the element of prayer is strongly present; indeed the whole paragraph is a prayer, the kind of prayer which springs from a sense of wonder and adoration at what God has done, is doing and is going to do. It is a situation in which homage and prayer are inseparable. Characteristically, God is named as **Father** (see 1:2–3, 2:18), but it is used here with a special purpose. He is **the Father from whom every family in heaven and on earth is named.** The translator is in two difficulties here. He has no word to indicate the very close connexion in the Greek between the word **Father** and the word **family.** In addition, it is not clear what precisely is meant by 'family'.

The Greek word for **family** (*patria*) is derived directly from the word for **Father** (*patēr*) and ideally an English translation should indicate this close connexion. The *RV* marginal translation tried to do this, and suggested 'fatherhood' instead of 'family', but this of course changes the meaning of the word. *patria* means a large family group derived from a single ancestor, all of whom feel their unity with the whole group because of their common origin. It would, however, normally be a much larger group than is indicated in English by the word 'family'. It is perhaps what we mean by a clan or a tribe. This is the only occurrence of the word in Ephesians, and the only two other uses of it in the *NT* (Lk. 2:4, Ac. 3:25) do not make its meaning precisely clear. The difficulty in English is to indicate the fact that a *patria* is called a *patria* because of its link with the *patēr* (father).

If we translate it as 'fatherhood' (as *RV* margin), the sentence would mean that all human fatherhood is derived from the Fatherhood of God. One could support this by recalling the way Jesus linked the two. If human fathers, he said, know how to give good gifts to their children, how much more the divine Father (Mt. 7:11). Knox follows this course and translates here: 'from whom all fatherhood takes its title'; and so also does Phillips: 'from whom all fatherhood derives its name'. But the Greek, properly translated, should mean 'every fatherhood' and not 'all fatherhood'. One could perhaps argue that it means 'every instance of fatherhood'; if so, it provides a certain link between the divine Father and the human father. In the abstract this translation is perhaps attractive, but it does not seem to fit the context here. What is an even more formidable obstacle is that *patria* in Greek does not in fact mean 'fatherhood'.

If 'family' is the nearest equivalent to the Greek *patria*, the translation here ought to be 'every family'. The wording of the Greek really does not permit the translation 'the whole family', although the *AV* adopted it and *NEB* allows it as an alternative in a footnote. The grammatical problem is like that in 2:21, where the Greek strictly requires 'every building', but *RSV* translates as 'the whole structure'. This translation, as also 'the whole family' here in 3:15, is possible only on the assumption that the writer has either failed to express himself accurately, or else allowed a Semitic idiom to supersede normal Greek grammar. If we do translate it as 'the whole family', it must mean the whole human family or possibly the whole family of the Church, those privileged to know God as Father.

The *RSV* represents the Greek better when it translates it as **every family.** What does this mean? It could mean every human family; or else every separate group of Christians within the total community of the Church. It could be, that is, a word for the local congregation. This is the more probable, because in Ephesians the word *ekklēsia* is used only for the Church universal, never for a local congregation, and the writer may have felt the need for a separate word for the local congregation. Interestingly enough, at 2:21, where the same grammatical question was forced on our attention, this also was the very point at issue. 'Every structure' there, as 'every family' here, probably indicates the local congregation within the total family of the whole Church.

If this is so, is there any better way of representing the link between the Greek word *patēr* and *patria* than by using 'Father' and 'family'? One wonders if the word 'brotherhood' might serve the purpose, since this word in English can have the double meaning of 'the status of being brothers' and also 'a company of people regarding themselves as brothers'. Christians soon learned to speak of each other as 'brothers' (cf. Mt. 5:23; Rom. 14:10) because they recognised each other as sons of the same Father in heaven. It is possible that here we could render the words as 'the Father from whom every brotherhood of Christians derives its name'.

The reference to 'every family' **in heaven** as well as on earth poses a problem. Masson (p. 180) quotes Rabbinic texts where angels are called 'the family above' in contrast to Israel, the family below. If, however, *patria* means the local group of Christians, would a *patria* in heaven mean a company of departed Christians? If so, then this is an early anticipation of the doctrine of the communion of saints. *do they stay together as a long. ebm?*

16. according to the riches of his glory: the 'glorious' (dazzling) **riches** of God are not different from 'the unsearchable riches of Christ' (3:8). From these resources of divine grace Christians may find themselves **strengthened with might** (equipped with courage and vitality for all the tasks ahead) **in the inner man.** This is very close to the thought of 2 C. 4:16: 'We do not lose heart ... our inner nature is being renewed every day.' The **inner man** or nature is the real man, the centre of our spiritual and psychological life. If all is well in this inner citadel, external difficulties can be met and overcome. This constant inward renewal is brought about **through his Spirit.** The **Spirit** is the mode in which God communicates himself to men and women.

17. and that Christ may dwell in your hearts through faith. 'Heart' is here another way of expressing what was meant by 'inner man'—the centre from which comes the will and intention by which a life is directed. It is the quality of the heart which determines the quality of the life (Mt. 12:34–5, 7:21). The whole life is significantly changed when obedience to God springs from the heart (Rom. 6:17; cf. also 'the circumcision of the heart' and 'the new covenant in the heart'). If Christ dwells in the heart, it means that he controls that which directs the whole course of a man's life. This phrase from Ephesians about Christ 'dwelling in the heart' has become so well known that it is a surprise to find that this is the only place in the *NT* where it is found, though there are, of course, many similar expressions. Paul, for instance, speaks of 'Christ in us' (Col. 1:27; Gal. 2:20) and John of Christ 'abiding' in us (Jn 14:23, 15:4).

This writer faithfully represents the thought of Paul when he makes no clear-cut distinction between the indwelling Christ and the Spirit of God in man. The Spirit in the inner man cannot be differentiated from Christ dwelling in the heart, just as in Rom. 8:9 Paul speaks of the *Spirit of God* dwelling in the Christian, and in the next verse of *Christ* being 'in you'. (There the Greek word for 'dwell' is similar but not identical to the word for 'dwell' in Eph. 3:17—*oikeō* and *katoikeō*.) Again, the writer stresses that this intimate relationship with Christ is not an automatic privilege mediated by a sacrament or conferred by official membership in the Church. It comes **through** personal **faith** (as at 3:12).

The consequence of Christ's dwelling in their hearts is that they can be described as **rooted and grounded in love.** The verbs in the Greek are in the perfect passive, which means that they describe something which has already taken place and is continuing as a stable and constant condition. The two words introduce a mixed metaphor, **rooted** being taken from plant life and **grounded** from building. A deep-rooted tree can remain firm and healthy in spite of hurricane and persistent drought; and a building with strong foundations reaching down to the rock can withstand the onslaughts of wind, rain, and flood. *NEB* combines the two happily: 'with deep roots and firm foundations'. The whole phrase means that the controlling spirit is one of **love.** This is the result of Christ's dwelling in the heart. He is in control of the springs of life, which means that self is no longer the master, and Christlikeness, an unselfish concern for others (**love**), has taken its place. The first-named fruit of the Spirit is love (Gal. 5:22). A Christ-directed life is one which is expressed in love.

The words **in love** in the Greek precede 'rooted and grounded' and some scholars contend that they should be understood as linked with the preceding clause. In that case they would describe Christ as dwelling in our hearts 'in love'. In either case the rule of Christ in the human heart is marked by a life of love (cf. 1:5, 1:15, 2:4).

18. It is as love for others takes control of our lives that we are enabled to sense the reality of the love of Christ. Hatred and resentment form a spiritual fog in which even the love of Christ is obscured. 'In so far as you advance in love, you will grow surer of the reality of God' (Dostoievsky, in *The Brothers Karamazov*). Christ awakens in us love towards others, and in turn that love

enables us to grasp the love behind the universe. To be reconciled to our brother enables us to be reconciled to God (Mt.
5:24; Mk 11:26). The presence of love for others in the heart is
that which makes it possible to **have power to comprehend . . .
the love of Christ.** Ill-will, self-pity, and self-indulgence dull
and even extinguish spiritual insight. Love is a kind of extra eye
to enable us to see spiritual truth. This vision of the reality of **the
love of Christ** is an experience shared **with all the saints,** all
one's fellow Christians (not just a privileged few). Nor is it just a
passing, partial glimpse; it is a sense of the love of Christ in all its
fullness, as something which reaches into every corner of life, something from whose grasp we can never slip. It is as inescapable as
the very presence of God's Spirit (Ps. 139:7–12). It reaches higher
than heaven and lower than hell, and further than the limits of
both east and west. The writer tries to express this all-embracing
quality of the love of Christ by speaking of its **breadth and
length and height and depth.** Some commentators express uneasiness that four dimensions are mentioned when in fact there
are only three. But the words are very expressive, even if not
precise. It is as though he said: whether you go forward or back-
ward, up to the heights or down to the depths, nothing will separate us from the love of Christ. The thought is very similar to that
in Rom. 8:37–39.

Somewhat fancifully, some commentators have related these four
dimensions in the love of Christ to the cross on which he died, two
dimensions covered by the upright post of the cross and two by
the cross beam; but though good homiletic points may be made
by this kind of ingenuity it is most improbable that any such
thought was in the mind of the writer.

19. Though a Christian may be enabled to sense the boundless
nature of **the love of Christ,** he knows that he has grasped only
a little of the total truth. It is a love which **surpasses knowlege.**
This means probably that it is too wonderful for us to take in (cf.
Ps. 139:6) in its entirety. There is always more than we had
reckoned. Some, however, see here a contrast between **love** and
knowledge, such as is sometimes found in the Christian challenge
to Gnostic teaching. The Gnostics tended to suggest that some
form of knowledge was the supreme qualification for the full
relationship to God; in contrast the *NT* emphasises the importance of love as compared with knowledge. 'Knowledge

puffs up, but love builds up' (1 C. 8:1; cf. 1 C. 13:2, 12). But
what is contrasted here is not so much love and knowledge as
possible pathways to God, but rather **the love of Christ** and
the inadequacy of human **knowledge** fully to comprehend
it.

that you may be filled with all the fullness of God. The
Greek literally means *to* **all the fullness of** God—that you may
come to possess not just some but all the gifts which God means
you to have. These include, as just indicated, inward strength
from the gift of the Spirit, Christ dwelling in your hearts and there
creating enduring love for others, a sense of the reality and complete adequacy of Christ's love towards you. The *NEB* margin
seeks to represent this emphasis: 'Up to the fullness which God
requires'. It could mean, however, not so much being filled with
God's gifts as with God himself. Phillips (1972) takes it this way
and translates: 'So you will be filled through all your being with
God himself.' Some think that the meaning is that each Christian
should long to be perfectly equipped as a Christian just as God
himself is perfect as God (Mt. 5:48).

20-21. This impressive doxology clearly indicates that one
main section of the epistle here comes to an end. The first three
chapters, overflowing with gratitude, have enumerated the
privileges which now belong to the Christian through what God's
grace in Christ has achieved for him. They have expounded the
long-hidden purpose of God for man which has now been disclosed through Christ and which has already reached a measure
of fulfilment in the new reconciliation of Jew and Gentile within
the Church. The chapters have underlined the outstanding part
played by Paul in the understanding and spread of the gospel.
Now this section of affirmation and praise is ended. A new section
whose primary note is that of 'exhortation' is about to begin. The
first word indeed in 4:1 is literally 'I exhort'.

Though the doxology is impressive, it is somewhat wordy and
indistinct in meaning. Like the similar doxologies in Rom. 16:25–
27 and Jude 24, it begins (in the Greek) with the phrase **to ...
him who ... is able ...** Indeed the doxology at the end of
Romans is so much like this one in style (see *EE*, p. 148) that
some have argued that they are the work of the same post-Pauline
author, perhaps the editor of the corpus of letters in its collected
form, Ephesians representing a kind of introductory summary of

the gathered letters and the doxology in Romans its concluding benediction right at the end of the corpus.

the power at work within us (cf. 1:19, 3:7), by means of which God achieves his victories in human life, is the Holy Spirit (see 3:16). By means of this **power,** active in the lives of individuals and in the community of the Church, God **is able to do far more abundantly than all that we ask or think,** more than the actual requests in our prayers, more even than our fondest imaginings. The Greek word translated **far more** is an extremely emphatic one, meaning 'far, far more'. The name of God is not mentioned, but only implied in the phrase often applied to him: He who is able. **to him be glory in the church:** within the community of the Church let there be proper recognition of what God has done and will do, and in consequence let praise be offered to him. It seems rather odd to have **and in Christ Jesus** added after 'in the church'. If both are to be mentioned surely 'in Christ' should come first. This difficulty was felt from very early days. In some of the earliest MSS the copyists reverse the order, or else omit the word **and** so that the passage could be translated 'in the church through Jesus Christ'. But, as is usually the case, it is the more difficult text which must be regarded as the genuine one, even if we cannot offer a satisfactory explanation of it.

Masson seeks to surmount the problem by insisting that since there is no main verb (**be**) actually expressed in the Greek, the whole sentence is not a wish but an affirmation. The verb understood should be expressed as 'is': 'glory is offered to God in the Church and in Christ Jesus.' He feels that this approach removes the difficulties: 'If glory is due to God in the Church, it is also due to him in Jesus Christ.' This may provide some mitigation of the difficulty, but cannot be said to have removed it.

It is not surprising that some commentators seek to gloss over the difficulty by abandoning the attempt to find a precise meaning in every single word and phrase. They claim that it is characteristic of this writer to accumulate words of an imposing nature in order to convey a general sense of impressiveness without analysing their particular significance. So Houlden writes of 'the sonorous language ... whose precise sense is hard to find'; and Allan comments: 'The rich liturgical language of the epistle should not be pressed too closely.'

to all generations, for ever and ever is an approximate translation of a somewhat imprecise accumulation of Greek words.

THE UNITY OF THE CHURCH 4:1-16

There is a recognisable pattern in several of Paul's letters: the early chapters deal largely with matters of experience and belief, and the later ones with conduct appropriate to the beliefs. He says in effect: You *are* Christians in belief and experience; then *be* Christians in the way you behave. This pattern is very clear in Romans (see 12:1), Colossians (3:1) and 1 Thessalonians (4:1). It is reproduced here also in Ephesians.

1. I therefore ... beg you are the same words as those used in Rom. 12:1. The word **therefore** shows that the ethical instructions are seen as a logical consequence of the doctrinal affirmations of chapters 1-3. The writer strengthens the appeal of his words by referring to Paul as **a prisoner for the Lord.** In the Greek this phrase is not the same as that in 3:1, though the English translation suggests that it is. There it was literally 'the prisoner *of* Christ Jesus'; here it is 'the prisoner *in* the Lord'. It is doubtful, however, if any difference of meaning is intended. Both imply that it is Paul's devotion to Christ which has led to his imprisonments. **lead a life worthy of the calling to which you have been called. lead a life** correctly translates the Greek word 'walk', since in the Bible 'walk' means 'conduct oneself', 'behave' (cf. 2:2). The conduct of a Christian should be such as matches his commitment to Christ, his **calling.** Here again is the emphasis that the Christians have entered this new life as the result of God's initiative in their lives. God has **called** them, as at 1:18—just as God 'chose' (1:4), 'destined' (1:5), and 'appointed' (1:12) them. But a Christian's response to God's call implies a willingness to allow God to control the quality of his life.

2. The words which follow describe something of this life. They are all taken from Col. 3:12: **with all lowliness and meekness, with patience, forbearing one another.** In Colossians they are associated with the establishing of peace and harmony in the community (cf. 'perfect harmony' in Col. 3:14, 'peace ... in one body' in Col. 3:15). Here in Ephesians they prepare the way for an even stronger emphasis on unity in the

Church. They are the qualities in individual Christians which make possible the continuing unity of the Church. **lowliness and meekness** are often associated together because of a basic similarity. Jesus himself brought them together in the description of himself as 'meek and lowly in heart' (Mt. 11:29). **lowliness** is the quality of one who does not seek to gain prominence for himself, does not insist on his rights and expect special consideration. It allows others to take precedence and receive credit. At Phil. 2:3 it is associated with 'counting others better than oneself'. We see the opposite of lowliness in those faults rebuked by Jesus in Mt. 23:5 where some Pharisees are described as loving the place of honour, the best seats, and honorific forms and titles of address. **meekness** is similar but not identical. It is the spirit of one who is so absorbed in seeking some worthy goal for the common good that he refuses to be deflected from it by slights, injuries, or insults directed at himself personally, or indeed by personal considerations of any kind. Provided the end in view is achieved, he cares little whether he or someone else is given the credit. It is the opposite of being touchy, resentful, retaliatory. It is not to be confused with weakness and may indeed be found in men of immense strength of character, men who can show complete personal disinterestedness in seeking some social good. Moses, for instance, is described as meek (Num. 12:3) even though he had the inward strength of character to lead a horde of demoralised slaves out to freedom and make of them the nucleus of a great and enduring nation. He was meek because in it all he was totally free from self-seeking, never reacting to a situation out of personal pique, always seeking first and foremost the good of the people with whom he was identified. **patience** is the ability to deal quietly and courteously with people who are awkward, difficult, and offensive. The Greek word literally means 'long-tempered', as opposed to short-tempered. It is a different word from the one which means 'steadfastness' in distressing circumstances (though this too may sometimes be translated as 'patience'). **forbearing one another in love.** This is not a separate quality from 'patience', but rather an amplification of what patience means. At 1 C. 4:12 this forbearance (there translated in *RSV* as 'endurance') is urged as the proper Christian response to persecution from non-Christians. Here, however, it is forbearance towards others within the Christian community. It is worth noting that the writer

has no rosy-eyed picture of this community as composed only of
perfect Christians. In the community are those with irritating
faults and idiosyncrasies, which can be extremely annoying to
others. These can be contained and prevented from disrupting the
fellowship only if other Christians meet them with good-humoured
tolerance. The Christian will seek to show this attitude to others,
because he knows that they, too, will need to show it towards *his*
faults. This writer then adds the words **in love** to the words he
borrows from Colossians. **love** means the consideration of other
people's welfare, the willingness to act for their good rather than
out of our own irritation. This forbearance was seen in Jesus
towards his disciples, though even for him it was clearly no easy
task (see Mk 9:19).

3. Any Christian who in the community life can constantly
show humility, meekness, and patient forbearance to others is
making a really solid contribution to the unity of the group.
Indeed the motive for their self-restraint is that they are **eager to
maintain the unity of the Spirit in the bond of peace.
eager** is hardly strong enough to represent the Greek word it
translates. 'Spare no effort' (*NEB*) gives the urgency of it better.
It is assumed that harmony is present in the Church, but that it is
threatened and that persistent and vigilant care is necessary if it is
to be preserved. It is called **the unity of the Spirit.** *RSV* prints
'Spirit' with a capital S because it interprets the word to mean
God's Spirit and not just the spirit of Christian people. Some,
however, take it this second way and translate as 'the spiritual
harmony of the community', its 'peaceful atmosphere'. But it is
more consistent with the use of Spirit in this epistle to understand
it here as the Spirit of God. The phrase then means 'the unity
which the Spirit gives'. **in the bond of peace: peace** is spoken of
as if it were a rope which can hold together within one secure
bundle separate elements which are not naturally cohesive. We
sometimes speak of peace as the goal to strive for in the Church.
Peace, however, is not so much an end in itself as a means by
which the greater end of the unity of the Spirit is continually
secured. Quarrelling and division destroy not just the pleasant
harmony of a congenial social group. It destroys **the unity of the
Spirit,** which was God's gift to his Church to enable it to be the
instrument of his purposes in the world. To allow personal irritation or resentment to sever the rope which holds this unity

securely is a responsibility too heavy for any individual to assume. Peace in the community is that which preserves the unity which God intended for his Church, both for the good of the individual members within it and for the furtherance of his wider purposes on earth.

It is sometimes asked whether this unity refers only to the local congregation or to the world-wide community of the Church as well. It would no doubt be a salve to our consciences to argue that it applies only to the single congregation and not to the whole Church, now divided into denominational separations which even prevent Christian sharing with Christian at the Lord's table. It is, however, quite impossible to restrict this insistence on unity and peace to the local congregation. It is the whole Church, not a local congregation, which is the body of Christ. God's intention for his universal Church to be one body has been sadly frustrated. How far, when denominational differences were set up, was the conduct of the protagonists on each side marked by humility, meekness, and patient forbearance towards others? How far is personal pride, touchiness, and impatient intolerance present in the perpetuation of these denominational differences? Is it not Christianly possible to have the widest degree of variations in method of worship, church government, and credal formulae, without allowing these things to break the unity of the Spirit? The writer of Ephesians clearly felt the unity of the Spirit to be of prime importance, of far greater importance than Christians of subsequent centuries have treated it.

4. Disunity among Christians is for this writer unthinkable. Wherever Christians are to be found they share the same basic treasures. Differences belong largely to the superficialities. The writer lists some of the underlying unities.

There is one body. The Church has already been called the **body** of Christ (see note at 1:23). It is so called because in the post-resurrection era its function was to continue to do for Christ what during his earthly life the body of Jesus did for him. It should provide hands, feet, eyes, and brain to serve the purposes of the Spirit of Christ in the world. As there was one body in the earthly ministry of Jesus, so there is one body in his continuing work. Though from widely different backgrounds Christians have found themselves unbelievably blended into one community. A deep sense of belonging together animated them. They were 'one body in Christ' (Rom. 12:5). It was as unthinkable that they should divide or mutilate this resurrection body of Christ as that they should 'crucify the Son of God on their own account and hold him up to contempt' (Heb. 6:6). The same emphasis on the unity of the body is found also at 1 C. 10:17, 12:4–6, 8:6). **and one Spirit:** this must surely refer to God's Spirit, whose coming into the Christian's life was a basic mark of his new experience. Some, however, have interpreted it of the human spirit, to mean harmony within the community. It was noted at 1:14 that Paul could assume that anyone who had become a Christian had received the Spirit of God. This belief was common ground among all Christians. When the Holy Spirit was given to Gentile Christians as well as to Jewish (as at Ac. 10:44–45) this was at first an occasion of surprise, but it never occurred to anyone to claim that this was a different Spirit. There is **one Spirit,** as Paul affirmed at 1 C. 12:13. It was so certainly the same Spirit that his presence in them all made of them a single community, in spite of all past prejudices which divided and alienated them. Associated with this shared gift of the Spirit is the hope into which **you were called,** and which **belongs to your call.** The word **called** once again underlines the God-given nature of this **hope.** At 1:14 the gift of the Spirit was called a foretaste and guarantee here and now of the fullness of life which awaits the Christian beyond death. The Spirit is the awakener of this hope. So, appropriately enough, **hope** comes to mind after mention of the Spirit. As it is the same Spirit who is given to all, so the hope he inspires is in all the same hope.

5. one Lord: For all Christians another basic element in their faith is their acknowledgement of Jesus as **Lord** (see 1 C. 12:1). This indeed is thought to have been the earliest and most widely accepted credal affirmation of the Church. **one faith:** At 2:8 faith is the willingness to open one's life to God, to receive whatever he sees fit to give, whether commands to be obeyed or healing of inward weaknesses. This was a factor in the experience shared by all Christians. It is possible, however, that in this verse something of the later meaning of faith, as an article of belief, is beginning to appear, and here **faith** may mean belief in Jesus as Lord, and the Spirit as renewer, and the Father as giver of all. If this is so, then faith is, as it were, the subjective element associated with the objective affirmation: Jesus is Lord. It is that in the

believer which enables him to make the confession. **one baptism:**
It was the universal practice in the Church that the faith of
believers was made public and corporate in the act of baptism.
The sacrament denoted their commitment to Christ and their
acceptance into the community of his followers.

It is not at all clear how baptism in water became a universally
accepted practice in the early Church. It was known that Jesus
had accepted baptism at the hands of John the Baptist, though it
is also made clear that the baptism which Jesus himself will give
is baptism in the Spirit. It is not clear how far Jesus himself ever
baptised disciples. The evidence in Jn 4:1 and 4:2 is incompatible.
For whatever reason, water baptism like John's was continued in
the Christian Church as the mark of initiation, but it was always
something more than just water baptism, which for John had
symbolised repentance. Full Christian baptism, even though
water was used in it, was understood to be also baptism by the
Spirit, by which new power from God was bestowed on the
believer.

It is often asked why, in the list of features which stamp the
Church with a basic and indivisible unity, the sacrament of the
Lord's Supper is not included, It is a strange omission, because this
gathering together at a common meal of great meaning was a
regular feature of all early Christianity. Some have argued that
perhaps a reference to it is implicit in the mention of the one Body,
since these gatherings were held for the sharing in the body of
Christ in the form of bread to be broken and distributed. But in
view of the earlier reference to the body as being the Church, the
use of the same word in a more narrowly sacramental sense seems
improbable. We do not know why there is no mention of this
sacrament, but its absence poses particular difficulties for those
who wish to interpret Ephesians as primarily a liturgical document framed for use in a sacramental setting.

6. one God and Father of us all. The Christian shared un-
questioningly in the Jewish affirmation that God is one. If others
spoke of 'many gods', they were only 'so-called gods', not really
God. The distinctive name by which Christians spoke of this one
true God was **Father.** This was the name which Jesus used of God
(see 1:2), and it became the characteristic mark of Christian
experience at its most profound that Christians were enabled
spontaneously to address God as '*Abba*, Father' (Gal. 4:6; Rom.

8:15). The word **us** is a recognition that it was only among Christians that God was confidently known as Father.

God is then further described in three prepositional phrases as **above** (or 'over') **all and through all and in all.** Some late MSS insert 'us' with **all,** but though this may accurately represent the meaning of 'all', the earlier texts which omit it must be regarded as the more accurate. Some commentators, however, take 'all' as a neuter to mean 'all things' (i.e., the universe); others take it as meaning 'all people'; still others think that it means 'all Christians'. Ronald Knox, in his translation, combines the three possibilities: God is 'above all beings, pervades all things, and lives in all of us'. The Greek does not make the meaning clear; we must allow the context to guide us to what appears to be the right interpretation. God is **above all,** supreme and transcendent. He is **through all,** actively at work throughout his creation, so that there is nothing which may not become an instrument of his purpose. He is **in all:** human lives may become his dwelling place, as God comes to us in Christ who 'dwells in our hearts' (3:17). Some (e.g., Masson) see here an anticipation of the doctrine of the Trinity as the three phrases describe the transcendence of the Father, the immanent activity of the Spirit, and the indwelling of Christ the Son. This, however, may be to find something the writer did not intend, though the three persons in the Trinity are in fact mentioned in verses 4, 5, and 6. If there is trinitarian thought here, it is in a somewhat indistinct form.

Houlden, who takes **all** to mean 'all *things*', describes these three prepositional phrases as 'simple Stoicism set in a Jewish-cum-Christian frame'. 'Above all', however, is Jewish more than Stoic (cf. Rom. 9:5), but to speak of God as 'through all *things*' and 'in all *things*' is not really characteristic either of the Bible as a whole or of Paul's letters in particular, though the phrasing has some similarity to items of the speech attributed to Paul on the Areopagus (Ac. 17:25). **in all** must here refer to people rather than things, or else we must say that the writer of Ephesians has allowed an un-biblical phrase into his writings at this point.

7. It is characteristic of the literary style of this epistle that the next ten verses (7–16) constitute in the Greek one single very long sentence. In translation, as in *RSV*, it is usually broken up into several shorter ones.

The essential unity of the Church could hardly have been more emphatically stated than it was in verses 4–6. Such unity entirely excludes any tendency to condone the possibility of two or three different churches in order to appease national or racial prejudices. Wherever a branch of the Christian Church has sprung into being, there it shares with all other parts of the Church a solid area of common ground. Whatever their national background or social origin, Christians know that in their experience and in their confessions of faith they acknowledge one Lord and one Spirit, one faith and one baptism, one Father-God. These shared certainties make all Christians and all Christian groups everywhere branches of the same one Church and parts of the one body of Christ.

Within this unity, however, there is rich diversity. Unity, but not uniformity, is the mark of this community. The individuals who become Christians bring with them the greatest possible differences of temperament and a wide variety of natural gifts, and all these are heightened and enhanced as the Spirit quickens them. Moreover, unguessed potentials in some Christians are stirred into activity and matured in unexpected ways. When this rich diversity of abilities is placed at the disposal of the Church, there is no proper function of the Church which is not provided for. The important point to be stressed is that all these abilities are really 'gifts' endowed on Christian believers by the grace of God in Christ: **grace was given to each of us according to the measure of Christ's gift.** Every single Christian is enabled to make some significant contribution to the common good. It is **grace,** God's enabling power freely and generously given, which brings this about. Nor is there any niggardliness or careful conservation of resources. God's gifts are not offered in 'carefully calculated less or more'. 'It is not by measure that God gives the Spirit' (Jn 3:34). So here the degree of God's generous endowment is described as being **according to the measure of Christ's gift.** If we ask what is meant by this **measure,** the answer is suggested in Rom. 8:32: 'He who did not spare his own Son but gave him up for us all, will he not also with him freely give us all things?' So **the measure of Christ's gift** means 'with a generosity which holds nothing back' (cf. also Lk. 6:38 for a description by Jesus of the bounty of God's generosity).

8. The writer then recalls a verse of Scripture which he quotes to confirm his emphasis on God's gifts through Christ. Scripture was God's Word and when some Christian truth, discovered in experience, could be shown to be affirmed also in the words of Scripture, then its reality was doubly vouched for. This verse of Scripture, as it is remembered, seems to be particularly applicable here, because it not only stressed God's gifts, but also other appropriate truths about Christ (such as his ascension and triumph). The quotation is introduced with the words: **Therefore it is said. Therefore** here means 'with good reason', or 'with complete appropriateness'. **it is said** refers to the Word of God spoken in Scripture. The quotation is, however, a very odd one. First, it is a striking misquotation which almost reverses the meaning of the actual text. Secondly, it is the misquoted words which alone make it applicable in this context. Psalm 68, from which the quotation is taken, is acclaiming a mighty victory won by God over his enemies. Verse 18 reads:

> Thou didst ascend the high mount,
>   leading captives in thy train,
>   and *receiving* gifts among men.

God is said to *receive* gifts from men as tokens of their homage and loyalty. But the writer of Ephesians in quoting the verse changes 'receive' to 'give': **he** *gave* **gifts** *to* **men.** There is no evidence that there was any variant reading in the earlier texts of the psalm which provided this alternative. It is clearly a mistake. Houlden regards it as a deliberate alteration on the part of the writer of Ephesians in order to make the quotation fit his need at this point: 'There is no need to suppose that the alteration was other than deliberate' (p. 310). In support he claims that Jewish expositors of that era took similar liberties with the text of Scripture, and adds: 'So here, the fact that Christian events tuned in better with the word *gave* than the word *received* not merely permitted but even demanded the change.' C. J. Ellicott (*St Paul's Epistles to the Philippians, Colossians, and Philemon*, 1857) took a somewhat similar line of explanation, claiming that Paul's apostolic authority gave him the right to adapt the words of Scripture to his purposes: 'The inspired apostle by a slight change of language . . . succinctly, suggestively, and authoritatively unfolds.' One does, however, find it difficult to think of a Christian writer as quite deliberately changing (so as to reverse its meaning) a word of Scripture to make it support his own contention. What is much more likely is that it was an unintentional misquotation. The writer's over-whelming sense of the wonder of God's gifts in Christ causes him to recall the psalmist's words in a form congenial to his own over-flowing gratitude instead of in the form they actually took in the psalm. The fact that the preceding word **ascended** was already associated in his mind with Jesus would make it easier for him to recall the later words in a form congenial to the Christian message. Psalm 68 is not one of the more familiar psalms and it is more than probable that the writer of Ephesians knew it only well enough to misquote it.

Strong and emotionally charged convictions can distort memory in this way. One remembers an old Christian man pray-ing that God would set him free from 'anger and hatred and pride'. He thought that he was quoting the words of a hymn, which in fact were: 'anger and falsehood and pride'; but 'hatred' slipped in for 'falsehood' because just at that time he was facing peculiarly difficult circumstances in which hatred was the sin he was then finding it hardest to withstand. Another misquotation from the *OT* is found at Mk 1:3. Isaiah 40:3 reads:

> A voice cries:
>   In the wilderness prepare the way of the Lord.

When it is quoted at Mk 1:3 it is changed to:

> The voice of one crying in the wilderness:
> Prepare the way of the Lord.

The phrase 'in the wilderness' is transferred from one clause to another, presumably because it was known that John the Baptist had in fact preached his message in the countryside away from the towns. The appropriateness of the change would lead to its being unconsciously (rather than deliberately) adopted by the later writer.

In the psalm 'the high mount' would probably be Mount Zion to which God comes in triumph. For the writer of Ephesians **When he ascended on high** speaks prophetically of Christ's ascension to the right hand of God. It is perhaps unnecessary to speculate who the **host of captives** were whom **he led.** Chrysos-tom suggested they were Satan, sin, and death (death being the 'last enemy' in 1 C. 15:24). Some recent writers suggest that they were not so much powers of evil which Christ had conquered as prisoners whom he had liberated from the domination of evil

and brought under the control of God. It may be doubted if the
writer had clearly thought out who the captives were. Certainly
there is nothing in the context to give us a clue. The form of the
gifts will be expounded in verse 11.

9. The word **ascended,** however, is a word to which he returns
for further elaboration. The sense of it has appeared already at
Eph. 1:20–22, where we read that God 'made Christ sit at his
right hand far above all rule, etc.' Here, however, the writer sees
the chance of emphasising still further the gracious gift of God
in Christ, not only in the ascension itself, but in that which preceded the ascension. For there to be an ascension at all, he argues,
there had first to be a previous 'descent', as Phil. 2:6–9 so movingly
expressed it: 'though he was in the form of God . . . he emptied
himself . . . Therefore God has highly exalted him.' The 'descent'
is then described: **he had also descended into the lower parts
of the earth.** As the *RSV* translation implies, this seems to refer
to the incarnation (as in Phil. 2:6–9). The **lower parts of the
earth** mean the earth which is lower than the heavens from which
he came. Calvin took it in this sense and quoted Jn 3:13 in
support of it. Had there been nothing else in Scripture to suggest
an alternative meaning, this would probably have been accepted
without question.

In 1 Peter, however, there is a clearly stated belief that Jesus,
between the time of his death and his resurrection, visited the
spirits of the departed in Hades: 'He went and preached to the
spirits in prison, who formerly did not obey' (1 Pet. 3:19). At
4:6 also we read: 'The gospel was preached to the dead.' It was
these passages which gave rise to the affirmation in the creed that
Christ 'descended into hell'. The purpose of this affirmation was
that it should be seen that no one who had died before the coming
of Jesus would be deprived of the privilege of hearing the gospel.
Once this belief had been established on the basis of these two
verses in 1 Peter, it was understandable that other texts should be
sought in the *NT* which would support it. Some have cited Rom.
10:7 to this end; but the one most commonly quoted is Eph. 4:9.
It was argued that the phrase translated in *RSV* as **the lower
parts of the earth** could equally well mean 'the parts lower
than the earth' (i.e., Hades), and certainly this could be the
meaning of the Greek. On the whole, however, it seems probable
that the reference here is to the whole story of the incarnation,

with all the gifts Christ thereby brought to human need. However important the doctrine of the descent into Hades may be, it is slight compared with the much greater wonder of the incarnation, to which it is only an addendum.

10. This verse explicitly insists that the one **who descended is** the same as **he who ascended.** There was an early heretical tendency to argue that the heavenly Christ was not the same as the human Jesus who wept and hungered and bled and died. These degrading humiliations could not be ascribed to God. The human Jesus who suffered was not to be wholly identified with the eternal Christ. This verse seems to be an explicit denial of this heretical trend.

G. B. Caird in *The Descent of Christ in Eph.* 4:7–11 (*Studia Evangelica* II (1964), pp. 535ff.) argues for a different interpretation of the word **descended.** Psalm 68, which is quoted in Eph. 4:8, is associated in Jewish liturgy with the celebration of the feast of Pentecost, and from this Caird argues that Christians may well have used it for their celebration of Pentecost, the time when the Holy Spirit was given. 'Descended' is, therefore, to be related to the coming of the Holy Spirit. In favour of this interpretation is the sequence of the words, since 'ascended' precedes 'descended'. Against this interpretation, however, is the fact that it was not Christ's return to the earth which was celebrated in the Christian Pentecost, but the coming of the Holy Spirit. It is true that both Paul and John on occasion somewhat blur the distinction between Christ and the Holy Spirit (e.g., Rom. 8:9f., 2 C. 3:17; Jn 14:16–18), but this is hardly sufficient to justify the interpretation of Pentecost as a descent of *Christ*. If so unusual a point was being made, it would surely have been indicated more clearly.

The odd phrase: **he . . . ascended far above all the heavens** is not easy to understand. It is true that in contemporary thought **the heavens** were regarded as a series of storeys or layers one above the other. Paul can speak of himself in an experience of spiritual ecstasy as being 'caught up to the third heaven' (2 C. 12:2). It is sometimes said that in Jewish piety it was customary to think of seven heavens, though occasionally the number is given as eight. The whole idea is very imprecise. Often heaven is thought of as the home of God, but here God's dwelling is beyond the heavens. In this context, therefore, **the heavens** are thought of as the abode of spiritual powers intermediate between men and

God. A similar thought to this is found at Heb. 4:14, which
affirms that Christ 'passed through the heavens'. God himself and
he who is at God's right hand are **above all the heavens,**
higher than the highest heaven.

The purpose of the ascension of Christ is **that he might fill
all things.** The ascension of Christ is thought of, not as an event
which removes Christ from the earth, but rather as that which
sets Christ free from anything that might localise him. It makes
him totally available to all men everywhere at all time. There is
no part of the universe where Christ is not.

11. The gift particularly associated in the *NT* with the action
of the ascended Christ is the gift of the Holy Spirit. In Ac. 1:7
this gift is promised as Christ ascends into heaven, and in Jn 7:39
it is stated precisely that the Holy Spirit had not been given
because Jesus was not yet glorified. Here, however, the **gifts** of
the ascended Christ to believers are endowments of special
abilities which will equip them for the Church's service. But this
is not at variance with the gift of the Holy Spirit, for in 1 C. 12:4
the 'varieties of gifts' are ascribed to the work of the Spirit.

At 4:7 it was stated that 'grace was given to each of us', and
the result was that special abilities were roused in believers—in
'each of us'. This clearly means that the writer is not thinking of
a small group of officials and leaders who make up the hierarchy
of the church (though some commentators argue for this). It is
the whole community of believers which is enriched by special
endowments. The writer then names some of the functions which
different people were thus enabled by God to fulfil. Some of these
correspond to those listed in the Pauline letters, but not all. There
are two in this list which are not named in Paul's lists: **evangelists**
and **pastors** (shepherds). These may be words more commonly
used in the writer's own day than in Paul's, though the function
they fulfilled may be similar to those described by other names in
Paul's lists. It will be useful to have the three main lists before us
for the purposes of comparison:

1 C. 12:28	Rom. 12:5ff.	Eph. 4:11
apostles		apostles
prophets	prophets	prophets
		evangelists
		pastors (shepherds)

1 C. 12:28	Rom. 12:5ff	Eph. 4:11
	ministry or service (*diakonia*)	ministry or service (*diakonia*)
teachers	teachers	teachers
workers of miracles	exhorters	
healers	contributors	
helpers	givers of aid	
administrators	merciful	
tongues		

apostles, prophets, teachers and **ministers** (servants) all occur in two of the three lists. The others occur in only one list, but some of them are probably different names for what are basically similar functions. **evangelists** and **pastors,** the two words peculiar to Ephesians, are probably functions carried out by some of the members in the community, rather than titles of permanent officials. There is no word in Ephesians for anyone whose primary function is administration or supervision.

Of the words which are found also in Paul's letters, **apostles** describes the original human founders of the Church. **prophets** were men of spiritual authority who spoke to their contemporaries messages which were recognised as 'words from God' (see note at 2:20). **teachers** were those equipped to give instruction in the faith—what was remembered about Jesus, what was believed and known about the living Christ, and what was the kind of conduct appropriate for those who accepted this faith and took their place in the Christian community.

The two descriptive words which are peculiar to the list in Ephesians are **evangelists** and **pastors.** It is probable that the date of Acts is fairly close to that of Ephesians, and certainly one notices similarities between these two writings in their use of names for functionaries in the Church. Evangelists and pastors appear in Acts as well as in Ephesians. In Ac. 21:8 Philip is called an 'evangelist' (cf. 'Do the work of an evangelist' in the post-Pauline 2 Tim. 4:5). The word probably describes those whose special gifts enabled them to take the gospel to those outside the Church. On the other hand the word **pastor** suggests one whose particular abilities were seen rather in caring for those already within the community: enquirers, beginners, falterers, those in need of love, encouragement, and a friend to talk to. If teachers

helped by verbal instruction, the pastor helped by personal friendship, wise counsel, and moral sympathy. In Ac. 20:28 Paul is
reported as telling the leaders of the church at Ephesus that the
Holy Spirit had appointed them 'bishops' (i.e., people with
responsible oversight of others, *episkopoi*) to shepherd (i.e., act as
pastors to) the church of God. Perhaps it was from this group of
people who excelled in pastoral care for others and ability to
build them up in the faith that the later office of 'bishop' sprang
(rather than from the 'administrator' of 1 C. 12 or 'the one in
charge' of Rom. 12:8—oddly in *RVS* 'he who gives aid').

12. All these different workers within the Church together
filled a double function. One was **to equip the saints for the
work of ministry** and the other was **for building up the body
of Christ.** Some commentators prefer to understand this as
indicating three rather than two functions: (i) equip saints;
(ii) do the work of a minister; (iii) build up the body. Indeed
RSV in its 1946 version suggests this threefold division. Our
preference would be to understand **for the work of ministry**
as going closely with the preceding phrase as representing that for
which the saints were being equipped, which is how the sentence
is translated in the *RSV* of 1973 known as *The Common Bible*. **the
work of ministry** is not something done by a special person in
the Church so much as that for which all Church members
(**saints**) are being prepared. The emphasis in **ministry** is not
so much on certain people with special status and official positions,
but rather on the fact that all who have gifts have them in order
that with them they may serve the community as a whole. The
first function of all those with special gifts is **to equip** God's
people (**saints**) for service—not to do their duties for them (as if
they were incapable), but to enable them to become themselves
God's ministers within and through the life of the Church. All
Christians are called to **the work of ministry** (*diakonia*). This
must mean something more than to hold the office of deacon
(*diakonos*). There is no hint of an official position here. The word
ministry had an honourable ancestry within the Christian circle
and was the antithesis of status. 'The Son of man came to minister
(render service), and not to be served' (Mk 10:45). The word may
well imply work of a practical nature. In the Gospels the same
word is used of Peter's mother-in-law serving the physical needs
of her visitors. In the parable of the sheep and the goats it

describes those who ministered to the hungry and needy. It is used also to describe the work of the women who made practical provision for Jesus during his ministry.

Sometimes Ephesians has been criticised for presenting a view of the Church as unduly preoccupied with herself and her own affairs rather than with the service which the Church may render to the world. It may well be that this writer felt that what was supremely needed at the time he wrote was that which would hold the Church together in unity, and so give it the strength it needed for these future tasks. If he neglected to emphasise the outward-looking tasks, it was because he was primarily concerned with the task of making the Church ready to fulfil them. If it had disintegrated through inward dissention, there would have been no Church to carry out the task later assigned to her.

Nevertheless, it should be noted that in fact the whole membership of the Church is to be prepared for service (**ministry**). The emphasis is on what the members should be *doing*. It is not clear whether this service is offered to those within the Church or outside it. One imagines that in these early days the numbers of those within the Church were so small compared with the surrounding society that the Church saw her responsibility to those outside largely in terms of the communication of the gospel (through the evangelists). Such responsibility as it felt for the physical welfare of others concerned primarily those who had come within the community, e.g., widows (Ac. 6:1, etc.). At that time and in their circumstances this was probably the wisest way to dispose their resources.

The second function of those whom God's grace has endowed is that of **building up the body of Christ,** that is to add to its numbers, to integrate newcomers harmoniously into the life of the body, to train them to become people who could themselves make their own contribution to the life of the Church and to their fellow members in it. **building up** would also include the maintenance of peace within the body, the encouragement of happy co-operation between all the various parts, and the prevention of rivalry, alienation, and division, which would weaken the body.

13. These two purposes are seen as the immediate task of the Church's community-life. Its ultimate goal, however, reaching far beyond the immediate present, is now stated. This ultimate aim of all work in the Church, whether of leaders or of the whole community responding to the promptings of the leaders, has already been described as the unity of the Spirit (4:3), the unity which the Spirit can bring even among people originally bitterly hostile to each other. This same unity is here described in different words as **the unity of the faith,** i.e., the unity inherent in their faith, that 'one faith' named in 4:5. It is also the unity which belongs to **the knowledge of the Son of God,** who is the 'one Lord' of 4:5, and 'Christ Jesus our Lord' of 3:11. The phrase **Son of God** has not so far been used in this epistle, but clearly it is a synonym for Jesus Christ which readers and writer alike would accept without question, since it was a title universally applied to Jesus in the Church.

It was characteristic of Jesus that he spoke constantly of God as Father, or even as *Abba*, so that his followers came to speak of God as they knew him through Christ as the Father of our Lord Jesus Christ (1:3). Even in Paul's Gentile churches the summit of Christian experience was an awareness of God through Christ and the Holy Spirit which led the believer spontaneously to speak of God as '*Abba*, Father', just as Jesus had done (see Gal. 4:16; Rom. 8:15). All men could through Christ become sons of God, but Jesus was **the Son of God** *par excellence*. At first this way of regarding Jesus may have arisen primarily from the recognition by the disciples that his manner of speaking of God as Father was something unique to Jesus. His happy intimacy with God and simple trust in him was something that made him different from other men. He was Son in a special sense. In addition, God was present to them in Jesus with a greater reality than anywhere else. 'God was in Christ' was how Paul expressed it. His followers also saw in him a consistent and compelling likeness to God. It was customary in Hebrew to express similarity in character by using the phrase 'son of'. 'Sons of Belial' were men of vicious character; Barnabas, 'son of consolation' (Ac. 4:36), was one whose chief characteristic was to encourage and inspire others. So **Son of God** meant one who reflected likeness to God (as at Mt. 5:45). As an aim likeness to God was something which all people were invited to adopt as their own, but as an actuality it belonged to Jesus uniquely so as to place him in a different category from others, especially as it was only through him that other men and women could hope to share some measure of these same spiritual privileges. So the title 'Son of God' came to be used of Jesus by

Christians to describe their sense of his uniqueness, both in the closeness of his relation with God and in his power to reflect the nature of God.

knowledge has already been used of our knowledge of God (1:17). Here it is knowledge of Christ. It is possible that **faith** as well as **knowledge** is attached to Christ, meaning 'faith in and knowledge of' the Son of God. It is more likely, however, that 'faith' is used independently, as at 4:5, to express all that the Christian is privileged to believe in.

The **unity** of the Church, with which this writer is so concerned, is given by the Spirit; it is inherent in their **faith;** it is a consequence of their deep awareness of Christ as **Son of God.** This unity is the goal to which we are all called to attain; it is the achievement after which every single member must aspire, and to which each must make his own proper contribution; it is also the treasured possession of the community as a whole.

That in the individual which enables him to make his full contribution to this unity is described as **mature manhood.** Proneness to quarrel is the mark of immaturity; the ability to hold diversity within a harmonious unity is the mark of maturity. Some commentators prefer to understand **mature manhood** as expressing the goal of the community as a whole rather than of each individual in it, but it is difficult to apply this very personal phrase to a community. It is the more difficult when we note that the Greek phrase does in fact mean, literally, 'a perfect man' (as *AV* rendered it). This is not a natural way to speak of a community.

The Greek word *teleios* may be translated as either 'mature' or 'perfect'. We naturally shrink from applying the word 'perfect' to our poor human nature, even as an ideal to aim at; but does not the translation **mature** rob it of some of its challenge? And there are some passages in the *NT* where to translate *teleios* as 'mature' is almost banal (e.g. Mt. 5:48, 19:21; Col. 1:28; Heb. 2:10).

What is meant by 'a perfect man'? How does one measure 'perfection'? The **measure** is that **of the stature of the fullness of Christ.** At 4:7 Jesus Christ is named as 'the measure' of God's grace. Here he is **the measure** of God's purposes for man. It is as though in Jesus Christ God is saying: 'This is human life as I meant it to be.' Perfect manhood, therefore, is the same as total Christlikeness, which includes a happy knowledge of God as

Father, utter obedience to his will at every point, an attitude of
loving concern for others at all times, complete loyalty to truth
and goodness, even when it provokes bitter opposition—this is
what we see in Jesus and it is what God planned for human life;
it is to this that he beckons his human children. All these qualities
added together make for **the fullness of Christ.** They describe
what is meant by perfect manhood. It is this which the company
of the Church seeks to bring about in every individual Christian.

14. This splendid, if inaccessible, goal is contrasted by the
writer with the disappointing quality of life which he sees in many
Christians, in consequence of which the unity of Christ's body is
threatened. One sign of this immaturity is the tendency to be
unduly impressed by new brands of teaching and new crazes.
Like **children** they are **tossed to and fro and carried about
with every wind of doctrine.** Children are easily attracted
by what is new and soon tire of what they have got used to. So
some Christians are attracted by newness by the mere fact of
its novelty. They lack stability. They are like flotsam **tossed** by
the ever-moving waves or **carried about** before the swirling
wind, now this way, now that. It is not made clear what these
crazes were (likened to winds) to which the readers were exposed
and which threatened to bring division within the Church. It is
known, however, that towards the end of the first century various
forms of Docetism and Gnosticism menaced the unity of the
Church, and it could well be something of this kind which the
writer had in mind.

The people are being swept along by the prevailing crazes and
new fashions of thought; but also they are being manipulated by
unscrupulous and clever men who by every trick they know are
trying to divert them from the main life of the Church into divisive
and sectarian movements. To attain their ends they are not above
the use of **cunning** and **craftiness in deceitful wiles.** That is,
they appeal to the selfish motives of others, to fear and pride, or
perhaps even to their idealism and devotion in such a way as to
twist it to their own ends. They are ready to manipulate the
human frailties of their hearers—jealousy, suspicion, antagonism,
resentment, personal dislike; and they themselves are motivated
by personal ambition, pique, and rivalry. They distort and mis-
represent the truth, and are unconcerned about the true welfare
of the people they deal with and use for their own ends. It seems

likely that there is a similarity here to the situation of which Paul
gives warning in Ac. 20:28f., and which is reflected later in 1 Tim.
1:3–4, 6:3–5, 20.

15. In contrast, the qualities of the stable, mature (perfect)
Christian are then described, the one whose influence will uphold
unity and peace. His essential quality is characterised as a combination of **truth** and **love**—utter loyalty to the truth about
human life and God's purpose for it as revealed in Christ, combined with a loving concern for individual people and their
personal welfare. It is all too easy for responsible Christians to
become so firm in their loyalty to what they see as the truth ('a
matter of principle') that they can show themselves quite harsh
in their treatment of people who seem to have transgressed against
it. But concern for individuals is no less important than devotion
to principle, though it is not always easy to do full justice to both.
John saw the two perfectly harmonised in Jesus whom he described as 'full of grace and truth' (Jn 1:14) and able to communicate both qualities to his disciples (Jn 1:17). The truth is of
fundamental importance. It must not be distorted to gain personal or sectional advantage. On the other hand it must not be
wielded as a weapon to inflict hurt on people we dislike or dis-
agree with or condemn. Even truth, for all its basic importance,
must be applied in love.

Truth is much more than verbal accuracy. The Greek word
here translated as **speaking the truth** does in fact not make any
reference to speaking. The word means 'being utterly genuine,
sincere, and honest'. Abbott suggests the word should be translated as 'cherishing truth'. It includes 'doing the truth' (Jn 3:21)
as well as speaking it.

We should not assume that all the faults leading to disunity are
to be found in the dissidents who feel themselves to be at variance
with the main body of the Church. The main body, by subordina-
ting love to truth, can alienate those it ought to conciliate and
persuade, and whose enthusiasm and vitality, even when embarrassing, ought to be retained within the continuing life of the
Church. The disposition, whether in dissidents or traditionalists,
which makes for unity in the Church is that which can hold in
proper balance both truth and love. Of any proposed action or
word we ask not only 'Is it true and right?' but also 'Is it kind and
loving?'

speaking the truth in love is the means Christians use. The end they seek is that **we are to grow up in every way into him who is the head.** The pathway from immaturity to maturity may be described as 'growing up'—growing up into Christ. Each decision on the way should be a decision in favour of that which brings us closer to Christ, as we 'look unto Jesus, the author and perfecter of faith' (Heb. 12:2). As each individual is potentially a member of the body of Christ, his aim is to become both fit and competent to play his part, by being totally obedient to the head (1:22)—not an undeveloped, infantile, or spastic limb (see note at 1:22).

16. The concern in the preceding verses has been primarily with the individual Christian, now committed to Christ and learning to become an effective part of Christ's living body, avoiding all that may separate him from the community or lead to sectarianism. Now the emphasis returns to the **body** rather than the individual member of it. Christ is the head, and obedience to him is the means of integrating all the members into one co-ordinated unit. It is from Christ that there comes the energy which makes for proper spiritual growth, and the right spirit which welds the separate parts into a single whole.

The human body has very many members and each member has smaller component parts within it. There is the arm, and within the arm biceps, forearm, wrist, hand, fingers. All these separate parts are held together by joints and muscles, and thus enabled to fulfil their separate functions within the whole (they are **joined and knit together by every joint with which** the body **is supplied**) but remain under the single control of the head (brain). There is disruption in the body when any member is unco-ordinated with other members or independent of the central control. So it is in the body of Christ. **each part** needs to be **working properly,** and it does this only in harmony with the other members and in obedience to the head. The whole body **makes bodily growth and upbuilds itself in love** as each part takes its full share in and contributes to the whole.

One has seen unhappy people whose limbs move without proper co-ordination and independently of the unifying control of the brain. The whole body is pathetically ineffective. The Church sometimes appears to be in such a condition. But that was not what God planned for it.

The body of Christ in God's plan is a united whole, well directed by the head and skilfully harmonised to work as a single unit. And the spirit which permeates its internal life and its impact on the outside world is described as **love.** The health of this body is measured by the circulation within its life of love, that is unselfish understanding and concern for others and their welfare. Love is its life-blood. This is not by any means the first time that the word **love** has occurred in this epistle. It appears seven times in all and in four of them it has been used in this same brief phrase **in love.** At 4:2, 15; 5:2 it is used to indicate the quality which controls each part in its relation to other parts. At 4:15 each individual is urged to 'speak the truth in love'. The repetition of **in love** yet again here at the end of the paragraph suggests that this is what is supremely needed within the life of the Church at the time this author is writing. Paul had declared such love even more important than faith and hope (1 C. 13:13); this writer sets it even higher than truth.

THE NEW LIFE IN CHRIST 4:17–32

In Eph. 4:1–16 the writer has been pleading for those Christian qualities in individuals which make for stability and coherence in a community, and for the avoidance of those tendencies, to which even convinced Christians are prone, which make for division and disunity. The writer now turns to more general matters of conduct. As at 2:11 and 3:1 he makes it clear that he is addressing Christians who have come from a Gentile background, where standards of moral conduct were low. The Jews usually maintained a higher standard because they acknowledged the authority of the Ten Commandments and the law of Moses as a whole. But the Gentiles had no such recognised standards, and their behaviour, particularly in sexual matters, was very casual. The writer insists that Christians from such a background must make a complete break with the kind of life they used to live. Moreover, they would need to be consistently on the alert lest pressure from this environment seduced them from their newly accepted Christian way of life. In Rom. 12:2 Paul similarly warns such Christians against the danger of allowing themselves to be 'conformed to this world', instead of allowing the new life in Christ to 'transform' all their conduct.

17. The writer insists that what he writes is **in the Lord,** that is, he writes it as a Christian with Christ's authority. It is not just his own idea of propriety. To add weight to his words he uses two somewhat solemn expressions: **I affirm and testify. testify** is a term taken from the law courts, applied to words spoken under oath. *TEV* indicates its significance in ordinary language: '. . . and I insist on it'. **you must no longer live as the Gentiles do: live** here translates the Greek word for 'walk', which means 'behave'. The words **no longer** imply that those addressed once themselves practised the moral carelessness of their Gentile environment.

Verses 17–19 contain many echoes of Paul's description of the Gentile world in Rom. 1:21–24. In that passage Paul describes the corruption of pagan life. Though pagans are not without a sense of God and a knowledge of right and wrong they do not let this rule their actions. They follow instead the promptings of their own appetites and desires. Such behaviour inevitably leads to evil consequences. Degradation leads to greater degradation. In a moral universe happiness and social harmony are not achieved by immoral conduct. The general tenor of this passage in Romans is reflected here, and also several of the actual words and phrases are reproduced:

Romans	Ephesians
1:21: they became futile in their thinking	4:17: in the futility of their minds
1:21: their senseless minds were darkened	4:18: they are darkened in their understanding
1:24: God gave them up to . . . impurity	4:19: they have given themselves up to licentiousness

in the futility of their minds: In Rom. 1:21 this **futility** is the direct result of their rejection of God. In consequence, life becomes empty and purposeless. For them there is no longer a creator who has invested the whole of life with meaning and direction. Without such a God, there is no answer to man's persistent question about life: 'What is the point of it all?' Everything appears pointless and futile. Nothing seems worth bothering about. Goodness is no better than badness. The only thing left to be done is to snatch at what pleasure one can and try not to think about the meaning or lack of meaning in it all. In Rom. 8:20 we read that 'the creation was subjected to futility', in the hope that this very hopelessness would turn men's minds back to God.

18. The phrases that follow indicate the further consequences of men's exclusion of God from their thinking, and their disregard of moral standards which deep down they know to be right. **they are darkened in their understanding:** their sense of moral distinctions became blurred. Having done again and again what originally they knew to be wrong, they find that they cease to think of it as wrong. The inward signals which once warned against the approach of evil have ceased to operate. This loss of power to distinguish between good and evil is called 'darkness', because where there is no light at all even the difference between white and black is blotted out. They are **alienated from the life of God.** Some have taken **life of God** to mean 'life as God wants men to live it'. But the Greek word here used for **life** (*zōē*) does not usually bear the meaning of conduct. It refers rather to the vital aspect of life. It is this word which is always used in the phrase 'eternal life'. Probably here it means life, not in the sense of moral conduct, but 'the new life', filled with significance and joy, life as re-created by God. It is the quality of life indicated in Jn 1:4: 'In him was life and the life was the light of men', the quality of life which Jesus came to bring to men (Jn 10:1). **because of the ignorance that is in them:** the **ignorance** is probably that referred to in Rom. 1:28: 'They did not see fit to have God in their understanding.' It was a self-induced ignorance, a deliberate rejection of the one clue which could make life meaningful and wholesome. **due to their hardness of heart:** this is an underlying cause of all the trouble—insensitiveness to spiritual truths such as the claims of goodness and the reality of God. This insensitiveness is produced by the repetition of wrong choices. Paul speaks of a similar 'hardening' which affected the people of Israel as a result of their persistent rejection of God's approach to them in Jesus (Rom. 11:7, 25). Similar 'hardening' is mentioned in the Gospel, e.g., Mk 3:5, 6:52.

19. This condition of 'hardness' is further characterised in the words: **they have become callous.** Literally, this means 'insensitive to pain'—in this case the pain inflicted by a sensitive conscience when evil has been done. Because of this insensitiveness they can now take part in indecencies which once would have disgusted and repelled them. The writer says: they **have given themselves up to licentiousness.** There is a clear reference here to the similar words in Rom. 1:24, but there is also a significant change of wording. Paul had written: 'God gave them up to impurity' (Rom. 1:24, 26; cf. also Rom. 9:13, 17). Modern readers feel a certain harshness in these words of Paul, as suggesting an attitude in God less than fully in harmony with the God and Father of our Lord Jesus Christ. It seems as though the writer of Ephesians felt something of the same hesitation, for he changes the words to: **they have given themselves up.** The cause of their degradation is given as their own deliberate disobedience to truth and goodness as their conscience at first had been able to recognise it. It is true that God has made the world in such a way that human disobedience would produce such consequences, and that a process of retribution (the wrath of God) is built by God into the very fabric of the universe. There is, therefore, a sense in which God is the ultimate cause of what has happened. But the immediate cause is the human disobedience which violates God's laws. In their disobedience they abandoned themselves to **licentiousness** (debauchery). In the *NT* this word primarily describes sexual licence (as at Rom. 13:13 and 2 C. 12:21). One of the first consequences of a loss of a sense of purpose in life is the weakening of basic decencies which normally control sexual activities. Sexual activity in itself is one of God's good gifts to his children. Not only is it the means by which children are born and family life made possible, but it is capable of wonderfully enriching life and of investing the personal relationships of man and woman with deep significance. But for this to be achieved there is need for its use to be controlled by a strong sense of responsibility, responsibility for the true welfare of the other person involved in the relationship, and for any child who may be born in consequence of it. The Christian insight which has evolved from this deep respect for the personal life of others, and for lives yet unborn, has led to the Christian standard in sexual behaviour which is normally summed up as chastity before marriage and faithfulness within marriage. The use of the sexual relationship merely for pleasure or excitement without any real sense of responsibility degrades personal life and personal relationships. It is this attitude to sex as nothing more than a means of pleasure devoid of any sense of responsibility which is described as **licen-tiousness.** Whereas within a truly happy marriage sexual rela-tionships are capable of bringing ever-renewed joy and happiness, in licentiousness they easily begin to pall or produce a sense of disgust. New devices may then be sought to maintain the excite-ment. It leads to a state where those involved become **greedy to practise every kind of uncleanness.** Normal sexual relation-ships give place to all kinds of perversion in the endeavour to stimulate jaded interest. In Rom. 1:24-32 Paul describes in some detail this swelling tide of debauchery, with one perversion fol-lowing another, as men and women devise new ways of sustaining the failing pleasure. The phrase translated **greedy** consists of two Greek words which literally mean 'with covetousness'. 'Covetous-ness' in modern English is used mainly of greed for money, but in the *NT* it is often associated with sexual sins, and means a ruthless appetite for more and more of what you want, without regard for the consequences it may have for the lives of others. *NEB* catches this well: 'They stop at nothing to satisfy their foul desire.'

20. You did not so learn Christ! Had it been a Jew writing to Gentiles who had become proselytes or 'God-fearers', he might have reminded them: That is not the kind of behaviour you learned in the Mosaic law. For the Christian, however, Christ has replaced the Jewish law as the standard of conduct, the inter-preter of God's will. In the Gospels we meet the phrase 'learn of me' (spoken by Jesus), but never elsewhere is the word **learn** followed as here by the direct accusative of the person. Some think that **Christ** is here used to mean 'the way of Christ' or 'the teach-ing of Christ'. Abbott sees it as the complement to 'preaching Christ' (Gal. 1:16; 1 C. 1:23). To accept the plea of the preacher and respond to it was to 'learn Christ'. Masson, however, under-stands it as the counterpart not to 'preach' but to 'teach'. Teachers and teaching (*didachē*) played a big part in the life of the early Church. To **learn Christ,** therefore, means to understand the will of God as it is embodied in Christ. Whatever else this means, from the context it is clear that it is a way of life in sharp contrast to the licentiousness which has been condemned.

21. assuming that you have heard about him: this seems an odd expression when the readers are converted and com-mitted Christians. The same phrase was used in 3:2 about their acquaintance with the apostle Paul. It must be, as Allan suggests,

that the Greek should be translated: 'for, of course, you have heard
of him', though, even if we allow that meaning, it still remains a
strange expression to use here. Masson suggests a different approach and renders the words: 'at least, if it is he you have
listened to', that is, 'if the one you have accepted as Christ is the
real Christ and not some fictitious alternative thought up by man's
imagination'. As we have seen, one of the dangers of the early
Christian communities was that mythical ideas about a divine
Man should be imposed upon 'Christ', so that Christ became more
like this mythical figure than the Jesus of the Gospels. The actual
Greek uses the words: '. . . you have heard him' (not 'about him').
This is an unusual expression in the Greek and perhaps it has
been influenced by 'learn Christ' in 4:20, or 'receive Christ' in
Col. 2:6. The writer may have merely substituted 'heard' for
'learn' or 'receive'. It may, however, imply that for the writer
Christ is to be heard speaking within the voice of the Christian
preacher who proclaims the gospel. **and were taught in him:**
this suggests that there are two stages in the early life of the Christian: his recognition that in the preaching of the *kerygma* Christ is
calling him, and his submission to a course of instruction (*didachē*)
by which he is prepared for acceptance into the Christian community through baptism. The substance of the instruction would
then be 'the truth as it is in Jesus' (*NEB*) or **as the truth is in
Jesus** (*RSV*). The change from **Christ** to **Jesus** must be quite
deliberate. **Christ** apart from Jesus is a vague elusive concept
with nothing to delimit the meaning read into it. **Jesus** may not
be defined with complete precision, but at any rate the word
certainly had some degree of agreed content and many speculative ideas about 'Christ' would be immediately excluded as inconsistent with what was known of Jesus. What we believe about
Christ must be moulded by the known truth about Jesus. As
Masson rightly insists: 'The man who bore in history the name of
Jesus provides the moral content of what is meant by the Christian
use of "Christ".' He adds: 'The Sermon on the Mount and the
cross for ever excluded the union of faith and immorality.' An
important element in the early catechetical instruction (*didachē*)
appears to have included information about the historical figure
of Jesus and his teaching; and these would form the basis for
further teaching about the character and conduct appropriate to
the Christian disciple and Church member.

22. In *RSV* verse 22 starts a new sentence: **Put off your old nature,** as though this were a direct command to the readers. In the Greek, however, the same sentence continues from verse 20 to 24, and 'putting off the old nature' is an element in what is 'taught in Christ'. *NEB* retains the meaning: 'Were you not taught the truth as it is in Jesus?—that, leaving your former way of life, you must lay aside that old human nature.'

Verses 22–24 show a close dependence on Col. 3:8–10. The following ideas occur in both passages: put off, old nature, be renewed, new nature, after the image of its creator. It was a common figure of speech in early Christian ethical teaching to speak of discarding (putting off) evil habits as if they were old clothes. Perhaps this metaphor became established in association with the practice of the candidate at baptism discarding his old clothes before baptism and clothing himself with new ones afterwards. This same Greek word meaning **put off** is used in a context of ethical requirements in many passages in *NT* epistles, e.g., Rom. 13:12, Col. 3:8; Heb. 12:1; Jas 1:21; 1 Pet. 2:1. Clearly, therefore, it represents an accepted form of Christian instruction widely used in the Church, and not only by Paul. So here this writer requires that they **put off** their **old nature** (literally 'old man'). Sometimes Paul uses stronger metaphors to express the same idea. In Rom. 6:6–8, for instance, the old nature is to be 'crucified' and 'done to death' with Christ. Whichever metaphor is used, it indicates a radical change of character. The old nature **belongs to your former manner of life and is corrupt through deceitful lusts.** *RSV* translates with present tenses, as though the old nature still lingers on within the new one, causing all kinds of former evils to reappear. This, of course, corresponds to a common human experience, but it is not what the writer intends. *TEV* does better justice to the Greek words when it translates them as referring to the past: 'So get rid of your old self, which made you live as you used to—the old self which was being destroyed by its deceitful desires.' The lusts are described as **deceitful** because they trick us about their true nature. Strong desires can so swamp every faculty of discernment that at the time they seem to bring with them their own justification. Only later do the actions to which they prompted appear disgusting and shameful. In the days of the 'old nature' these tyrannous desires exercised far too strong an influence, and were destroying (corrupting) the lives that obeyed them.

23. Jesus taught that an evil spirit which has been cast out must
be replaced immediately by a positive good or it will return reinforced. So here, it is not enough to discard the old nature: the
positive replacement is insisted on. It is that they are to **be
renewed in the spirit of** their **minds.** The power of Christ
can 'renew' poor human nature. Paul in 2 C. 5:17 writes: 'If any
one is in Christ, he is a *new* creation.' John makes Christ say: 'You
must be born *anew*' (Jn 3:3). This indicates a radical process of
renewal similar to that used in 1 Pet. 1:3. If we take **spirit** here
to mean the human spirit, it is perhaps pointless to ask how spirit
differs from mind. The two together are used to indicate man's
innermost self, the real self within. That is, the change is not just a
superficial one affecting outward conduct, but an inward one
transforming the very springs of a man's being, his desires, attitudes, and values. Houlden argues that elsewhere in Ephesians
spirit always means God's Spirit, and therefore it probably carries
the same connotation here. The translation he recommends is:
'Be renewed by the Spirit in your mind.' What makes this unlikely, however, is that the phrase here translated **in your minds**
is in the Greek literally 'of your mind', and one doubts if there is
any way at all to make it carry the meaning 'in your minds'. And
it is improbable that God's Spirit would be described as 'of your
mind'.

24. This renewal is then expressed in another way. The writer
reverts to the metaphor of the changing of clothes: **put on the new
nature.** The verb 'put off' or 'discard' is found in many different
writers in the *NT*, but this word **put on** is found only in the
Pauline letters (Rom. 13:14; Gal. 3:27; Col. 3:10). At Gal. 3:27
what is to be 'put on' is Christ himself ('You have put on Christ').
Here it is **the new nature.** This, however, is only a different way
of saying the same thing. Christ ruling in our lives is the new
nature. It is **created after the likeness of God.** The word
created reminds us that this change is God's doing, not our own.
The new creation of 2 C. 5:17 is 'all from God' (i.e., 'all God's
doing'). Those who are born anew are born of God (Jn 1:13).
The new nature is created by God in us and for us, and it is **after
the likeness of God** (literally, 'according to God', i.e., according
to his will for us). The wording here in Ephesians differs from that
of Col. 3:10, but clearly the meaning is intended to be the same.
Col. 3:10 reads: 'You have put on the new nature, which is being

renewed in knowledge after the image of its creator.' There is a clear reference to Gen. 1:27: 'God created man in his own image.' That is, man was made to be in the image of God. But in the course of human history that image has been so sadly disfigured as to be almost effaced. When Jesus Christ lived on earth men came to see in him two related truths: the reality of God was present in his life as in no other life, and also men recognised in him and the quality of his life the picture of what God had originally meant human life to be like. They expressed the first of these truths by saying that Jesus was the image of God (2 C. 4:4; Col. 1:15; Heb. 1:3). The second truth could also be expressed through the same concept, since man in God's intention was made to be in the image of God. This true image of God for which man was made was seen in Jesus Christ, but, more than that, it was also in his power to enable men and women to recover in themselves this **likeness of God** (godliness), which is the chief mark of the new nature.

The quality of this new nature is characterised as consisting of **true righteousness and holiness.** Literally, the phrase is 'the righteousness and holiness of truth'. *RSV* takes 'of truth' as an Hebraic genitive used with an adjectival sense. There is, however, another alternative, which is adopted by *NEB*: 'the just and devout life called for by the truth'. In that case **truth** would mean the Christian message which had been accepted by them and allowed to rule their lives.

righteousness and holiness appear together again in Lk. 1:75. **righteousness** in Paul usually means first and foremost being right with God, and then that moral righteousness of life appropriate to one who is right with God. It is the second of these two meanings which predominates in *NT* writings other than those of Paul, and here its meaning is probably that of moral obedience to the will of God as known in his commandments. **holiness** is the quality of that which belongs in a special way to God and so here is the quality of life appropriate to one whose life is wholly ruled by God, the quality of a temple in-dwelt by God.

25. Verses 17–24 have urged Christians to abandon totally all the practices of Gentile society which spring from unredeemed human nature, and instead to let their new, Christ-given nature, control all they do. The writer now moves on to indicate some of the positive directions in which the new nature will express itself differently from the old one. The counsel given falls predominantly into a series of contrasts. First, that aspect of the old nature is named which is to be avoided, and then, to offset it, the corresponding good which must replace it. Lying must be replaced by truthfulness, stealing by supplying the needs of others, cynical and depressing conversation by words which bring encouragement and hope. In this contrast we see something of the genuinely Christian attitude in matters of conduct; it starts from the assumption behind the Jewish law that evil things which hurt others must be avoided, and passes on to the insistence on the practice of positive goods which benefit others. It is an example of the counsel to overcome evil with good, not merely by opposing it but by replacing it.

Therefore, putting away falsehood. The **Therefore** provides a link with the preceding section. If the 'old nature' is to be put off and the 'new nature' put on, what in terms of actual moral conduct does this mean? The writer proceeds to explain. **putting away** is the same Greek word as that used for 'putting off' the old nature in 4:22. Its use again here indicates that these verses are intended to explain what this means. **falsehood** can mean any distortion of the truth whether in act or word. Here, however, the emphasis seems to be on *spoken* falsehood, i.e., lying. The same word, however, is used at Rom. 1:25 where Gentiles are accused of 'changing the truth of God for a lie', and here the word 'lie' (= falsehood) means a false idea of God rather than a spoken word. The positive counterpart to falsehood is truthfulness and the need for this is emphasised by what is substantially a quotation from Zech. 8:16: **let everyone speak the truth with his neighbour.** The fact that the plea for truthfulness can thus be reinforced by words taken from Scripture invests it with added authority. In Zechariah the quotation continues by noting that what is true 'makes for peace' (a concern with which this writer has closely identified himself). Some commentators indeed argue that all the moral exhortations of this section are included just because they further the cause of harmony within a community. But this, indeed, applies to every aspect of goodness—it strengthens unity, whereas evil disrupts. In fact, these exhortations of 4:25–5:2 do have a wider validity than merely their ability to strengthen the communal life. They apply to all aspects of Christian behaviour, and affect conduct directed towards non-Christians as well as to fellow Christians within the Church. At least, one would assume that the command to refrain from stealing (4:28) would be applicable outside as well as within the community. In verse 25, however, it is clear that it is the welfare of the community which is primarily in the writer's mind, since the motive he gives for truthfulness is: **for we are members one of another.** The word **members** relates this verse to the thought of the Church as the body of Christ (unless conceivably the whole world-wide human family is in the writer's mind—which is unlikely here). Indeed, the words are taken exactly from Rom. 12:5, where they follow 'we, though many, are one body in Christ'. In Ephesians, so far, the main emphasis has been on the need for every individual member of the body to be obedient to the head. But there has been also the implication that members depend on one another and need to contribute to each other's welfare (e.g., 4:16). Here, even more precisely, the emphasis is also on the importance of full co-operation between the members because of their mutual interdependence.

At many other points in the *NT* we meet the emphatic insistence on the need for scrupulous honesty in word. Jesus himself at Mt. 5:37 taught that simple 'Yes' or 'No' must be as binding on a Christian as the most solemnly reinforced oath (or, in modern terms, as a legal document duly signed). Jas 5:12 repeats this word of Jesus. Col. 3:9 has: 'Do not lie to one another,' and Eph. 4:15 requires 'speaking the truth in love'.

26. Be angry but do not sin is another quotation from the *OT*, Ps. 4:4. It is quite wrong to take it as a command or even a permission to **be angry.** The imperative in Semitic idiom is often used to represent the protasis of a conditional sentence. 'Do this and you shall live' means 'If you do this, you will live.' So here the quotation means: 'If you do get angry, don't let it lead you into sin.' The wording does, however, seem to be intentionally different from the comprehensive prohibition of anger which we find in Col. 3:8 (on which this passage in Ephesians is largely dependent) and Gal. 5:20. It may be that behind the more cautious words of Ephesians there is a recognition that anger, though commonly just an evil thing, may on some occasions be appropriate even in a Christian. So James commands: 'Be slow to anger' (1:19). But anger, though on a rare occasion appropriate, does not often serve God's purposes (see Jas 1:20), since it is usually compounded with some degree of human sin. Only if this can be excluded can anger be justified in the Christian. There were indeed occasions when Jesus was angry (Mk 3:5, 10:14), and some of his words have the note of anger in them (Mk 9:42). Anger, therefore, *may* be free from sin, and this seems to be allowed by this writer. A Christian's anger must be of that kind—directly wholly against evil things which hurt others rather than ourselves. This is a rare kind of anger in human life. Usually, even in what we call 'righteous indignation' there is more than a little thwarted self-interest or injured pride and touchiness. It is very difficult to be angry and not to sin. For anger not to be sin, it must be totally disinterested. If we look at the instances where anger is recorded of Jesus, we see this illustrated.

Unhappily, however, anger, even if in the first place it was justified because it was directed against what injured others, can often build up into something marked by selfishness and ill-feeling. If it lasts, it becomes what we know as resentment or hate, the kind of thing which Jesus explicitly forbids in Mt.5:22 (where *NEB* translates to represent Jesus as rebuking those who 'nurse anger'). This seems to imply that if there is good reason for anger, the best thing is to get it over and done with quickly, not to 'nurse' it. So the writer of Ephesians: **do not let the sun go down on your anger.** It must not be allowed to disturb one's night's sleep by smouldering painfully in one's thoughts, nor to reawaken again into the new day that follows.

27. To allow anger to linger on until it grows into an enduring resentment gives **opportunity to the devil,** by providing him with—as it were—an ammunition-dump laid ready within the stronghold he plans to conquer. Anger in a Christian is a kind of 'fifth-column' available for co-operation with the enemy. For 'the anger of man does not work the righteousness of God' (Jas 1:20).

The word **devil** is not found in Paul's writings. He uses the name Satan for the power of evil. Probably **devil** should be regarded as arising from the vocabulary characteristic of a time later than Paul.

28. The man, who before he became a Christian was a **thief,** is told to abandon his stealing habits as belonging to the old nature he has laid aside. The Christian substitute for it is to **labour, doing honest work with his hands.** The aim of this is not just the mundane one of earning enough money to live on honestly and so gain a position of respect in the community, but rather the totally unselfish one of having something over and above his own basic need to be able **to give to those in need.** This is not just Christian idealism, but sound common sense. To win a permanent victory over an evil habit of long endurance one needs something more than just a bad conscience about the evil of the past. There must be a generous incentive which reaches into the future. A man wishes to give up a lifelong habit of smoking because he realises that it is destroying his health. He provides himself with powerful and positive motivation by putting aside week by week the money he saves by giving up smoking and uses it to provide a television set for someone else too poor to afford one. The joy of being able to do this generous action for someone else makes possible the abandonment of something which otherwise he might have been unable to master.

The phrase **with his hands** is puzzling. Any honest work providing money and occupying his mind would seem to be adequate, without its needing to be manual work—unless a manual sin like stealing needs a manual 'sublimation' to offset it. What makes the phrase the more puzzling is that the Greek words in fact mean 'with his *own* hands', with special emphasis on the word 'own'. The fact of the matter is that the whole of this phrase occurs in exactly the same words in 1 C. 4:12, and one has the impression that the writer inserts these remembered words without noticing that the phrase 'with his own hands' is not particularly appropriate for his purposes here.

29. Let no evil talk come out of your mouths. Already dishonesty of word has been forbidden. **evil talk,** therefore, must be other than lying. The word **evil** here literally means 'rotten', as of fish or fruit no longer fit to eat. Jesus uses the same word for a rotten tree which cannot produce good fruit (Mt. 7:17). As applied to talk it is perhaps represented by the word 'foul'. This, however, in English may put the emphasis on indecency to the exclusion of other 'rottenness'. It means anything which lowers the moral tone of the community. This may include such things as ascribing bad motives to other people's apparently good actions, or putting a sinister interpretation on quite innocent conduct. This is the more probable because in Col. 3:8 'evil talk' is linked with 'slander'. **Evil talk** may, therefore, include within its scope

words of a complaining, sneering, cynical, sarcastic type, all of
which spread demoralisation in a community. The kind of conversation to be encouraged is that which **is good for edifying,**
that is, that which raises morale, creates a spirit of goodwill, builds
up confidence and courage among all concerned. This means
words of appreciation and hope and faith in other people's
ability and loyalty, words which make someone in the community
more ready to take up bravely the tasks his Christian commitment
has laid upon him. The Greek word for **edifying** literally means
'building'. Its significance here is brought out by adding that its
purpose is **that it may impart grace to those who hear.** That
is, our conversation should aim at adding something good to the
situation in which we are. A word which confers **grace** is one
which brings special strength from God to make good things
possible. It aims not just at not doing evil, but adding something
positively good.

30. do not grieve the Holy Spirit of God. In the Pauline
letters every Christian is regarded as one who has received the
Holy Spirit, either at his conversion or at his baptism. His body
is a temple of the Holy Spirit which he has from God (1 C. 6:1).
It is because the Holy Spirit comes from God that here he is
described as **the Holy Spirit of God.** He is indeed God himself
at work within the life of the Christian as he seeks to enable his
new nature to shape all his conduct, and produce the fruit of the
Spirit. There are, however, forces, both within and outside the
Christian, which work against the Spirit. They resist him (Ac.
7:51) and even 'quench' him (1 Th. 5:19). It would be easy in
these contexts to write 'it' rather than 'him' of the Holy Spirit,
because 'resist' and 'quench' readily applied to physical forces
such as wind or fire. But **grieve** is movingly personal. God's
Spirit within us can be disappointed and saddened by carelessness
and lack of response on our part, just as the right response can
bring 'joy in heaven' (that is, to the heart of God, Lk. 15:7).

At 1:14 the reality of the Holy Spirit in the life of a Christian
was described as a foretaste and guarantee of the life beyond death.
Here he is the one **in whom you were sealed for the day of
redemption.** It is customary to relate the metaphor of 'sealing'
to baptism, the baptism giving as it were official seal or confirmation
to what definitely but less officially had already taken place in
conversion (see note at 1:13). Some, however, think that it was

the gift of the Spirit himself which was the seal upon the experience of conversion. **the day of redemption:** At 1:7 (see note) the word **redemption** is used to describe the *present* privilege of the Christian, equivalent perhaps to 'the glorious liberty of the children of God'. Here, however, there is a future significance in it. As opposed to the present foretaste of deliverance at 1:7, it seems to mean the final completion beyond death of that deliverance or salvation. The phrase would not have been unexpected in the letters of Paul who looked for an imminent consummation of future hopes in the parousia. But in Ephesians there is no expectation of this kind, and the phrase here seems to refer to the fullness of life which awaits the Christian in heaven beyond this present life. *NEB* translates: 'final liberation'. **redemption** in Ephesians, therefore, carries a double meaning: sometimes it refers to the existential reality of a present deliverance from crippling powers in the experience of conversion; sometimes its reference is to the completion beyond death of that of which conversion was the foretaste. Paul in Romans uses 'adoption' in a similar twofold way (Rom. 8:15 and 23).

Masson argues that 4:30 should be taken closely with 4:29, so that the 'evil talk' of 4:29 is understood as that which grieves the Holy Spirit (4:30). Perhaps this is to press their association too much, though clearly they are all part of the same context. The closer link, however, seems to be between 4:30 and 4:31. We avoid grieving the Holy Spirit when we **let all bitterness and wrath and anger and clamour and slander be put away from you, with all malice.** These faults both grieve the Holy Spirit and disrupt harmony within the fellowship.

31. all bitterness means every expression of bitterness. Abbott defines **bitterness** as 'the temper which cherishes resentful feelings'. It is that which harps on past grievances, real or imagined. *NEB* translates as 'spite', **wrath** (*thymos*) is anger expressed violently in an outburst of temper (whereas **anger** (*orgē*), that which is forbidden in 4:26, means persisting resentment which will nor forget, with the antagonism and even hatred it gives rise to). **clamour** (*kraugē*) indicates voices uplifted in quarrelling, so that people forget the normal courtesies which govern Christian conduct and even shout at each other. **slander** (*blasphēmia*) may mean irreverent words spoken about God, but here clearly means abusive and sneering words spoken about other people in their absence, whereas **clamour** is used of words shouted to their face. **malice** in *RSV* appears to be slipped in at the end, almost as an afterthought. If it is to be translated **malice,** as though it were something different from the preceding faults, it does have the appearance of an afterthought. But here the word is used not so much to add a new dimension of forbidden evil, but rather to offer an inclusive word to gather up all that has been specified and anything else of a similar kind not precisely mentioned. *NEB* has 'bad feeling of every kind'.

32. The writer then turns to the positively good things which should replace and leave no room for the evil things to be discarded. **be kind to one another.** The word **kind** which in the Greek is *chrēstos* is more precise than our very vague word 'kind'. Its similarity to the Greek word for Christ (*Christos*) led to a play on the two words. To be *chrēstos* is to be like *Christos*. It is in fact the word used to describe the yoke which Jesus asked his followers to take up and which is called 'easy' (*chrēstos*) (Mt. 11:30). The yoke is easy when it fits comfortably on the shoulders of those who wear it, enabling them to carry heavy burdens without pain, friction, or soreness. So when it is used of a person it means one who fits into the community life easily and happily, so that others do not find him difficult to work with and live with. Perhaps the word **kind** is as near as any single word can get to the meaning, but it describes a person who is kind in the sense of being considerate to others and ready to accommodate himself to their interests—the opposite of awkward, stubborn, and self-assertive. **tenderhearted** means compassionate, ready to feel sympathy for others in their distresses. **forgiving one another:** the word 'forgive' here is only an approximate translation of the Greek word which includes forgiveness, but is also much wider. It is derived from the word for 'grace', and it means to treat others with the same grace, or generosity of heart and act, with which God has treated us. It describes that treatment of others which is generous to the point of being uncalculating and free from all hesitations imposed by ill-feeling or self-interest. **as God in Christ forgave you:** i.e., with the same unbelievable generosity (including forgiveness) which God showed to us in Christ. The tense of the Greek verb suggests that one particular occasion in the past is being referred to—either conversion or baptism—the occasion when they realised that, in spite of all their past offences against God, they were accepted by him, reconciled to him, and forgiven. This generous attitude of God to totally undeserving people would have been incredible had they not seen it visibly embodied in Jesus Christ. It was **in Christ** that they found themselves able to believe with unquestioning confidence in God's forgiving love and continuing grace towards them. It is this which is the measure of the love and kindness they in their turn should show to others (Mt. 18:33; 1 Jn 4:21, etc.).

PUTTING THE NEW LIFE INTO PRACTICE 5:1-20

1. The fact that not only a new paragraph but also a new chapter begins at this point may obscure the very close link between these verses and those which precede them. 5:1 may indeed be said to give a wider application to the basic thought of 4:32. There the readers were bidden to allow the generous kindness of God, especially as seen in Jesus Christ, to be the pattern for their own treatment of one another. 5:1 then gathers up this plea in a more general principle of conduct: **Therefore be imitators of God, as beloved children.**

To instruct human beings to 'imitate' God sounds at first almost grotesque. The translators of the *AV* seem to have felt this because they translate the words as: 'Be followers of God.' But the Greek word unmistakably means 'imitate'. *The Jerusalem Bible* and *RSV* retain this translation, but *NEB* and *TEV* paraphrase with: 'Try to be like God.' It is true that elsewhere in the *NT* imitation is appealed to as a motive for good conduct. Paul invites his converts to imitate him as their father in Christ (2 Th. 3:7, 9; 1 C. 4:16, 11:1), and he insists that he himself is an imitator of Christ (1 C. 11:1; cf. 1 Th. 1:6), and even though the precise word 'imitate' may not be used he can still appeal to Christians to allow the conduct of Christ to be the pattern which shapes their lives (cf. Phil. 2:4–5). This verse in Ephesians, however, seems to be the only passage in the *NT* where human beings are called upon to 'imitate' God. The thought behind the word is, however, implicit in the teaching of Jesus. He appealed to the utter generosity of God both to the deserving and the undeserving ('he sends his rain on the just and the unjust', Mt. 5:45, 48; Lk. 6:35; and 'is kind to the ungrateful and the selfish', Lk. 5:36) as the example which Christians should follow, as the example which should lead them to love their enemies and to do them good, expecting nothing in return (Lk. 6: 35).

The authority of Jesus, therefore, may be said to support this surprising exhortation to **be imitators of God.** Perhaps the phrase is made easier in this context because the writer can assume that the nature of God has been made visible in Jesus. In Colossians, from which Ephesians borrows so largely, Jesus is precisely called 'the image of God'; what is true about God is, within the limits set by the incarnation, true of Jesus. To imitate Jesus is to imitate God. To imitate God is, therefore, a little more accessible to human reach because in Jesus we can see what God is like.

In 1 C. 4:14–16 the readers are called to be imitators of Paul because they are 'his beloved children'. Here it is **God** they must imitate, but on the similar ground that they are now God's **beloved children.** The inward renewal brought about in them by the Holy Spirit established a new relationship of happy trust and obedience towards God which enabled them to address him in the same word of intimacy as Jesus himself had used: '*Abba*' (Mk 14:36; Rom. 8:15; Gal. 4:6), 'Father'. They knew themselves to be God's children, as it were younger brothers in the same family as Jesus (Rom. 8:29). But the phrase 'child of' was used among the Jews to indicate not only a closeness of relationship, but also a similarity of character. A child of God is one who is like God. Mt. 5:45 invites disciples to be 'sons of their Father' by acting as he acts. The proverb 'like father, like son' should be true within the family of God (cf. also Mt. 5:9).

2. walk in love: that is, conduct your lives in a spirit of **love,** the spirit which can subordinate self-interest to a genuine concern for the welfare of others. God is love, and it is to the practice of this love that Christians are called. Here, as elsewhere in the *NT*, this love is found most clearly in God, and is pre-eminently disclosed in what God did in Christ: 'In this is love, not that we loved God but that he loved us and sent his Son . . .' (1 Jn 4:10). Here the same truth is appealed to. We know the meaning of love because **Christ loved us and gave himself up for us.** The hall-mark of love is the willingness to give oneself for the sake of another. Love is not just a warmth of feeling for another; it is the readiness to renounce self and sacrifice self in costly action for the good of the other. For Christ this love meant not only the acceptance of human flesh in the incarnation but the readiness to tread the hard way to the cross and the sacrifice of life itself (Phil. 2:5–8).

The Greek word for 'give up' (*paradidōmi*) is used in the *NT* of the death of Jesus in a curious variety of ways. Judas 'gave him up'; the high priests 'gave him up', and so did Pilate. It is also said that God 'gave him up' (Rom. 8:32). Here (and at Gal. 2:20) it is Jesus who **gave himself up.**

The association of 'giving' with 'love' is also characteristic of the *NT*. 'God so loved the world that he gave . . .' (Jn 3:16). 'Christ loved the church and gave himself up for her' (Eph. 5:25). At Gal. 2:20 Paul writes: 'He loved me and gave himself up for me,' a form of words echoed here in Eph. 5:2. Whatever the object of the love, whether it be the world, the church, or the individual, the love is proved in the readiness to give.

This self-giving of Christ in death is then described, in the strange language of the ritual of *OT* sacrifice, as **a fragrant offering and sacrifice to God.** The **sacrifice** in the Temple of living creatures played a big part in the religious rituals of the Jews, in spite of the angry protests of some of the prophets; but this was one of the features of the Jewish faith which was not perpetuated into Christianity. Animal sacrifice altogether ceased. The one and only **sacrifice** which made all others unnecessary was found in the death of Christ. All that the Jews of that time claimed to be assured to them through animal sacrifice, Christians believed had been much more effectively made theirs through the self-giving of Jesus on the cross. The Jewish words for sacrifice were still used, but they were applied only to the sacrifice of Christ, or, occasionally, to the sacrificial self-giving of Christians for the benefit of others (Phil. 4:18). The two words **offering** and **sacrifice** are often found in combination (e.g., Ps. 40:6), and there is no gain here in trying to distinguish their meaning. The word here translated **fragrant** was rendered more literally in the *AV* as 'for a sweet smelling savour'. It is probably a survival from the very primitive practices of sacrifice when it was believed that the god actually enjoyed the smell of the burnt offerings (cf. Gen. 8:21). Such an anthropomorphic idea had no doubt long been discarded by Jews, but the word was still used to describe, in a metaphorical way, a sacrifice which was particularly pleasing to God (cf. 'pleasing odour' in Exod. 29:18; Lev. 2:9; Ezek. 20:41).

It is not easy to detect any orderly progression of thought in the passage 4:17–5:14. In Col. 3, which provides the background to this passage, there is a discernible pattern. First, Christians are urged to renounce the gross sins characteristic of the pagan world (3:5), and then the more subtle sins which continue to mar the lives even of professed Christians (3:8). Then at 3:12 there follows a list of the positive qualities of goodness which Christians should aim to practise. Here, however, in Ephesians, there is no such developing sequence. At 4:17–19 there is a general denunciation of the wickedness of Gentile paganism, which the Christian discards when he puts on the 'new nature'. Then there follows an exhortation to renounce those sinful tendencies which persist into the Christian life and are of a kind (so Masson argues) to hurt one's neighbour and disrupt the peace of the community. Then at 4:31–5:2 there is an appeal for Christian goodness to replace these faults. It is surprising, therefore, to find the writer at 5:3 returning to upbraid again the outrageous vices characteristic of pagans. It is true that the emphasis here at first is on the need not even to mention them in speech, but in verses 5–7 it is the vices themselves which are again condemned with special severity.

One possible explanation of this reiterated denunciation of pagan vices is that at the time when the epistle was written a Gnostic type of teaching was beginning to exert a demoralising influence in the Christian community. This teaching put its central emphasis on the gaining of a special illumination of mind, often accompanied by ecstatic experiences. This was said to bring with it a special quality of freedom, freedom from anything that was sinful. Believers were said to have risen into a mode of life which was immune from sin. This did not mean that they did not do evil things, but that their new state of spiritual light and exultation meant that for them merely physical indulgences did not register as sins. Their inner life was with Christ, and it was totally unaffected by what their body did. The body was a wretched thing made of matter and suffused with evil. It would perish in the grave. What this poor body did, however, need not affect the spiritual rapture in which one lived. In such circumstances Christians, who at first had turned from 'immorality and impurity and filthiness', may have found these things creeping back into their lives, as they listened to those who argued that bodily sins were a matter of complete indifference to the truly spiritual

Christian to whom a Gnostic illumination had been granted. If some such situation as this were threatening the church addressed in this epistle, it would account for the writer's repetition of his earlier condemnation of the sexual sins of paganism.

3. The word translated **immorality** in the original *RSV* of 1946 means 'sexual immorality' and the revised translation of 1973 (*The Common Bible*) substitutes for it **fornication** (as also *NEB*). This is better since **immorality** is something far wider than sexual offences. The Greek word *porneia* covers a wide range of sexual evils, and in a Christian context would mean any sexual indulgence outside the permanent relationship of marriage, in circumstances where the sexual appetites are used merely as a means of pleasure without any sense of responsibility and care for the partner. **impurity** would include sexual perversions of various kinds. At first it seems odd to find **covetousness** standing in the midst of a list of sexual sins, but this in fact occurs often in the *NT* (cf. 1 C. 5:10-11, and see note at Eph. 4:19). Here it may mean making money through prostitution, or—more widely—ruthlessly seeking one's own satisfaction in sexual indulgence with a callous disregard for the welfare of others.

The writer is not so much forbidding these three evils, as prohibiting even the discussion of them (as also at 5:12), though this may be mainly a device for emphasising their extreme wickedness from the point of view of Christians. But conversation about them must not be indulged in. There is a danger that by talking about evil activities, even though disapprovingly, one can come to enjoy a perverted pleasure in them, even while ostensibly condemning them. These gross misdemeanours are best not even talked about among those whose lives are wholly committed to the way of God. It is **not fitting**; that is, it is inappropriate among those who are **saints** (see on 1:1).

4. There follow some other words descriptive of what is out of character in a Christian. **filthiness** means anything that is shameful. **silly talk** literally means the talk of a fool. The 'fool' in biblical contexts means a man who acknowledges no standards of morality and has rejected belief in God. The talk characteristic of the 'fool' could, therefore, be conversation of a kind which shows a total disregard for decency and honourable behaviour. **levity** means clever witticisms with nasty insinuations which raise a laugh at the expense of someone's good name. It would include

cheap jokes about sexual matters, but also cruel sallies against
other people's frailties, errors, or simple goodness. This kind of
conversation which cheapens human relationships is not appropriate to those whose lives are supposed to be Christ-controlled.
It is a rare and commendable Christian skill to be able to chat
happily and entertainingly without speaking of those things which
imply discredit or bring pain to others, or achieve laughter by
implied indecency. **instead let there be thanksgiving. thanksgiving** may seem to be an odd alternative with which to replace
these evil things. Allan has an attractive alternative suggestion.
The Greek word for **thanksgiving** is derived from two Greek
words which mean 'good' (*eu*) and 'grace' (*charis*), and he asks if
it is possible here that the derivation is dominant in the meaning.
Could it here mean 'gracious speech' rather than 'thanksgiving'?
As he says, this would 'fit the context excellently'. But it is difficult to find any parallels to such a use and we must accept the
normal meaning of the word. Understood in the widest sense of
the word, thankfulness would here mean that the subject of our
conversation should be those things we can thank God for, our
'blessings', things positively good and wholesome, rather than the
things we should be ashamed of, if we remembered that Christ were
present. Some commentators link the word **thanksgiving** with
the sexual content of the sins forbidden earlier, and suggest that
thanksgiving here implies that sexual appetites should be allowed
satisfaction only in circumstances where we can thank God for it.
For the Christian this would mean within a faithful and enduring
marriage relationship. It has been pointed out that thanksgiving
is recommended as an alternative to evil-speaking in the Qumran
Rule (see Vermes, p. 91), but the parallel is not in fact close.

5. The very emphatic reminder, **Be sure of this,** is consistent
with the suggestion that the writer is here seeking to counter the
danger threatened by Gnostic ideas. He states with the clearest
possible emphasis that those who are sexually **immoral** (forni-
cators) and **covetous** will fail to secure a place in the kingdom of
God. He seems to be deliberately contradicting those who contend that the satisfaction of bodily appetites is a matter of little
importance so long as the inner spirit is 'pure'.

One who is covetous is here equated with **an idolater.** This
is one of the many places where Ephesians seems to be largely
reproducing words from Colossians (see Col. 3:5). Idolatry as

such is forbidden by Paul, but not elsewhere identified with covetousness. Covetousness, whether just greed for money and posses-
sions, or, more widely, as ruthless greed to get whatever one wants
without regard for other people's rights or feelings, can come to
dominate a man's life to the exclusion of all other considerations.
It becomes his god, as we say.

Some scholars have remarked on the recurrence of lists of moral
evils in the different books of the *NT*, and have claimed that there
is a marked similarity (indicating dependence) between them and
similar lists found in Jewish and Stoic writings. If there is any
such dependence at this point, it must be on Jewish rather than
Stoic sources, since the word 'idolatry' would be more likely to
appear in Jewish writings. It is probable, however, that the evidence for the mutual interdependence of such lists has been
greatly exaggerated, and even the evidence for the supposed
standardisation among the Christian lists is less than wholly
convincing. In the *NT* such lists of moral evils are to be found in
the following contexts: Eph. 5:3; Col. 3:5; Rom. 1:29; 1 Pet. 4:3;
Rev. 21:8; Mk 7:21 (cf. also Wis. 14:25ff.). In consequence of
these lists and their internal similarities, Houlden, for instance,
writes of 'a pattern of moral teaching in the early Church' (p. 204).
There is no doubt about a basic similarity in the good qualities
advocated and the bad qualities condemned, but one wonders
whether this amounts to evidence for 'standardised lists' which
people merely memorised and repeated parrot-wise. In fact, the
lists, when compared, are curiously dissimilar, in spite of some
common features. Certainly they do not present a common
pattern which is regularly reproduced. For example, in the eight
passages listed above there is not one single word which appears
in all eight. The most frequent is the Greek word for sexual
immorality (*porneia*) which occurs six times, covetousness five
times, idolatry four times, and uncleanness (*akatharsia*) three
times. Even if the list of evil attitudes had been made up on the
spur of the moment, the degree of similarity might have been
equally high.

The person who practises immoral acts has no **inheritance
in the kingdom of Christ and of God.** The phrase **the kingdom of . . . God** (or 'of heaven') is exceedingly common in the
teaching of Jesus as recorded in the Synoptic Gospels, but much
less frequent in the other books of the *NT*. It occurs only ten times

in the genuinely Pauline letters, eight times in Acts, and only twice in the Fourth Gospel. In Paul it appears to be used as a phrase well-established in the tradition of the Church rather than as a phrase which is of particular significance in his own thought. The words in Eph. 5:5 are closely similar to Paul's words in Gal. 5:21, which also follow a list of evil actions ('those who practise such things will not inherit the Kingdom of God'). There is also a similar sentence in 1 C. 6:9–10. The kingdom is here described as both the kingdom of God and of Christ. This combination is not found elsewhere, except in Rev. 11:15, though in 1 C. 15:24 it is said that in due time Christ will 'deliver the kingdom to God the Father'. In the teaching of Jesus the kingdom may be spoken as something confronting men in the here and now, as well as something which is still to come. One cannot be sure whether in Ephesians the kingdom is thought of as entirely in the future. But probably there is a future reference here, just as when the word 'inheritance' is used in 1:14 it refers to the blessedness of eternal life awaiting the Christian beyond death. The word 'inherit' is constantly used in connexion with the phrase 'kingdom of God', both in Paul and in the Synoptic Gospels. It had probably become a conventional usage, and did not mean more than 'acquire possession of' or 'gain a place in'. Those who are sexually immoral or indulge in sexual perversions of any kind, and those who allow their own personal advantage to dictate their whole course of life (as though this were their god), are not the people over whom God rules as king. They have no place in that kingdom whose marks are 'righteousness, peace, and joy'.

6. Let no one deceive you with empty words, that is, with arguments which sound plausible and attractive, but which run counter to true reasoning and intuitive insights. This warning also could well be addressed to Christians who were exposed to Gnostic-type teachers who insisted that it was the inward spirit of a man which mattered and that the mere satisfaction of a physical appetite was unimportant. This attitude undermined standards of morality and ordinary decency. It was a falsehood to be exposed and rejected. **it is because of these things that the wrath of God comes upon the sons of disobedience.** The **wrath of God** is the enduring hostility of God to all that is evil. It is to be seen in the punishment which often follows wrong-doing even within human history. In Rom. 1:18 Paul writes that

God's wrath is being revealed, that is, one can now see it at work. Sometimes, however, it is 'the wrath to come', the punishment to be faced when life on earth is over (1 Th. 1:10). C. H. Dodd, in his commentary on Romans at 1:18, argues that the wrath of God at work within human history is very similar to what may be called the principle of retribution, which has been built into the very fabric of the universe. Retribution is recognised not only in Christian teaching but also in many of the other great religions of the world—the deep conviction that sooner or later men get what they deserve. Since this is not always evident within this world, the principle is usually understood to work also beyond this life. Wrongdoers who incur this wrath are called **sons of disobedience.** This is a further example of the familiar Semitic idiom: it means those who are disobedient to God's will (cf. 'children of wrath' at 2:3).

7, 8. The readers are called upon not to **associate** with such people, and not to listen to their specious arguments, because 'bad company ruins good morals' (1 C.15:33). The very actions which they argue are morally neutral are in fact the very evils in which they had lived in their pre-Christian days and from which they had been rescued by the power of Christ. Looking back on this former life from the vantage point of their Christian conversion, they recognise it as **darkness** (see 4:18) in contrast to which their Christian experience brought **light.** The writer, however, is not content to say 'you lived in darkness and then entered into light'. He writes: **you were darkness, now you are light.** The **darkness** enveloped and penetrated their whole life, inwardly as well as outwardly; they felt themselves identified with it, not merely surrounded by it. **darkness** and **light** are familiar contrasts often used symbolically with religious significance, **darkness** representing evil and Satan, and **light** standing for goodness and God. These words are used in antithesis by several writers in the NT (cf. Mt. 6:23). John is particularly fond of them. Jesus is God's true light (Jn 1:5–9) which the darkness cannot extinguish (cf. Jn 8:12, 9:5). The life of purity and goodness lived in fellowship with Christ is also spoken of as 'light' (1 Jn 1:5–7, 2:9; cf. 2 C. 4:6, Rom. 13:12, etc.). The sacrament of baptism, which confirmed the Christian in the life of obedience to God, came later to be known as 'enlightenment'. This contrast between light and darkness is also found in the writings from

Qumran. Since, however, the same contrast is found widely throughout religious writings, this alone cannot be taken as evidence of any literary connexion between Qumran and the *NT*.

now you are light in the Lord. 'You are the light of the world,' said Jesus to his disciples (Mt. 5:14–16). It is **in the Lord,** through his power in bringing men to conversion, that the change from darkness to light is accomplished. It is not so much that some imprisoned and obliterated element in their own nature has been released. Rather, it comes as a gift from Christ and is dependent upon the presence of Christ.

walk as children of light. children of light is another Hebraism, meaning 'enlightened people'. Jesus uses the same phrase (at Lk. 16:8) to describe his own followers, in contrast to the 'children of this world'. The readers are to **walk** (i.e., behave) in conformity with their new character. This is an instance of a mode of exhortation often found in Paul's writings: 'Be what you are'—the indicative of a spiritual experience providing the basis for an imperative of appropriate action.

9. This is a parenthesis in which the writer comments that **the fruit of light is found in all that is good and right and true.** The word **fruit** is a common metaphor in the *NT*. Just as the seed or the plant fulfils its own nature in producing fruit, so the **light** of Christ's presence in the human heart is a seed from which grows everything **that is good and right and true.** Jesus used the word 'fruit' in this sense (Mt. 12:33), and Paul also speaks of the fruit of the Spirit (Gal. 5:22). Some commentators refer to a similar threefold description of the content of obedience to God as 'truth, righteousness, and justice' in the Community Rule at Qumran (Vermes, p. 72). It is characteristic that here in the *NT* 'goodness' replaces 'justice'. Righteousness may be understood as the avoidance of those evil things which God has forbidden; goodness is an attitude of generous kindliness to others, which is happy to do far more than is required by mere justice; truth implies sincerity, genuineness, the absence of sham and pretence.

10. try to learn what is pleasing to the Lord. It is characteristic of the *NT* that though it offers guide-lines of conduct, it does not attempt to provide precise rules to cover all the varied situations that may arise in life. It prefers to awaken, cleanse, and instruct each man's conscience, so that he himself may achieve insight into what is God's will in any moment of decision (cf.

Rom. 12:3). So Jesus said: 'Why do you not judge for yourselves what is right?' (Lk. 12:57). The essence of Christian obedience is not in the keeping of rules, but in obedience to the living presence of Christ and the development of an intuitive sense in each changing situation of what will gain his approval. Paul declared it to be his personal ambition 'to please Christ', i.e., to gain his approval. **try to learn** (*RSV*) may give the wrong impression of what the writer actually says. He is not suggesting anything at all like memorising prepared instructions. The meaning would be represented better by the words 'try to find out'. And the standard to aim at is 'what will please Christ'.

11, 12. The readers are urged to **Take no part in the unfruitful works of darkness.** Evil actions are **unfruitful** in the sense that they do not lead to *good* results. It is the Christian's duty to **expose them.** Mere neutrality or unprotesting toleration is not enough. Evil must be actively opposed by being exposed. Those who love the Lord are called upon to hate evil (Ps. 97:10), not just to pretend it is not there. Evil prospers when good men are content to ignore it and do nothing about it. It is not clear exactly what is meant by **expose.** The word could be translated as 'rebuke' or 'convict'. One might have thought that it meant a verbal denunciation of evil, so that all may be able to recognise it for what it is, if it were not that the following verse deprecates even so much as speaking of the evil deeds. Phillips suggests that **expose** here means 'show up', not so much by verbal protest as by actions of a totally different quality. He then introduces a link with the following verse, by adding: 'you know the sort of things I mean', and then continuing in verse 12: '—to detail their secret doings is too shameful to mention.' The evil things which are being done are so deplorable and shocking that it is wrong, not only to participate in them, but even to talk about them. It is a similar thought to that of 5:3.

Some commentators have seen in this instruction to expose evil a parallel to the Rule of Qumran (see Vermes, p. 8), where members of the community are required to rebuke or challenge a fellow-member whose conduct they regard as blameworthy (cf. Mt. 18:15–17). Here, however, the 'sons of disobedience' whose sins, too evil to be spoken about, are to be 'exposed', must surely be pagans outside the life of the Church rather than defaulting members within it.

13. This verse, especially the second part of it, is obscure. Literally translated it would be: 'When everything is exposed by the light, it is brought into the open; for everything which is brought into the open is light.' Any translator who is determined for the sake of the reader to produce some clear meaning is almost compelled to introduce an element of interpretation into his translation. Some interpretation is present even in the *RSV* translation: **When anything is exposed by the light it becomes visible, for anything that becomes visible is light.** It is not easy to see what the writer means when he says that even evil things, once they have been **exposed,** become **light.** It might conceivably be a vivid way of saying that they are shown up for what they are. A second possibility is this: that even evil things, once seen for what they are and mastered in the life of the Christian, can prove to be an asset in his witness as a Christian. Another possibility is this: that an evil man fearlessly confronted with his own evil deeds will 'yield to the power of light and be won over' (Allan). Phillips in order to bring some clearly intelligible meaning out of the Greek, allows a large degree of interpretation in his translation: 'Light is capable of showing up everything for what it really is. It is possible (after all it happened to you) for light to turn the thing it shines upon into light.' It is not possible to make a firm choice between these various possibilities.

14. Therefore it is said: the quotation following is introduced by the same formula as the quotation from Scripture in 4:8. The words could possibly be translated: 'Therefore, God says' (an impersonal passive being used out of reverence, in order to avoid introducing the word 'God' unnecessarily). This quotation, however, is not from Scripture. From earliest times commentators have tried to identify its source. Some suggest that it is a free translation of Isa. 60:1: 'Arise, shine; for your light has come, and the glory of the Lord has risen upon you.' The similarity, however, is not close enough for it to be a direct quotation, even though the recollection of this passage may have been in the mind of the writer. Others have thought that it may come from some Jewish apocalyptic writing which has been lost, but the use of the word **Christ** makes this unlikely. The common interpretation today is that the words come from a Christian hymn, and this seems the most probable origin. Some claim further support for the theory by arguing that there is a rhythmic quality in the words. The fact that it can be introduced by the same formula as is used elsewhere to introduce words of Scripture (4:8; cf. Jas 6:4) may indicate the high status which some hymns had come to have in the thought of early Christians.

The hymn calls upon the non-Christian, as a **sleeper, to awake . . . and arise from the dead,** that is, to come to see the vanity and worthlessness of his evil life and turn from it. The life of sin has earlier been spoken of as a kind of death (cf. 2:1: 'dead through trespasses and sins'). If they take this step, **Christ shall give them light.** The word **light** provides an effective link-up with verses 8–13. The Christian pleads that his own happy experience as described in verse 8 may become also the experience of the non-Christian to whom the quotation is addressed.

C. F. D. Moule, in his book, *The Birth of the New Testament*, p. 25, notes some curious parallels between this quotation and Ac. 12:7 where Luke describes Peter's escape from prison: 'A light shone in the cell . . . the angel woke Peter saying: Get up quickly.' The three Greek words translated as 'light', 'woke', and 'get up' ('arise') are the same as those which appear in this quotation from the hymn. It is hardly likely that there is a direct literary connexion, but the association of these three words in two separate contexts in the *NT* suggests that they reflect a recurring sequence of thought in the evangelism and worship of the early Church.

NEB is so certain that the quotation comes from a hymn that it introduces it with the words: 'And so the hymn says: . . .' but there is nothing in the Greek to justify this insertion (which may be misleading). A. R. C. Leaney in fact protests against this presumption on the part of the *NEB* and insists that it is a debatable point whether its source was in fact a hymn (*The New Testament*, p. 154).

Some modern commentators argue that the quotation fits most suitably into a baptismal occasion. A. R. C. Leaney, in the same context, comments that the quoted words 'magnificently express the situation of someone just baptised and bidden to awake from the sleep of spiritual death into the life and light of Christ . . . Eph. 5:14 may well have been spoken to those baptised on such an occasion.' The words would, however, appear to be more appropriate as addressed to a catechumen who has been prepared for Christian baptism and is now awaiting the moment of baptism, rather than one who has been baptised. Such a one sees baptism

as the step by which he responds to the call of Christ to rise from
his moral torpor (death) and enter into the light of Christ. It is
true that the words translated **awake** and **arise from the dead**
are also used in passages about Christ's resurrection, and that
baptism was interpreted as symbolic of dying and rising with
Christ (see Rom. 6:5–11). The reference may, therefore, be to a
baptismal situation, but it could also apply rather to the conversion–experience of which baptism is the outward sign and seal,
than to the ceremonial element in a baptismal service.

15. The writer has already insisted that Christian experience
should lead to Christlike conduct (5:8). Exalted spiritual awareness must not be regarded as a substitute for Christian behaviour.
Rather, it should prove to be the driving power which produces
in a Christian actions appropriate to his profession. Here the
writer returns to this same important emphasis: **Look carefully
then how you walk.** That is, you must take very special care
about your conduct. This is noted as the mark of the **wise** person,
in contrast to the **unwise** one.

A **wise** man is one who can anticipate the likely consequences
of an action, and who so acts as to avoid what will bring trouble
and later regret. So the wise Christian is one who will seek to avoid
any action of which he may be later ashamed, or which will
bring disgrace on the Christian community of which he is a
member. The *OT* in several places insists that 'the fear of the
Lord is the beginning of wisdom' (*NEB*: 'the first step to wisdom').
This means that the recognition that we live in a world where evil
actions are followed by evil consequences is the first step towards
wise conduct. If that is the beginning of wisdom, the source of
mature wisdom is indicated in verse 18. True wisdom comes to
those who are 'filled with the Spirit', by whom goodness is sought
not out of mere prudence, that is, fear of the consequences that
follow evil doing, but because the inner life has been changed so
that the man 'loves what God has commanded' and finds himself
empowered to do what God approves. To want to do what one
knows one ought to do is one of the qualities of the 'new nature'
(4:24). See also 1 C. 1:30.

16. One mark of Christian wisdom is to be **making the most
of the time,** that is, of every opportunity that comes our way.
The word used for **time** suggests that what is meant is not so
much the need to fill every unrelenting minute with useful activity,

but rather to be ready to seize every opportunity to practise Christian love and to bring others to the knowledge of the Christians' Lord. If one is pre-occupied with one's own spiritual excellence to the extent of becoming indifferent to down-to-earth actions of simple Christian goodness (such as helping to relieve the distresses of others, carefully avoiding evil talk, ill-will, and hostility), that will mean wasting God-given opportunities of serving him.

In 1 C. 7:29, where Paul is advising his readers about the wisdom or folly of actions they are contemplating, he reminds them to bear in mind that 'the appointed time has grown very short', that is, the end of the present world-order is very near. Soon men will be standing before God at the final judgment. Inevitably such a belief must have a strong bearing on the conduct of those who hold it. Here, however, there is no hint of urgency on the ground that the end of all things is near. The plea for serious-minded conduct is based on the fact that **the days are evil.** It is true that this also could be related to thoughts of the coming end of the world, even though that is not specifically mentioned as imminent. In some apocalyptic expectation it was believed that the actual end would be preceded by a period of tribulation (cf. Mk 13:7ff.), and it is possible that this is in the mind of the present writer when he writes **the days are evil.** But there is nothing in the context here to suggest such an interpretation. This seems rather to suggest that the evil in the world is so widespread and arrogantly powerful that this provides even added reason why Christians should not add to it by their own conduct, but rather aim to inject into the world some compensating goodness.

17. Therefore do not be foolish, but understand what the will of the Lord is. The **foolish** are those who act selfishly, and foolishly, regardless of the evil consequences which may follow. The writer pleads that his readers will not fall into this class, but instead will be concerned to find out first and foremost what is **the will** of God for them. This recalls 5:10 where the same plea is expressed in different words. True wisdom is the ability to discern what is the will of God, the belief that in it lies man's truest welfare, and the willingness, with God's help, to do that will.

18. do not get drunk with wine. Alcohol and other drugs are a means by which people seek to escape from the drabness and monotony of life, or from the aching regrets and disappointments within their own hearts. Man feels deep within himself that life was meant to be something significant and joyous, even though it so often falls far short of this. Sometimes outward circumstances make a joyful life wellnigh impossible, such things as extreme poverty, uncongenial work, the misery caused by broken personal relationships or by loneliness and the absence of friends; sometimes, however, the cause of the trouble is within one's own heart—a sense of guilt, frustration, resentment, hatred, defeat, and inward division. Men often turn to drugs and drink to try to find some quick relief from these aching sorrows. Aldous Huxley, who himself experimented with drug-taking, speaks of the power of the drug 'to abolish solitude' and 'to attune us with our fellows in a glowing exaltation of affection' and to make life appear 'divinely beautiful and significant'. But the relief and excitement they bring is only short-lived. When the effect of the drug has worn off, the same desperate situation is still there to confront us once again, and we are even less well equipped to meet it with wisdom and courage. Drunkenness and drug-taking, moreover, diminish one's sense of responsibility. Under their influence shameful things are done (**debauchery**) which would be quite out of character in normal circumstances. And these irresponsible actions make a bad situation even worse.

Sometimes also alcohol and drugs are taken in a deliberate attempt to induce or heighten mystical experiences of the nearness of the divine and our oneness with it. They have the effect of reducing the sobering effect of self-criticism and rational assessment, and of producing a sense of uninhibited freedom and expansiveness which appear to make these experiences more intense and wonderful. Paul tells us that drunkenness took place at Corinth during the celebration of the Lord's Supper, but this seems to have been merely careless excess rather than an attempt to induce a higher spiritual sensitivity. Here, too, the drunkenness which is deplored seems to be the ordinary drunkenness into which men slide in their attempt to escape from some of the harsh facts of their daily existence, not a device to stimulate mystical rapture.

The writer is well aware of man's longing for that which can make life wonderful and significant, in spite of the grim realities of human existence. He knows, too, that in the Christian life there is that which can bring joy, peace, happiness, hope, and love, replacing despair, misery, unrest, and bitterness. It is all given to one who allows himself to **be filled with the Spirit**. This is the Christian equivalent of drunkenness, the alternative to alcohol and drug-taking. 'This is a pleasant kind of drunkenness,' was the comment of Erasmus.

It may at first seem astonishing, even improper, to associate the gift of **the Spirit** with intoxication. Our own religious life on the whole has become so sober and restrained that exuberant and thrilling joy seems out of place. But this writer is not the only one in the *NT* to associate the gift of the Spirit with intoxication. Luke tells how the disciples on the day of Pentecost were 'filled with the Holy Spirit' and in consequence behaved with such joyful abandon that the bystanders sneered: 'They are filled with new wine' (Ac. 2:13). They had indeed found those qualities of life the lack of which, according to Aldous Huxley, leads men to drugs. Their loneliness had been replaced by a warm comradeship which the *NT* speaks of as the fellowship created by the Holy Spirit; love, peace, joy—the fruit of the Spirit—had come to life within them. Life, eternal life, significant, authentic life had become theirs. They felt that they had been lifted out of themselves, out of their normal imprisoned lives into a triumphant freedom.

Some exponents of these passages in Acts and Ephesians have argued that the phrase 'filled with the Holy Spirit' indicates a stage in the Christian life beyond that which is just described as 'having received the Holy Spirit'. But this is unlikely. It is not so much a further stage as a different way of describing the same experience. The only writers in the *NT* to use the phrase 'filled with the Spirit' are Luke in Acts and the writer of Ephesians. It is predominantly a Lucan manner of speech. Some scholars have wondered if Ephesians took it over from Acts. At any rate it is noteworthy that in Ac. 2 there occurs the phrase 'filled with the Spirit' (2:4) and also the contrast between this and drunkenness (2:13), both of which are found in Eph. 5:18. Is it possible that the writer of Ephesians was aware of this passage in Acts, whether in its present form or some earlier version? Or is the similarity due rather to the fact that they both drew on the same strand of tradition within their common Christian heritage?

19. This spiritual joy and exultation, more evident today in Pentecostal movements than in more established churches, is treated here as something characteristic of the corporate life of the community rather than just an experience of individuals in isolation. This verse certainly implies a gathering of the community for fellowship. We notice, however, that the gathering is marked by a considerable degree of informality. If it is to be thought of as a meeting for worship, then it is worship characterised by spontaneity rather than a solemn observance of a fixed liturgical pattern. In 1 C. 14:26 Paul writes about Christians 'coming together' in a gathering in which 'each one has a hymn, a lesson, a revelation, a tongue, or an interpretation'. The situation assumed here in Ephesians is somewhat similar. The members of the group are seen as **addressing one another.** There is, therefore, a considerable degree of congregational participation rather than formalised worship where clergy and choir predominate. Here everyone present takes an active part, and what is spoken or sung is offered as a contribution to the whole community. It is not an abstract exercise in the worship of God, but fellowship controlled by the Spirit of God for the mutual benefit of all present.

Congregational participation consists of **psalms and hymns and spiritual songs.** It is perhaps futile to attempt to draw a sharp distinction between these three items. If, however, distinctions are to be sought, perhaps the **psalms** are those derived from the *OT* and the worship of the synagogue, **hymns** are verses to a musical setting addressed to God, and **spiritual songs** are songs of Christian aspiration and exhortation in which the members of the fellowship are **addressing one another** rather than God.

It may be that this wording in Ephesians suggests a gathering for fellowship which has become slightly more formal than the one pictured in 1 Corinthians. There is, for instance, in Ephesians no reference to teaching, revelations, or tongues in the corporate worship. The stress on individual initiative is not so pronounced, though it appears to be implied. Nevertheless the gathering is still marked by spontaneity and flexibility. Probably, too, we should think of a small group rather than a large congregation. In the early Church small fellowships in the homes of members were the order of the day, rather than meetings in large special-purpose buildings. We read of churches which meet in so-and-so's house. In Ac. 19:7 the group which Paul visits at Ephesus consists of about twelve men. The formal liturgical worship probably developed at a later time, and was practised probably in larger gatherings in which the smaller, scattered 'house fellowships' of an area met together for a corporate act of witness and worship. In such large gatherings informality and spontaneity were less appropriate and a larger degree of formality and planned order-liness were felt to be necessary. It is probable also that it was in such larger groups where members were less intimately known to each other that the formal liturgical type of worship began to develop with its set prayers, lectionaries, and sermons. Perhaps in the first place this formal worship of the larger congregation was looked on as supplementary to the meeting of the smaller group of more intimate, friendly, informal fellowship, and was never intended to become a substitute for it, as has largely happened today.

Even when their **singing and making melody** is addressed **to one another** (that is, meant for mutual encouragement) it is still directed also **to the Lord,** since it is he who is being honoured in their fellowship and worship. Music and singing are prominent in their worship, as has so often been the case in lively Christian revivals. Indeed, wherever people in community find themselves moved by strong positive emotion, whether of a religious nature or not, it readily finds expression in song. This singing, according to *RSV*, is to be **with all your heart.** This translation suggests that the phrase means 'enthusiastically' or 'heartily'. The Greek words, however, translated literally, mean simply 'with your heart'. This could mean simply 'in your heart' (as the similar phrase in Col. 3:16 does). Indeeed at this point *NEB* joins with the older translations and gives 'in your hearts'. This suggests not so much 'heartiness' as that the outward singing should be an ex-pression of what is felt deeply with one's heart, that is 'with sincerity' or 'conviction'.

20. always and for everything giving thanks. The Greek word for 'I give thanks' is *eucharisteō*. It is the normal term for thanksgiving, and there is little reason here for ascribing to it any 'eucharistic' significance. This sacramental meaning was not ascribed to the word until times later than the *NT*. The idea of giving thanks **always,** though difficult enough in practice, is one which is met with elsewhere in the *NT*. In Eph. 1:16 the writer has already said: 'I do not cease giving thanks for you,' just as Paul in 1 C. 1:4 wrote: 'I give thanks always for you.' It is

understandable that an attitude of continuous gratitude is characteristic of the Spirit-filled Christian. It is less easy to understand
how even the sincere Christian can be expected to give thanks not
only **always** but **for everything.** Even if we may learn how to
keep a thankful heart *in* all circumstances, it is not easy to see how
one can be grateful *for* everything. It presupposes a deep underlying faith that God can produce good out of even the most
unpromising situation, and that thankfulness, therefore, can be
felt because of the confident hope that in some wonderful way God
will make even disaster and suffering an occasion for later blessing.
It is possible, however, that these difficulties which we feel in the
passage arise because the writer of Ephesians is quoting from
memory words which he recalls in the letter to the Colossians
which he knows extremely well; but his recollection is faulty and
he quotes inaccurately in a way that distorts the original meaning
of the words. This is something which Paul himself could hardly
have been guilty of, though one can understand it happening if the
one who wrote Ephesians was one other than Paul who wrote in
Paul's name and tried to represent Paul's thought, recalling where
possible the actual words Paul had used.

We make a comparison of these two passages in Ephesians and
Colossians, indicating the words they share in common, which
prove beyond question their mutual interdependence:

Col. 3:16–17	Eph. 5:19–20
. . . sing psalms and hymns and spiri- *tual songs* with thankfulness *in your* *hearts to God.* And whatever you do, in word or deed, do *everything* *in the name of the Lord Jesus, giving* *thanks to God the Father* through him.	*. . . in psalms and hymns and spiri-* *tual songs, singing* and making melody *to the Lord with all your* *heart,* always and for *everything* *giving thanks in the name of our Lord* *Jesus* Christ *to God the Father.*

In Colossians the two phrases 'everything' and 'in the name of
the Lord Jesus' are attached to the command 'do'. That is, our
whole activity is to be controlled by what is appropriate in a
Christ-directed life. The word 'giving thanks' occurs quite
separately in the following clause, and is totally unconnected with
these phrases. The writer of Ephesians, however, recalls the words
as belonging to the same general context, but forgets their actual
sequence and their precise significance in the sentence. So in-
appropriately he associates 'thanksgiving' with 'everything' and

'in the name of Jesus' in a way which is not only much less apt than in their original use in Colossians but is even hard to explain convincingly.

The writer here is clearly reproducing material from Colossians in a somewhat mechanical way, associating in meaning words which in Colossians were only adjacent in physical position but totally unconnected in meaning. Many scholars feel that Paul himself would have been unlikely to do this, though a later Paulinist might have done.

CHRISTIAN STANDARDS IN THE HOME 5:21–6:9

In this passage the writer offers guidance about Christian conduct to different groups of people within the community—wives and husbands, children and fathers, slaves and masters. There are similarly instructions for the same six groups in Col. 3:18–4:1. 1 Pet. 2:18–3:7 and 5:1–5 offers moral guidance to somewhat different groups—servants, wives and husbands, elders and younger people. It is customary to refer to these lists of particularised instructions as *Haustafeln*, the German word for rules for members of a household. A. M. Hunter in *Paul and His Predecessors*, pp. 55–7, summarises what has been written about them. Claims have been made that these lists in the *NT*, show evidence of borrowing from Jewish or Stoic *Haustafeln*, but the similarities are not very close, and quite apart from non-Christian antecedents it is the kind of material which could have arisen spontaneously in the Christian community. New converts would quickly ask, not only for general instructions about behaviour appropriate to a Christian commitment, but also for precise instructions relating to their particular station in life, especially at those points where Christian behaviour differed from generally accepted standards. How does one's acceptance of Christ as Lord affect relations between husband and wife, between slave and master, etc.? We cannot be sure that Paul originated these items of advice, though his letters preserve the earliest Christian instances of them. There may have been antecedents for him to follow within the Christian community. But in fact there is no actual proof that Col. 3:18–4:1 had earlier patterns to follow, and 1 Peter was probably written in the light of both Ephesians and Colossians, and may well have borrowed from them.

21. Be subject to one another out of reverence for Christ. This verse has been interpreted in different ways. (i) It may be the final clause of the preceding paragraph. The verb **Be subject** is, in the Greek, a participle, not an independent imperative, and therefore some argue that is is dependent on the preceding main verb 'Be filled with the Spirit', and parallel to the other preceding participle 'giving thanks'. Both *AV* and *RV* treated it in this way. (ii) It may, however, be an independent sentence, serving as an introduction to the following paragraph. This is how both *RSV* and *NEB* understand it. The fact that in the Greek the verb **Be subject** is a participle may seem to favour (i), since a participle is usually dependent on a main verb in the same sentence. It has, however, been shown that in the Greek of the *NT*, in a context of exhortation, a participle may be used as if it were an independent verb and carry the force of an imperative. This allows the possibility of alternative (ii).

Another difficulty is that the general instruction **Be subject to one another** is not in fact applicable to all the six groups that follow, but to only three of them—wives, children, and slaves. The other three—husbands, fathers, masters—are addressed as those who expect subordination from others, rather than submit to it themselves. This is not surprising, since in the first century wives were expected to show deference to husbands, children to their fathers, and slaves to masters. What is unexpected is that this whole section is introduced by the general instruction, apparently including all Christians, that they should **Be subject to one another.** There would be no difficulty if the subordination asked for was to be offered to the Lord, but it is, strangely enough, **to one another.** The Greek word translated as **Be subject** is a strong one, stronger indeed than the similar word used for 'obey' in the directions to children and slaves (6:1, 5). Here it is used only of the subordination of wives to husbands and of one Christian towards other Christians (**one another**). It is in fact the same strong word which is used in Rom. 13:1 to describe the appropriate attitude of Christians to their secular rulers. It is indeed surprising to find this same word used of a Christian's attitude towards his fellow Christians, though Clement of Rome (38:1) repeats it in his letter: 'Let each one be subject to his neighbour.' It may be that the instruction does not so much mean that every Christian must be subject to every other Christian, but rather that

among Christians there should be an agreed willingness to accept
the Christian conventions about the deference one group should
pay to another, showing honour to whom honour is due, etc. (as at
Rom. 13:7). It is, however, very doubtful whether this gives due significance to the writer's words. One recalls the incident where Jesus
washed his disciples' feet (Jn 13:14–15) and the instruction that
they should do the same for one another. Similarly in Phil. 2:3–4 we
read: 'In humility count others better than yourselves.' So here,
'subject yourselves' must mean at least that Christians should be
willing to subordinate their own interests to those of others. Allan
suggests that this verse is recommending 'a principle of mutual
consideration'. But the word **Be subject** does in fact imply something stronger than that. It means at least the attitude of treating
another Christian's welfare as more important than one's own.

However, even if Christians are being asked thus to subordinate
their personal interests to those of others, it is a carefully qualified
subordination. His submission to others is to be offered only in so
far as it is compatible with **reverence for Christ.** We are not
asked to yield to the wishes of others, no matter what they wish,
but only when what they ask of us is in line with **reverence for
Christ.** Actually these words, if translated literally, mean 'the
fear of Christ', a phrase which is clearly parallel to the familiar
'fear of the Lord'. It is not without significance that the writer
can slip in the name of **Christ** for the more commonly used
'God'. It is an indication of how closely God and Christ are
associated (almost equated) in the writer's mind. God is to be
feared in that disobedience to him is fraught with hurtful consequences for the wrong-doer and for his community. We have
come to identify Christ only with the gentler aspects of God's
nature, so that 'the fear of Christ' sounds almost self-contradictory.
We easily overlook the fact that Jesus himself spoke some extremely
severe words. There is that in Christ which is to be feared, since
he fully represents God, and there is in God that which is to be
feared. The phrase 'the fear of Christ' recognises humbly the
element of judgment in the Christian faith and the part assigned
to Christ as Judge in Christian thinking. This Judge may, at the
last, say: 'I do not know you,' 'Depart from me.' This is a verdict
to be feared. The first requirement of Christians, therefore, is to
be obedient to God as we know him in Christ, so that at the last
they may hear from him words of commendation, not condemna-

tion. Our deference to the will of others, therefore, is asked of us
only if it does not run counter to the prior claim upon us of obedience to Christ. Provided, however, that it does not entail disobedience to Christ, the Christian is required to subject himself
to his fellows. This means, at least, that he should show the utmost
consideration to their wishes and preferences, and a willingness to
let their interests take precedence over his own.

22. Wives, be subject to your husbands, as to the Lord.
The first of the six groups to be addressed consists of **Wives.** The
words here are very similar to the parallel passage in Col. 3:18
which reads: 'Wives, be subject to your husbands, as is fitting in
the Lord.' The phrasing in Colossians is in fact much to be preferred to that of Ephesians. One feels that the writer to Ephesians
has been influenced also by Paul's words on this topic in 1 C. 11
and 12:34ff. Paul never seems to have quite resolved the conflict
between the view of women consistent with his new Christian
insights and the view which he inherited from his Jewish past.
His Christian insight prevails when he writes: 'In Christ there is
neither male nor female' (Gal. 3:28). He recognises that the
marriage relationship has been transformed for real Christians.
For them the wife now has the same claims upon her husband as
the husband has upon her (1 C. 7:4), and both man and wife
are equally interdependent on one another (1 C. 11:11). But
Paul seems to have been aware of another responsibility besides
that of explaining to Christians the radical change which Christ
brings into all human relationships, including marriage. As a wise
pastor he had to try to see to it that the new freedom and status
of the Christian woman within her own home and marriage
relationship was not so practised as to create dangerous misunder-
standings and resentments among pagan neighbours, especially if
these misgivings would militate against these neighbours feeling
able to listen to the gospel and to respond to it. In the ancient
world a man's right to expect obedience from his wife was so
universally conceded that a movement which seemed to coun-
tenance and approve a wife's insubordination towards her husband
would rouse many prejudices. Such behaviour on the part of
Christian women would have prevented their neighbours from
hearing sympathetically the message of the gospel. Paul said of
himself that he was ready to endure any deprivation rather than
put an obstacle in the way of the gospel of Christ (1 C. 9:12), and

for this reason, if no other, he asked wives not to provoke antagonism to the gospel by insubordination to their husbands. In a
similar way Paul asked Christian women to continue to wear the
veil in Corinth, lest their abandonment of it should lead to their
being mistaken for women of loose moral character and to the
Christian faith which they represented being understood as a
society which permitted sexual licence.

It is doubtful, however, whether either Paul or the writer to
Ephesians asked women to be subject to their husbands merely
as a temporary expedient, a way of avoiding unnecessary offence
to potential converts from pagan society. In spite of the new freedom which women enjoyed within the Christian community, and
in spite of the transformation which this would ultimately bring
within Christian marriage, it is probable that Paul continued to
feel that obedience was the proper attitude of the Christian wife
to her husband. Indeed, until recent times it was almost universally expected that a Christian bride would promise obedience to
her husband, and indeed may still feel that this is appropriate.
Apart from Christian considerations, there are among psycholo-
gists those who believe that many women are happier within a
marriage where ultimate responsibility for decision-making is not
shirked by the husband, and that children are less likely to be
emotionally stable if they come from a home where the mother
dominates over the father. Today we should not wish to continue
the use of the word 'subordination' or 'subjection' within marriage,
and within a truly Christian marriage there is real equality
between partners, consultation with each other and consideration
for each other. It is, however, possible that the idea that the husband is the rightful head of the home is based on more than old-
fashioned custom.

Whether this is so or not, it must be conceded that both Paul and
the writer of Ephesians believed that it was, and, moreover, both
expressed it in ways which few Christians would regard as accept-
able today. Moreover, both try to find arguments to support
their attitude not only from contemporary custom, but also from
the very constitution of things and from Christian faith and
experience, which today sound less than convincing.

We have suggested that the wording of Col. 3:18 is preferable
to that of Eph. 5:22. Colossians claims that it is *appropriate* (fitting),
among those who acknowledge Christ as Lord, for the wife to be

subject to the husband. In Ephesians, however, wives are bidden
to **be subject to** their **husbands, as to the Lord,** to offer the
same obedience to their husbands as to Christ their Lord. This
seems to be assigning a degree of wisdom and authority to the
Christian husband beyond anything that is reasonable. But both
Paul and this writer seem to have believed in a kind of hierarchy
of authority within the Church: God, Christ, husband, wife. The
head of Christ is God, the head of every man is Christ, the head of
a woman is her husband, wrote Paul in 1 C. 11:3. Eph. 5:23
partly reproduces this sequence, but modifies it by introducing
into it the concept of the Church.

23, 24. Already in Ephesians the Church has been spoken of as
the body of Christ (4:12) and Christ has been described as the
head of the Church (1:22, 4:15–16; cf. Col. 1:18). Here the idea
of Christ as the head of the Church is combined with the thought
of man as the head of the woman (from 1 C. 11:3). Here, however, it is not so much the idea of delegated authority, descending
in three stages from the highest to the lowest (as in 1 C. 11), but
of two parallel ideas, each of which is used to interpret the significance of the other. The authority of a man over his wife helps
to interpret the authority of Christ over his Church; and the
relationship of Christ to his Church throws new light on the relationship of husband to wife within Christian marriage. **the
husband is the head of the wife as Christ is the head of the
church, his body.** Therefore, **As the church is subject to
Christ, so let wives also be subject in everything to their
husbands.** The Church is not actually called the bride of Christ
in Ephesians. That occurs only in Revelation. But the relationship seems to be there by implication. (For a discussion of the
Church as 'the body of Christ' and Christ as the head of the body,
see notes 1:22 and 4:15).

The writer, however, seems to feel that there is something
missing in the description of the relationship between Christ and
his Church, as corresponding to that between **head** which commands and **body** which obeys. So he slips in the word **Saviour**
to supply what is lacking. To speak of Christ as head of the body
(especially in relation to such a phrase as **subject to**) puts the
emphasis on the duty of obedience which the body owes to the
head. But the fact that Christ as the head commands the obedience of the body, his Church, is not the whole truth about their

relationship. The missing truth is that the Church derives her whole
life and vitality from the head. The writer does not attempt to
express this by further development of the anatomical metaphor.
Instead he simply adds: Christ **is himself its Saviour.** 'Lord'
and 'Saviour' became the two words which together were felt to
sum up the significance of Christ, one asserting his right to command total obedience, and the other his power to rescue, heal,
renew, and revitalise. The word **head** is here equivalent to
'Lord', and the word **Saviour** is added to make it clear that he
who commands is also the one who upholds, sustains, and em-
powers. It is something of a curiosity that in Paul's genuine letters,
though the verb 'save' and the noun 'salvation' are found, there is
no instance of the word **Saviour.** Its use is more characteristic
of later writings such as Luke–Acts, the Pastoral Epistles, and
2 Peter.

25. Wives have been instructed to 'be subject' to their husbands,
since the husband is the head of the wife (23), the immediate
authority to whom she must offer obedience as a disciple of Christ.
We should expect the instruction to the husband to correspond
to this, and require him to exercise his authority with consideration. But there is no reference to the husband's right to require
obedience. His responsibility towards his wife is gathered up in
the word **love.** The Greek language has several words which in
English may be translated 'love', and one of these has special
reference to a love with sexual content, such as the love between
husband and wife. But this is not the word used here. This word
for **love** is the one which the Christian community made especially its own. It is the word used in the Gospels for the Christian
duty of loving both neighbours and enemies. It is a word which
signifies a constant concern in thought and action for the welfare
of the other person. It is the verb which corresponds to the noun
'love' as used in 1 C. 13. It means not only a practical concern for
the welfare of the other, but a continual readiness to subordinate
one's own pleasure and advantage for the benefit of the other. It
implies patience and kindliness, humility and courtesy, trust and
support (1 C. 13:4–7). This love means that one is eager to understand what the needs and interests of the other are, and will do
everything in his power to supply those needs and further those
interests. This is the love with which **husbands** should **love**
their **wives.**

To make clear the quality of this love the writer introduces the perfect example of this love at its best—the love of **Christ** for **the church.** The word 'love' in this full Christian sense derives its meaning not from any human love but from God's love for man (1 Jn 4:10), or from Christ's love for his disciples: **as Christ loved the church and gave himself up for her.** The close link in the *NT* between God's love and God's giving was emphasised in the note on 5:2.

It is a little unexpected to find here the verb **loved** in the past tense, rather than 'loves' in the present tense. It refers to some definite action of Christ's in the past rather than his continuous attitude. This action must be the self-giving of Christ in his death. It is not that his love is confined to this action, but rather that its quality and extent is demonstrated and proved by what he did there. Christ's death is also seen as the inevitable end of a course of action upon which Jesus entered voluntarily. He **gave himself up.** It was not his enemies who robbed him of life, nor yet God who forced the sacrifice on an unwilling victim. He laid down his life of his own accord, as Jn 10:18 insists. Since Christ has gone to this ultimate limit of self-giving in his love for man, there is nothing that love will not do. 'He who did not spare his own Son but gave him up for us all, will he not also give us all things with him?' In this passage from Rom. 8:32 it is God who 'gave up Christ' and it was done 'for us all'. In Ephesians, however, the object of Christ's sacrifice is the Church. In so far as 'for us all' in Rom. 8:32 may have meant 'for all the world', the use of the word **church** here may seem to introduce a limitation on the extent of his love. But this need not be so. The Church consists of those who have recognised Christ's action as God's outreach to them, and who have responded to it. Christ has a special concern for those who have thus responded, because they, as the Church, are now to be the instrument of his wider purpose to make his love known and effective amongst all men.

This emphasis may seem to give ground to those who complain that in this section, and indeed in the letter as a whole, the writer is unduly pre-occupied with the Church, and not sufficiently outward looking with a concern for the Church's mission to the wider world. It is true that the main concern here is with the quality and responsibilities of those who are already Christian. But the Church is to Christ as the plough, the harrow, and the harvester are to the farmer—the means by which his tasks are effectively fulfilled. It would be a false enthusiasm which led the farmer so to concentrate on his fields that he neglected the tools by which the fields could be made productive. So the Church, to be God's effective instrument in the world, must be kept fresh, vigorous, obedient, and totally committed in her devotion to Christ.

26. The immediate purpose of Christ for his Church is **that he might sanctify her.** The word **sanctify** (like 'saint' in 1:1) carries a double meaning. Basically, it means to mark off something as belonging wholly to God. In a derived sense, however, it means also to produce that quality of life which is appropriate to that which is controlled by God, that is, moral goodness. Again, the tense of the Greek verb (aorist) indicates that this 'sanctifying' refers to some specific action by God in their lives. The words that follow suggest that this was their baptism, the open act by which all Christians expressed their penitence for past sins, their total commitment to Christ for the future, their openness to receive the gift of his Spirit and to accept full participation in the life of the community of the Church. It was in baptism that all who belonged to the Church were marked off as 'holy' or 'sanctified'.

This 'sanctification' in baptism is referred to as Christ's action—not something the converts did themselves, not even what the Church did. It was his action also which **cleansed her by the washing of water with the word.** Part of the bride's preparation for her marriage was careful bathing. So the Church is prepared for Christ by the cleansing of baptism, which in the early days of the Church was normally administered by total immersion in water. It is clear, however, that the writer does not think this immersion by itself is in some magical way the effective element in the baptism. It is not the application of ceremonial water which produces moral cleansing. The cleansing needs also **the word.** Similarly in 1 Pet. 3:21 baptism means not only 'a removal of dirt from the body, but an appeal to God for a clear conscience' (which implies some spoken word). When the **word** is used along with the **water,** then there is 'cleansing'. This moral cleansing includes both forgiveness for past sins and the actual purification of life and conduct for the future. This combination of 'cleansing' and 'sanctification' is found also at 1 C. 6:11: 'You were washed, you were sanctified.'

The phrase **with the word** clearly implies that the spoken word had an important place in the baptismal ceremony. Commentators differ in their understanding of what precisely it means. Some take it to refer to the words of a baptismal service spoken by the officiant. Others think it is the preaching at such a service for the purpose of awakening faith. But faith in fact has already been awakened in the baptised person and indeed his faith was a condition of his acceptance for baptism. It could possibly refer back to the preached word which had at an earlier stage led to his conversion (cf. Jn 15:3: 'You are already made clean by the word which I have spoken to you.'). It seems much more probable, however, that **the word** here is the spoken witness of the convert himself, declaring his faith in Christ as Lord and Saviour and his personal commitment to him (cf. Rom. 10:8–9: 'The word is near you, on your lips and in your heart ... because, if you confess with your lips that Jesus is Lord and believe in your heart that God raised him from the dead, you will be saved.'). Many scholars think that the earliest Christian affirmation of faith consisted of the words: 'Jesus is Lord,' and an appropriate time for such a declaration was at the time of baptism. The affirmation is both an expression of faith in Christ as God's representative and at the same time a promise of personal obedience to him as Lord. It seems probable that in 1 Pet. 3:21 (quoted above) the words translated in *RSV* as 'an appeal to God' do in fact mean this personal avowal of commitment to God. Indeed *TEV* in that context translates as 'the promise made to God'.

27. that the church might be presented before him. This is the translation of the *RSV* 1946. But in the 1952 and 1973 versions it becomes: **'that he might present the church to himself'** (as also *AV, RV, NEB*). The simile of marriage, to interpret the relationship beween Christ and his Church, is appropriate enough for expressing the devotion which the Church owes to Christ and the loving care which Christ has for his Church. But there are difficulties if the comparison is pressed further, and these begin to be felt in this verse. It is inappropriate to the marriage metaphor that the bridegroom should present the bride to himself. The bride's parents or a family friend would do this. Perhaps this explains the action of the 1946 *RSV* in violating the meaning of the Greek in order to avoid so obvious a departure from marriage customs. Clearly what is here being expressed is

what is appropriate in a baptismal context (not any longer in a
marriage context). In baptism the Christian would wish to
emphasise that at every point the initiative had been with Christ.
In 2 C. 11:2 Paul himself reflects more accurately the marriage
customs of that time when he speaks of himself (as if acting as
father or family friend) as presenting the Church to Christ as a
'pure virgin'. The writer to Ephesians struggling to be true to the
baptismal emphasis in this passage writes as though it is the
bridegroom who rather oddly presents the bride to himself.

A bride should come to her husband pure and untainted, and
by universal custom dressed in clothes of special beauty. So the
Church is presented to Christ **in splendour, without spot or
wrinkle or any such thing.** She is free from all disfigurements
or deformities. As befits what is offered to Christ, she must **be
holy and without blemish.** At 1:4 God is said to have chosen
individual Christians that they may be 'holy and without blemish'.
Here these words are applied to the whole Church. Christians are
indeed the Church, and Christ's aim for Church and for Christians is that they shall be completely Christian in outward obedience as well as inward faith.

**28. Even so husbands should love their wives as their
own bodies.** Christ loved the Church, and the Church is his
body. **husbands should love their wives** in the same way.
Some commentators insist that the Greek words can only mean
that **husbands should love their wives** because their wives
are, in a sense, **their own bodies.** One might claim that this
understanding of the words is required by the quotation from
Gen. 2:24 which appears in Eph. 5:31, where man and wife are
said 'to become one flesh'. Support is sometimes found for this in
some words of Plutarch which speak of a man as ruling his wife
in the same way that the 'soul' rules the 'body' (see *ICC* p. 171).
The words, however, can readily be understood to mean, not
that a wife is the body of her husband, but that husbands should
love their wives as they love their own bodies. *NEB* takes it in this
sense. The words would then be an application of the command
approved by Jesus that we should love our neighbour as we love
ourselves.

This lofty Christian duty is then provided with a very prudential,
if not actually selfish, motive. **He who loves his wife loves
himself.** The command to love neighbour as self assumes the

basic fact of love of self and seeks to widen its scope to include
others as well, but—though accepting self-love as a fact of life—
it does not commend it as a praiseworthy thing. Here, however,
the husband's own love for himself is given as a motive for loving
his wife. It is, of course, a plain fact of human nature that if a man
can by his love for his wife enable her to become a truly happy
person, his own life in her company is likely to be all the happier
for it. But the wife would not feel she was being treated with real
love if the motive for that love were the husband's desire to make
life pleasanter for himself. Perhaps, however, even for the Christian
the conduct of life is a curious blend of high idealism and prag-
matic self-interest. It is easier to do what is right and good if one
can see at the same time that it will also produce something
beneficial to ourselves.

29. The basic self-concern of every human being is here asserted quite bluntly. **For no man ever hates his own flesh,
but nourishes and cherishes it.** He does not deliberately hurt
or maim his own body, but makes it a primary aim of his life to
provide it with all that it needs for health and comfort, and with
protection against every threat of injury. Similarly, Christ cares
for his body, the Church, providing all that is needed for its health
and well-being. The reference to 'nourishment' has been seen by
some as an oblique reference to the Eucharist, but the meaning
here is probably more general than that.

30. One would expect the next sentence to read: Because we,
the Church, are his body. It is difficult to assess what was in the
writer's mind when, instead, he wrote: **because we are members of his body,** unless he purposely wished to incorporate this
phrase, borrowed as it is from 1 C. 6:15. Perhaps he chose to use
these words to remind the readers that the Church, which is being
spoken of in such high terms, is in fact just the aggregate of themselves. If man cannot avoid love of his own body, then we can be
sure that even more Christ will be concerned for the welfare of *his*
body, the Church, and indeed for every single member of it.

31. This verse is simply a quotation from Gen. 2:24, which
concludes the story about the creation of Eve from a rib in Adam's
body. Adam acknowledges her as 'flesh of my flesh', and Gen.
2:24 follows: **For this reason a man shall leave his father
and mother and be joined to his wife, and the two shall
become one flesh.** The closeness of the union of man and wife

is such that it may be described as becoming **one flesh.** The intimacy of this bond, established by their sexual union, led to the thought of marriage as creating out of two individuals a kind of new single personal entity. The writer of Ephesians quotes this verse from Genesis because of the strong support it gives to the close unity, almost identity, of man and wife within marriage. This unity is the ideal for all marriages, but not all achieve it. The ideal of unity is seen only in the marriage of Christ and his Church, which itself sets a pattern for human marriage to emulate.

32. This verse applies the quotation to Christ and the Church, and some commentators have sought to discover a deeper christological significance in it than the writer intended. Jerome, for instance, suggested that it meant that Christ, as man, had left his Father (God) and his mother (the heavenly Jerusalem), in order to unite himself with his Church. To modern readers this sounds fanciful, perhaps even offensive, but Abbott quotes some 'moderns', such as Alford, Ellicott, and Mayer, as agreeing with Jerome. Abbott, however, rejects it resolutely as out of keeping with the thought of the *NT*. The quotation from Gen. 2:24 must primarily refer to man and wife in their married relationship. The reference in Eph. 5:32 to Christ and the Church is introduced only incidentally, because the whole context in Ephesians is interpreting their mutual relationship as a parallel to that between husband and wife. Gen. 2:24 interprets God's intention for marriage as a relationship between man and wife marked by a mutual loyalty even greater than that of the man and the woman for their parents (whom Scripture commands them to 'honour'). The same words from Gen. 2:24 are also quoted by Jesus at Mk 10:7, where the insistence on man and wife being 'one flesh' is quoted as indicating that God's intention in marriage was its permanence —even against the law of Moses which allowed divorce and listed the grounds on which it was permissible.

This is a great mystery (*RSV* 1946). There are two difficulties here: (i) Is this a legitimate translation of the Greek? (ii) In what sense are we to understand the word **mystery**? In relation to (i) it is sufficient to note that the 1973 *RSV* revised its former translation to: **This mystery is a profound one** (cf. the earlier *RV* 'This mystery is great,' which is a very literal translation of the Greek words). It is, however, not easy to see what significant difference in meaning the more accurate translation makes. (ii) In Ephesians the word 'mystery' has already been used significantly to describe God's purpose for mankind in Christ, a purpose long hidden but now disclosed through Christ (e.g., 1:9, etc.). This purpose is to bring together into unity through Christ all the disunited people of the world—to reconcile all things. It is impossible, however, to read anything of this meaning into the word here—though the idea of 'unity' is present in both cases. The word is used here in a more general sense than it was earlier, to describe some deep truth which is not immediately obvious or superficially likely. So *NEB* translates: 'It is a great truth which is hidden here,' and *TEV*: 'There is a great truth revealed in this Scripture.' Phillips keeps the word 'mystery' and refers it primarily to human marriage, and only in a derived sense to Christ and his Church: 'The marriage relationship is doubtless a great mystery.'

Most commentators, however, refer the 'mystery' to the relationship of Christ and his Church. But it may equally refer to human marriage at its best. In a truly happy and complete marriage there is a deep richness which seems to transcend merely rational explanations. Each partner can contribute much to the fulfilment of the other. The sexual appetite, instead of being a disturbing selfish drive, finds itself expressed and satisfied within a relationship of deep mutual respect and affection, where each partner seeks the true happiness of the other and accepts full responsibility for the other. It is a relationship in which sexual intercourse heals and comforts and unites, and proves itself one of God's most wonderful gifts to his human children. Here friendship can grow into something sensitive and enduring, through co-operation in various duties, services to others and shared achievements. Here is a relationship which can be incalculably enriched and deepened through the gift of children and the interchanges of family life—and, all in good time, by the immense privilege of happy grandparenthood. In all this there is a dimension that awakens wonder and overflowing gratitude. If a mystery is an experience of life which is inexplicably wonderful, significant, and enriching, then marriage can indeed prove to be 'a profound mystery.'

I take it to mean Christ and his church (1946) is changed in 1973 to: **I am saying that it refers to Christ and the church.** The 1946 translation implies that the whole purpose of the writer in quoting Gen. 2:24 is because he saw it as a disguised allusion to Christ and his Church. This seems to us improbable. The 1973 revision suggests that the initial reference in Gen. 2:24 is to the relationship of man and wife, but that it may also be applied to Christ and his Church in a secondary sense. This is to be preferred, and *NEB* makes its preference quite clear: 'I for my part refer it to Christ and his Church.' That is, the interdependent unity of man and wife in what may be thought of as a kind of single personality is an illustration of the unity between Christ and his Church. He is the head, the Church is the body. Together they constitute a single entity. The Church is the true partner of her Lord, sharing fully in his life and work. Christ is to the Church the one whose strength and wisdom supplies her every need and directs her energies, the one who shares fully in her fellowship and her mission.

The Greek word here translated **mystery** was rendered in the Vulgate by the Latin word *sacramentum*, which led to its being translated in English as 'sacrament', as though marriage were being explicitly described as a sacrament. But this is a most misleading translation.

33. The writer has allowed this section, which began as a set of instructions to Christian husbands and wives, to become a kind of allegory of Christ and his Church. In this concluding verse he returns to the practical counsels with which the section had begun. The word **however** suggests that the writer acknowledges the digression and returns to the main point at issue. **let each one of you love his wife as himself.** The Greek makes it clearer than the English that it is the husband who is here addressed. *TEV* rightly translates: 'Every husband must love his wife as himself.' This is a reiteration of verses 25 and 28. **and let the wife see that she respects her husband.** The word translated 'respect' is actually the Greek word 'fear' (as also in 5:21), which is far stronger than seems appropriate in the twentieth century.

It is clear in this passage, as in so many others in Ephesians, that the writer has derived many of his words and thoughts from Colossians. Eph. 5:22 is similar to Col. 3:18: 'Wives, be subject to your husbands as is fitting in the Lord.' Eph. 5:23 recalls Col. 1:18: 'Christ is himself the head of the body, the church.'

Eph. 5:25 reflects Col. 3:19: 'Husbands, love your wives,' and
Eph. 5:27 is parallel to Col. 1:22: '. . . to present you holy and
blameless'. Interwoven with this material from Colossians are
other materials from *OT* sources. Eph. 5:31 is a verbatim quotation of Gen. 2:24, though there are no words introducing it as a
quotation. Eph. 5:28–29 indicates an awareness of the command
to love neighbour as self (Lev. 19:18), though the word 'neighbour' is not explicitly used. The implication that, in a symbolic
way, the Church, the new Israel, may be thought of as the bride
of Christ, owes something to the *OT* thought of Israel as the bride
of Yahweh, which is found in such passages as Hos. 2:19–20: 'I will
betroth you to me for ever' (cf. Ezek. 16:8–14). This blending of
materials from different sources leads Käsemann to claim that not
only this passage but 'the entire letter appears to be a mosaic
composed of extensive as well as tiny elements of tradition and the
author's skill lies chiefly in the selection and ordering of the
material available to him' (*Studies in Luke–Acts*, ed. by Keck and
Martyn, p. 288). J. P. Sampley has written a substantial book on
this passage entitled: '*And the Two shall become One Flesh*': *A Study
of Traditions in Ephesians 5:21–33*. The fact that not only Ephesians but other *NT* writers show an awareness of the *OT* materials
used in this passage is made the ground for arguing that all these
materials here used in Ephesians were already in common use
within the Church. His claim (though he concedes it is only an
'hypothesis') is that Ephesians is 'a unique, syncretistic collection
of a variety of tradition in the early Church'.

We have given reasons for doubting whether Ephesians as a
whole (or even large parts of it) was ever meant to be used as a
liturgical document or was derived largely from liturgical materials. What is demonstrable is that Ephesians borrowed largely
from Colossians (and also from the other Pauline letters) and any
claims to establish liturgical dependence must be in harmony with
this prior and more basic conclusion. The writer, as he presented
Paul's message to his own day and used for that purpose materials
from Paul's letters, clearly incorporated other material familiar to
him from the *OT*, and from the preaching and hymns of the
Church at that time. But whether this proves as much as Käsemann and Sampley claim may be doubted.

It cannot be determined with any degree of certainty whether
the writer of Ephesians borrowed these three *OT* items direct

from the *OT* or found them in the worship of the Church. One cannot help feeling, however, that the writer's combination and use of these materials is not one of the more successful parts of the letter. They are related to each other in a laboured and unnatural way. They present real difficulties for the commentator who tries to establish a logical sequence between them. It is true that this is a passage which many have felt to be extremely impressive and it has certainly exercised a considerable influence upon doctrine. But if it is studied in detail, it is found to be lacking in systematic construction and in strong internal connexions. If it is read in public with oratorical skill, it can sound most impressive. If it is studied item by item and analysed in detail, it is less satisfactory.

6:1. In the moral instructions of 6:1–9, relating to children and parents, slaves and masters, the writer is following closely the material in Col. 3, both in the categories of people he addresses and in the order in which he addresses them. In each case, however, he makes his own modifications and additions. He has just dealt with the Christian obligations of wives and husbands, and in that context added further teaching about Christ and his Church. Now he turns to **parents** and **children.** In Col. 3:20 Paul had written: 'Children, obey your parents in everything, for this pleases the Lord.' Eph. 6:1 slightly modifies this to: **Children, obey your parents in the Lord, for this is right.** Colossians requires total obedience to parents, since this is a Christian duty. Ephesians requires obedience to parents, provided this is **in the Lord,** that is, consistent with Christian commitment. Paul in Colossians writes with the assumption the children concerned are the children of Christian parents, who would not ask of their children conduct inconsistent with obedience to Christ. This would be true of children attending Christian meetings in Paul's lifetime. Ephesians, however, appears to have in mind a situation where the children addressed may have pagan parents. Their obedience to them, therefore, is not to be 'in everything' without qualification. It is rather to be an obedience which does not contravene a primary obedience 'to the Lord'. This adaptation of phrasing is consistent with the understanding of Ephesians as belonging to a later period in the development of the Church.

The phrase **in the Lord** is, in fact, missing from some early MSS, but the majority of the more reliable ones retain it and on their authority *RSV* includes it in the translation. We have treated the

words as implying that obedience to parents is subject to an over-
riding obedience to Christ. Others, however, understand the words
differently. Houlden, for instance, treats **in the Lord** as meaning
'as a Christian should'. The disadvantage of this interpretation is
that it makes the following phrase **for this is right** largely repeti-
tive, and also it ignores the possibility that a pagan parent may
ask a child to do what, for a Christian, is wrong. The reason for
this instruction is because **this is right.** This may mean that the
obedience of children to parents is a moral obligation which is
everywhere accepted as right. Or it could mean that in the case
of a Christian it is right for him to put loyalty to Christ first, and
obedience to parents second.

If this writing, as some have contended, were prepared for a
baptismal occasion, and the moral directions intended for those
who have just been baptised into the Christian faith, then **children** must be included among the baptised. It would not be legitimate, however, to argue from this that the practice of infant
baptism was current at that time, since such infants would be too
young to understand instructions. It could only refer to older
children (perhaps what we should call teenagers) who were of an
age to make a personal commitment to Christ, but still young
enough to be living at home with their parents.

**2, 3. "Honour your father and mother" (this is the first
commandment with a promise).** These words do not occur
in the parallel passage in Col. 3. The commandment quoted is the
fifth of the Ten Commandments as recorded in Exod. 20:12. In
the original Ten Commandments it is addressed not so much to
younger children still in the care of their parents as to older
children, who are called upon to exercise a sense of responsibility
for the welfare of their parents who are growing old. This seems
to be its significance here in Ephesians also. To **honour** one's
parents implies obedience on the part of young children, but with
grown-up sons and daughters it implies rather an attitude of continued respect, consideration, and care.

Commentators find difficulty in understanding why this commandment should be described as **the first . . . with a promise.**
It is pointed out that the second commandment, which forbids the
making of graven images, is followed by a reference to God as a
'jealous God' who both punishes disobedience to his commands,
and also promises rich rewards to the obedient. Is not this second

commandment, therefore, the first 'with a promise'? But the
promise there, it may be argued, is not so much attached to that
particular commandment as part of an explanation of what is
meant by speaking of God as 'jealous'. It is, therefore, quite
understandable that the fifth commandment is known as the first
with a promise. This **promise,** addressed to children who do
honour their parents, is **"that it may be well with you and
that you may live long on the earth".** The Hebrews believed
that God rewarded those who obeyed his will with prosperity and
long life (Ps. 91:16). In Exod. 20:12 the long life which is promised will be lived 'in the land which the Lord your God gives
you'. In Eph. 6:3 this is replaced by **on the earth.** This makes it
applicable to everyone and not just to Jews. This is a command
which, if obeyed, makes for happiness here on earth. The reward
attached to it is not one deferred until an after-life. We today are
probably inclined to understand this not so much in an individual as in a community sense. A community in which the aged
are respected and cared for by their own children is a healthy
society in which men live happily together.

4. If children should obey and honour parents, **fathers** also
have their Christian obligations towards their children. They are
urged: **do not provoke your children to anger.** The fault most
to be avoided by parents in their treatment of children is that of
irritating and exasperating them. It is not made clear what kind of
behaviour it is to which this applies. Perhaps it was an unbending
demand for obedience in matters in which the child could see no
purpose at all; or treating an older child as if he were still an
infant; or it may be inconsistency, so that the same action by a
child may one day be greeted with amusement and another day
by angry condemnation. A Christian father will have a real
concern for his child's happiness and welfare and in consequence
will seek to see the child's point of view and to understand and
avoid those attitudes and actions which the child finds exasperating. Col. 3:21 indeed adds the words 'lest they become
discouraged'.

The positive alternative is to **bring them up in the discipline
and instruction of the Lord.** This is the opposite of just letting
them do what they want, because you cannot be bothered with
them. It is an attitude which expresses a deep and responsible
concern for their welfare. Some commentators try to make a sharp

distinction between **discipline** and **instruction,** suggesting that
the first means 'obedience enforced by punishment' and the second
'oral teaching'. This is a little strained, but the words together suggest both the inculcation of patterns of behaviour worthy of a Christian and also verbal instruction about the contents of the faith. Some
have asked if **instruction of the Lord** could mean 'teaching about
Jesus', but it is probable that **of the Lord** means that the discipline
and instruction will be truly Christian, compatible with loyalty to
Christ as Lord. What children should see in their fathers is what
Christ himself stands for in the conduct of life.

This insistence on the careful upbringing of children (absent
from Colossians) is another indication of the later date of Ephesians. When the end of all things appeared imminent, the educa-
tion of children for adult life must have seemed of small importance. But as the expectation of an immediate end of all things
diminished, it became increasingly the proper concern of Christians to win their children to a commitment to Christ and an
understanding of what it involved, and also to behave towards
them in such a way that the family unit would be kept intact.

5. What is clear beyond doubt is that, for this writer, loyalty
to Christ affects every relationship of life. This is pre-eminently
true in the intimate relationships within marriage and the life of
home and family. Where the 'family' includes **slaves** who do the
menial tasks for the household, these too become the object of
loving concern. Further, if they themselves are Christians, it
means that they also will see their relationship to their masters in
a new light. This passage, 6:5–9, seeks to help Christian slaves to
understand how their allegiance to Christ will affect the way they
do their tasks and treat those who are their **earthly masters.**
The words are very similar to those in Col. 3:22–25. The main
difference is that the recommendations in Ephesians are of a more
general nature, whereas in Colossians the words seem to have
particular reference to the case of the slave Onesimus and his
master Philemon, both of whom were known by the Christians
in Colossae.

Slavery was a common feature of the ancient world. A large
proportion of the population were slaves. These were not just
ignorant and ill-educated people, but sometimes included men of
scholarly achievements, who had been made slaves when their
country was overrun by military conquest. Debt also was a

common cause of slavery, when men and women were sold as slaves in order to liquidate the debts they themselves had been unable to pay. The complaint is sometimes made against the early Church that it did not at once condemn the whole institution of slavery as an evil thing and campaign for its immediate abolition. At first, however, the Christians were a small, uninfluential, and persecuted minority. Their expectation of an early end to the world made the achievement of social change seem unimportant. But even when this expectation faded, they still did not carry out an organised campaign against slavery. Perhaps they did not see it at first as something that could or should be abolished. We all accept customs and attitudes because we have grown up with them and are used to them and see no wrong in them, even though later generations are shocked by them and condemn as hypocrites those who did not see the wrongness of them earlier. Older people today have long accepted a life-style in which women and coloured people laboured under considerable handicaps, without being oppressed by the unfairness of it. But what the early Christians did was to revolutionise their own attitudes to slaves within their households, and the change of heart would in time lead Christians to demand the abolition of slavery as an intolerable evil. At the time this writer lived, the immediate concern he felt was to guide Christian slaves and masters to an understanding of the way in which their mutual Christian faith should affect their attitude to and treatment of each other.

In verses 5–8 the writer gives general counsel to Christian slaves on the kind of behaviour which is expected of them, now that they are Christians. Their main concern will be to serve Christ and bring others to honour him. It is not their primary aim to achieve material benefits for themselves. So the writer advises them: **Slaves, be obedient to those who are your earthly masters.** The **masters** are described as **earthly** because the Greek word for 'master' is here the same as that for 'Lord'. It was indeed the normal word for the owner of slaves. But for the Christian there is only one real Lord—the Lord Jesus Christ. Those who by social convention would be called their 'lord and master' are distinguished from the real Lord and Master by being called **earthly.** In Colossians there seems to be the assumption that Christian slaves will have Christian masters. This is not necessarily so in Ephesians, though some of the phrases used here would be more appropriate in a situation where both slave and master were Christians (e.g., **as to Christ,** 6:5). If the master were a Christian, there would be a danger that the slave would presume upon it and become careless. If the master were not a Christian, the slave might argue that he did not merit devoted service. But slaves are told to **be obedient** in either case to their earthly masters, and **with fear and trembling.** This appears to be a common phrase. Paul uses it several times (1 C. 2:3; 2 C. 7:15; Phil. 2:12). One does not need to take the words literally, though they do perhaps bring a reminder that in the last resort the earthly master had the power of life and death over his slave. Christian slaves should be obedient to their masters, partly because disobedience can be punished with the utmost severity, partly because good service on their part will reflect credit on their new allegiance to Christ. Their obedience should be **in singleness of heart,** that is, with complete sincerity; it should be offered not just when the master is watching or disobedience might be found out and punished, but on all occasions. The obedience indeed is to be offered **as to Christ:** if this means that the master is to be thought of as the representative of Christ in the slave's life, it can only mean that the master himself is a Christian (cf. the similar instruction to wives in 5:22). But more probably the writer means that all we do (including work done for an earthly master) should be done by the Christian as if he were doing it for Christ. His 'single' purpose is to please Christ. The writer is here apparently applying to slaves the more general direction of Col. 3:17: 'Whatever you do ... do everything in the name of the Lord Jesus.' Work so done will not only be done better and enjoyed more in the doing; it will also bring greater credit to Christ whom the slave now represents. A Christian slave who after his conversion is eaten up with resentment, and in his duties is unreliable and shirking, provides a poor commendation for his new faith.

6. Christian slaves are to do their work **not in the way of eyeservice, as men-pleasers.** They will work well not only when they are watched, but all the time, since their aim is not to please men but to please Christ (see 5:10). They regard themselves **as servants of Christ.** The Greek word here translated as **servants** is the same as that translated 'slaves' in verse 5. Today we seem to wish to avoid being called 'slaves of Christ', but in *NT* days Christians did not shrink from it. Paul used the phrase of himself frequently (e.g., Gal. 1:10; Rom. 1:1, etc.) and congratulated others who, though in civil life they were free men, had willingly made themselves 'slaves of Christ' (1 C. 7:22). Perhaps we ought to keep the word here. At any rate there is a sense in which 'servant' is misleading. A servant today is one who receives a wage, works agreed hours, and can give in notice and change his employer at will. A Christian is not to think of himself as possessing these freedoms in respect of his commitment to Christ. He belongs to Christ twenty-four hours a day; he looks for no material reward; his commitment to Christ is for ever. He is the property of Christ. Yet today the word 'slave' has serious disadvantages because it suggests a 'slave mentality', that is someone lacking in self-respect, initiative, and the will for courageous action.

As 'slaves' of Christ they do **the will of God.** This is stated without argument or explanation. This is because in the early Church Christ was believed totally to represent God. All he was and did, as well as what he taught, was an expression of the will of God. To be the slave of Christ, therefore, meant **doing the will of God.** This obedience to God's will, however, is not for them a task accepted as an imposition. Their lives have been inwardly so transformed that they now 'delighted to do the will of God'. They did it from free choice, gladly, spontaneously, that is, **from the heart.**

7. The service they render is done **with a good will,** or as *NEB* and *TEV* translate it, 'cheerfully'. This verse largely repeats the substance of the preceding verse. But repetition may be justified when it emphasises what is felt to be important. The duty carried out by the slave is done as for Christ his **Lord** and, therefore, is done not 'grudgingly or of necessity', but eagerly and happily (cf. 2 C. 9:7).

8. This course of action is followed primarily because it will please Christ, not to gain a reward; but it does in fact bring its own reward to the doer. That is how God intends it should be. Good actions are followed by good consequences. We reap what we sow (Gal. 6:7). This principle has been inbuilt by God into the universe. The commandments of God are for our good (Dt. 10:13). The good reward is to be seen as coming **from the Lord.** It is not just a mechanical, automatic process, but one which God created and sustains. The reward, of course, is not to be thought of as consisting in material gains. Indeed Paul had reminded the Galatians that spiritual good is rewarded by spiritual gains (Gal. 6:8). Those who sow 'to the Spirit' will of the Spirit 'reap eternal life'. All this applies to the **free** master no less than to **slave.**

9. Masters are next called upon to **do the same to them.** Slaves have been asked to make it their aim in all their duties to please Christ, and to pursue this aim cheerfully and with good will. Masters are now asked to put the same principles into practice in their particular situation: in their treatment of their slaves, it is Christ whom they must aim first to please, and their personal attitude also will be one of cheerfulness and courtesy. The fault which they are called upon to avoid above all else is **threatening** —the practice of trying to extort the last ounce of effort from their slaves by threat of punishment. This weapon of threatened punishment is not fitting in a relationship between Christians, which is controlled by the thought that both have Christ for **their Master.** Both seek to please Christ first. This verse clearly implies that both masters and slaves are Christians. Neither holds a more advantageous position in Christ's eyes than the other. **there is no partiality with him.** For Christ, as for God, social status among men is not a ground for preferential treatment. The master cannot claim an advantage because of his higher social standing. Distinctions of class, wealth, and race, such as are indicated by outward appearances, count for nothing with God (cf. 1 Sam. 16:7).

The word **partiality** in the Greek means literally the acceptance of people at their face value, the value accorded to them by other people and expected from others by the people themselves. This affirmation that God does not follow this man-made standard seems to have been one of the most widely accepted of early Christian affirmations. Four other *NT* writings also make it: Ac. 10:34; Rom. 2:11; Col. 3:25; 1 Pet. 1:17. In Jas 2:1 and 9 such impartiality is also a quality expected of the Christian in his treatment of others.

In Ephesians this emphasis on God's impartiality is placed in the paragraph addressed to masters. This seems appropriate, because the higher up the social scale a man feels himself to be the more likely he is to expect that God will accord him special consideration. Normally a slave would not be guilty of such presumption. In Colossians, however, this phrase—very oddly—occurs in the paragraph addressed to slaves. The explanation must be found in the special circumstances out of which Colossians was written. The case of Onesimus and Philemon was much in the mind of Paul when he wrote that letter, and in the mind of the readers who first received it. Paul seems to have felt in this connexion that it was slaves like Onesimus, guilty of serious misconduct and perhaps inclined to presume on the Christian gentleness of their master, who needed to be reminded that God acts towards men on a basis of strict fairness, and no one has a right to expect preferential treatment. So in Col. 3:25 it is emphasised that an offending slave will be punished for the wrong he has done. A person who has made a Christian profession has no right to plead exemption from the basic law that evil is punished and good rewarded.

In Ephesians, however, this particular local situation is no longer under consideration and so the insistence on God's impartiality is allowed, more appropriately for general circumstances, to slip into the section addressed to masters.

GOD'S EQUIPMENT FOR THE CHRISTIAN 6:10-22

This important section is the culmination of the epistle. In it the writer insists that the Christian life is a warfare, but the Christian may, if he will, be thoroughly equipped for it with the armour which God provides. The warfare to be waged is not primarily against other human beings who range themselves with evil intent against the Christian disciple, but against spiritual forces of evil. These may assault the disciple's soul directly, or seek to divert him from his commitment by provoking the hostility of human enemies.

This striking portrayal of the Christian life as a continuing struggle, the description of the equipment which is needed if this war is to be waged successfully, and the clarion call to 'fight the good fight', seems to break upon the reader without much warning. We have been moving fairly quietly through sober and serious passages of ethical instruction: Christians should show courteous deference to one another, wives submit to the authority of their husbands, and husbands show loving thoughtfulness for the wife's welfare; children should honour and obey parents, and fathers act with understanding towards their children; slaves should do

their work as if it were for Christ, and masters of Christian slaves
should remember that Christ is their standard of behaviour.
There is little to prepare us for the sudden rousing call for pre-
paredness, since the Christian is in fact actively engaged in a
fierce battle with supernatural forces of evil.

It is more than likely that the writer's mind is at this point
moving further back to the passage (5:3–20) which precedes the
sedate list of household rules, where the actions which belong to
'darkness and shame' are being denounced—fornication, covetousness, filthiness, drunkenness, debauchery (or perhaps even
earlier to 4:25–31, where the reader is exhorted not to allow any
opportunity to the devil). These blatantly evil things, always
threatening the life of the Christian from the surrounding pagan
world in which they flourish unhindered, seem to be more obviously the signs of the power of evil in human life than mildly
sub-Christian conduct within the family circle. Perhaps, however,
it is the writer's intention to insist that whether it be in flagrant
wickedness or in apparently slight unfaithfulness to Christ's high
standard for human life, it is the same power of evil which is at
work, seeking to outwit and defeat the unwary Christian.

The cause of all sin, whether blatant or subtle, is not merely
some inward carelessness or heavy pressure from a surrounding
hostile environment. The instigators to evil in all cases are
spiritual powers of wickedness. These powers are the enemies of
God and Christ and are bent on destroying the Christian quality
of lives which have felt the transforming touch of the Spirit of
God. They use our moods and appetites, our jealousies, resentment, and pride to gain an entry into our lives. It is they who
instigate other people (**flesh and blood**) to oppose and humiliate
the Christian, so that, angry and upset, he is the more likely to
allow evil impulses to gain control of his conduct. To meet this
constant onslaught, both insidious and overpowering, the Christian needs not only watchfulness and determination, but also the
extra reinforcement of moral strength and courage which only
God can supply.

10. The writer begins: **Finally.** This is the concluding exhortation of the epistle, that we shall avail ourselves of those rein-
forcements from God by which alone the Christian life can be
successfully lived. **be strong in the Lord: in the Lord** or 'in
Christ' has been a recurring phrase throughout the epistle. In

chapter 1 we met it constantly as the writer reminded his readers that all God's richest gifts had been made available to them 'in Christ'. In chapter 2 we learned that these gifts may be appropriated and made our own 'in Christ'. Ethical instruction is then offered, also 'in Christ' (4:17). Here it is **in the Lord** that the power to live this new life is provided. It is **in the Lord** that we are made strong.

The *RSV* translation **be strong** is perhaps misleading, since it suggests the rallying of our own inward resources. What, however, the Greek actually urges is that Christians 'be made strong', 'be empowered', that is, by this new relationship with Christ and the resources he makes available to us. *NEB* brings this out well: 'Find your strength in the Lord.' Phillips, to make sure this point is not missed, elaborates in a paraphrase: 'In conclusion be strong—not in yourselves but in the Lord.' The tense of the Greek imperative is present, which means that the 'empowering' is a continuing, day by day, moment by moment, experience. **in the strength of his might.** This combination of the same two words which are almost synonyms (a characteristic of Ephesians) has occurred already at 1:19.

11. Put on the whole armour of God. The Greek word translated **Put on** is frequently used in Paul's letters. He thought of conversion (and baptism) as the time when the Christian discarded his old nature like an outworn garment, and put on a new nature, as if it were a new outfit of clothes. This 'new outfit' may be described differently: in Rom. 13:14 and Gal. 3:27 it is the Lord Jesus Christ whom Christians are urged to 'put on'. At Col. 3:10 (as also at Eph. 4:24) the apostle writes: 'put on the new nature'—perhaps with no real difference in meaning. Here the writer to the Ephesians rephrases it as **put on the whole armour of God.** The tense of this Greek verb, **put on** (aorist), suggests that this is one definite step which the Christian must take, as he makes his own this offer of God's spiritual power. This would fit a baptismal occasion when the new Christian is ready to step out in his new venture of Christian discipleship.

The word translated **whole armour** is in the Greek a single word (*panoplia*) which is sometimes transliterated as 'panoply', as in Charles Wesley's well-known hymn:

> But take to arm you for the fight
> The panoply of God.

221 EPHESIANS 6:11

It means the total military equipment of the soldier who is ready
to go out to battle. It includes both defensive armour and offensive weapons. The English word **armour** may in fact be misleading at this point, because it has come to suggest almost
entirely defensive items. Indeed the *Oxford English Dictionary*
defines armour as 'defensive covering'. But the Greek word has no
such limitation. It means the soldier's total equipment, and includes the sword as well as the shield. We need to be protected at
every vulnerable point, and also to be able to make effective
counter attacks so that the enemy may be dislodged from areas
which he has made his own. The purpose of this armour is that
we shall not be overwhelmed by the enemy's attacks, but enabled to keep our feet (**to stand**) and hold the enemy at bay,
repel and overcome him.

The assaults are called **the wiles of the devil.** The word **wiles**
is the same as that used at 4:14 for 'the deceitful wiles of cunning
men'. The emphasis is on the cleverness and subtlety of the attacks of this enemy. The **devil** is an enemy who can win victories
by trickery as well as by frontal attack. He can cunningly dis-
guise himself as an angel of light (2 C. 11:14), or he can threaten
and fume like 'a raging lion' (1 Pet. 5:8), using whichever tactics
are best fitted to the object of his hostility. This epistle consistently
speaks of **the devil** (cf. 4:27) rather than Satan, which is the word
Paul uses to describe the directing intelligence behind the forces
of evil. Many theologians today regard this as a mythological way
of speaking, and demythologise the word 'devil' into a mere figure
of speech for 'evil'. Others, however, though acquainted with the
theological difficulties in acknowledging a supreme evil being who
is able to defy and thwart God, are also deeply aware of what
appears to them as the skill and intelligence with which this
mysterious force of evil campaigns to crush innocence and
uprightness. Even if it is only a metaphor, they find it easy to
speak as if it were all directed by a supreme intelligence, and,
therefore, to refer to it in personal terms. There is a sense in which
this power of evil may be said to have been already stripped of its
power by Christ. In Col. 2:15 Paul writes: Christ 'disarmed the
principalities and powers . . . triumphing over them'. Christ has
already won the decisive battle in the war. Nevertheless, the final
victory has not been achieved, and before this is accomplished
there is much hard fighting still for the Christian. Just as salvation

is ours partly now, and partly still in the future, so Christ's victory over evil has in one sense already been won, and in another sense has still to be achieved.

12. The Christian's struggle, therefore, is not ultimately against **flesh and blood,** that is 'human nature' or 'other people' (cf. Gal. 1:16, Mt. 16:17). The real enemies of the Christian, which seek to destroy his faith and seduce him from his obedience to God, are the **principalities** and **powers.** These two words are also associated in Col. 2:15, and in Eph. 1:21, where their meaning has been discussed. Here they are linked with, perhaps identified with, **the world rulers of this present darkness. world rulers** (one word in the Greek) is found only in Ephesians. It indicates the area where the authority of these evil powers is most effectively exercised. It is in the **world** where they seem to rule supreme as if they had temporarily usurped God's power, so that God's people live in the world as his representatives in a land under alien rule. This recognition that the world has fallen under the power of evil is common among *NT* writers. John speaks of Satan as 'the ruler of this world' (12:31, 14:30, 16:11), and in Matthew and Luke, Satan, as the tempter of Jesus, claims that 'all the authority' over the kingdoms of this world 'has been delivered' to him. In terms of modern metaphor it is sometimes said that Jesus came to establish on earth a bridgehead from which God could begin to extend his hold upon enemy-occupied territory, and ultimately to reclaim the world of men as his own dominion. This world, in its present condition, is here described as **this present darkness.** It is the presence of dominating evil which produces darkness. Already in Ephesians **darkness** has been used to indicate the evil-dominated life (5:8, 11). These evil powers are next described as the **spiritual hosts of wickedness in the heavenly places.** Though their present dominion extends over the earth, their origin and base of operations lie beyond this world. This sphere is called **the heavenly places.** The phrase probably means what we might express as 'supernatural realms', 'beyond this earth'. Similarly, Jesus, rejoicing in the successful mission conducted by his disciples, says that he 'saw Satan fallen from heaven', as though heaven had been his basic stronghold.

13. Therefore: that is, in view of the devilish subtlety and supernatural might of these evil powers ranged against the Christian, he will need supernatural equipment to be able to withstand them.

Moreover, he will need this supernatural strength at its maximum. He will need **the whole armour of God.** This alone will enable the Christian to **stand** firm **in the evil day,** when the struggle is at its height. Some relate this **evil day** to the miseries and exceptional distresses which were expected to precede the end of the age (cf. Mk. 13:20–27; Mt. 26:5–13), but apprehension about the end is not characteristic of Ephesians. Others suggest that it refers to the time of persecution which the Church had been warned to expect. This is not to be excluded, but probably the expression is used to indicate any experience when evil seems overwhelmingly strong and our own defence against it weak and crumbling (cf. *NEB*: 'when things are at their worst'). The equipment which God can provide will, however, enable the Christian to win through even the most severe ordeal, to **withstand** the onslaught and endure to the end (Mt. 10:22). When he has withstood this heavy pressure without yielding and won the day (**having done all**) he will then find that he has gained a new stability in the Christian life, and a new confidence in the effectiveness of the resources available to him. He will now be able **to stand** firm, and become a rallying point for others.

14. The writer proceeds to specify the items which together make up the full equipment of the Christian in this fierce and prolonged conflict with the powers of evil, and to show how this equipment is a kind of spiritual equivalent of the armour and weapons of a soldier on military service—belt, breastplate, footwear, shield, helmet, sword. The Christian's equivalents are listed as truth, righteousness, peace, faith, salvation, and the Holy Spirit. The writer skilfully combines these items in corresponding pairs. It is, however, a mistake to over-elaborate the precise correspondence in each case: for instance, to construct a detailed parallelism between the helmet and salvation. The emphasis is rather on the total equipment. Just as the soldier in physical warfare needs all six items, if he is not to be needlessly vulnerable at some point, so the Christian needs each piece of spiritual equipment for his struggle.

This writer is by no means the first to compare spiritual equipment with the physical accoutrement of the soldier. Isaiah, for instance, had drawn the parallel, especially at 59:17, though there is some echo of it also in 11:4. In Isaiah, however, it is God who wears the warrior's armour, which includes (like the armour in Ephesians) righteousness as the breastplate and a 'helmet of salvation'. Wis. 5:17 provides another parallel, including the same idea of 'righteousness as a breastplate', but in this context helmet, shield, and sword are made the equivalents of 'impartial justice, holiness, and wrath'. In Wisdom also, as in Isaiah, it is God who wears the armour. The differences between Eph. 6 and these *OT* passages make it unlikely that the writer precisely consulted them as he wrote. More probably he was aware of them and inexact recollections of them came to his mind. Paul also had used the same idea, though for him the equipment was that of the Christian, not of God, and in this the writer of Ephesians follows Paul. In 2 C. 10:4 Paul writes of the Christian's 'weapons of warfare' and in 2 C. 6:7 of his 'weapons of righteousness'. At Rom. 13:12 he summons the Christian to 'put on the armour of light'. It is, how-ever, only in 1 Th. 5:8 that individual items of the armour are specified, e.g., 'the breastplate of faith' and 'for a helmet the hope of salvation'. These are similar to the phrasing in Isa. 59:17, but not identical to it. Ephesians is nearer sometimes to Isaiah, some-times to 1 Thessalonians. This writer, with a greater degree of elaboration than the others, lists six items of military equipment with six spiritual equivalents.

Stand, therefore: with this full equipment the Christian is urged to 'stand firm', **having girded your loins with truth.** The girding would be done by a belt. *NEB* in fact translates: 'Buckle on the belt of truth.' The phrase 'gird the loins' is mean-ingless today for westerners with the kind of clothes they wear, but very appropriate for the first-century easterner with his flowing robes. His outer garment would be a long loose-fitting cloak reaching to his ankles. If he tried to run or fight in it, it would wrap itself round his legs and trip him up. If he needed to act quickly and with agility, this loose garment had to be lifted clear above the knees and fastened securely round the waist. So to gird the loins was the necessary preliminary to any vigorous action. For instance, the Israelites, at the time of the first Passover, as they waited for the signal to make their escape from Egypt, were at the ready 'with loins girded' (Exod. 12:11). Elijah, as a herald of the fulfilment of God's promise of rain, prepared to outrun on foot the horse-drawn chariot of Ahab, by 'girding up his loins' (I Kg. 18:46). Understandably the phrase came to be used metaphori-cally of mental and spiritual readiness for exceptional tasks. 1 Pet.

1:13 summons Christians to 'gird up the loins of your minds'. So
here in Ephesians the Christian is called to 'gird up his loins'
spiritually. This means getting rid of anything which might be a
hindrance in the struggle against evil, eliminating any easy-
going casualness which might make him less than ready for the
fray. The meaning is similar, though the language is different, to
that expressed in Heb. 12:1: 'Lay aside every weight, and sin
which clings so closely.' The 'belt' which prevents entanglements
and encumbrances from thwarting effective action against the
evil forces is equated with **truth.** We could represent its meaning
here by 'sincerity' or 'integrity'. Half-truths, prevarications, and
disloyal compromises may make for personal comfort and enable
us to avoid social awkwardness, but they are poor preparation for
decisive Christian action. They put us at a disadvantage when our
main concern is to defeat evil wherever it is encountered. Some
writers, however, dissent from this interpretation of the meaning
of **truth.** Allan, for instance, writes: 'Truth will not mean sincerity, but rather the truth of the Gospel.' Abbott, however, points
out that this 'objective truth' of the Gospel appears later as 'the
word of God' (6:17) and, concludes, therefore, that here 'truth'
means 'an element of character'. Houlden also understands it to
mean 'genuineness' or 'reliability'.

The **breastplate** is identified with **righteousness** (as in
Isaiah and Wisdom). The **breastplate** was worn to protect such
vital parts as heart and lungs. The equivalent defence for the
Christian is uprightness of conduct. **righteousness** is total
obedience to the known will of God. Any divergence from this
leaves a weak spot where the enemies' thrusts may penetrate and
mortally wound.

**15. having shod your feet with the equipment of the
gospel of peace.** Battles, historians tells us, have sometimes been
lost by inadequate footwear. Swords and helmets lose their
effectiveness if the soldier is footsore or crippled by ill-fitting
boots. A soldier for whom every step is a drudge or a misery is
not likely to win battles. The equivalent of strong, light, well-
fitting boots for the Christian soldier is that he is equipped with
the gospel of peace. Few things make a man feel agile and
mobile more than the confidence that he is the bearer of joyous
good news (**gospel**). So the Greek soldier who brought the splendid news of the victory of the small Greek forces at Marathon over

the masses of Persians could keep on running though his whole body was at the point of collapse through exhaustion. So the Christian is provided with tireless energy by the knowledge that he is the bearer of the best news in all the world. This good news is called **the gospel of peace** because it puts right broken relationships between man and God and also between man and man, even between those long separated by stubborn enmity. **equipment** may be rendered: 'readiness to announce' (*TEV*).

16. above all: even more important than integrity, uprightness, and the knowledge that we bear great good news is **faith**. This is described as **the shield of faith**. The **shield** here indicated is not the small round 'target' shield, but the large one measuring about four by two and a half feet, big enough to protect the whole body from missiles and blows. The **faith** which provides this over-all protection for the Christian is, of course, not to be identified with the mere acceptance of a statement of doctrine. It is the utter confidence that God is able to protect and provide in all circumstances. It is that openness to God which allows his enabling power free course within our lives. It is the faith of which Jesus spoke when he said: 'Your faith has saved you.' It is this saving faith which is named as the most important part of the Christian's equipment. Its effectiveness is measured by its power to cope with all that can be thrown against us, even when the missiles are the most destructive that can be devised—**flaming darts.** These arrows had doubly destructive power. They could pierce and kill the soldier; they could also set fire to clothing and baggage and so spread terror and panic. Even these faith can **quench:** this word alludes particularly to the incendiary flame the arrow carries. The shield can quench them because it is covered with non-inflammable leather (perhaps even soaked with water) and the burning arrows which strike it merely burn themselves out harmlessly. The Christian is told to take the shield of faith which can similarly extinguish the devil's missiles. The word 'take' means to receive it as God's gift to us, rather than seize by our own prowess.

17. salvation is likened to **the helmet** which protects the head. In 1 Th. 5:8 the helmet consists of the *hope* of salvation. Here it is salvation itself. It is characteristic of Ephesians that salvation is regarded not as something in the future to hope for so much as something already bestowed upon the Christian, a privilege he already enjoys (as at 2:5, 8). It is a glad awareness of having been put right with God, and the inward sense of 'wholeness', peace, and vitality which this brings.

The concluding item in the armour is **the sword,** the only one whose purpose is for attack as well as defence. It is described as **the sword of the Spirit.** This could mean either the sword which consists of the Spirit, or the sword which the Spirit provides. We have already seen that this writer believes that every Christian, by the mere fact of being a Christian, has received the gift of the Spirit, that is a new accession of inward power from God, with the confidence and assurance this brings. The Spirit provides the means by which the Christian not only defensively stands his ground and wards off evil, but also is enabled to go on to the attack and make new conquests in God's cause. The sword is then further identified as **the word of God.** The grammar in fact allows us to understand **the word of God** as identified either with the Spirit or with the sword (wielded by the Spirit). It would, however, be unusual in the *NT* for the word of God to be identified with the Spirit. The word of God appears to mean God's message in the gospel, whether written or spoken, and when this is personalized it is identified with Christ rather than the Spirit. There are, however, passages in Paul's writings where Christ and Spirit are not sharply distinguished (Rom. 8:9; 1 C. 3:17; cf. 1 Pet. 1:11). However, it is better here to regard **the word of God** as referring to the sword which the Spirit provides.

In Paul's writings those who spoke God's word under the impulse of **the Spirit** were called prophets. It was their function not so much to recall and expound written words from the past as to speak out what God was saying to them in the present. 'Thus says the Lord' was their characteristic utterance. The Spirit in a Christian can enable him to become God's spokesman to the situation in which he finds himself. The Spirit furnishes him with the word of God, the spiritual sword in God's advancing cause. In this cause the Spirit, it was believed, would provide the Christian with the word he needs to make an effective answer either as a witness or under interrogation: 'The words you need will be given to you . . . It will be the Spirit of God speaking in you' (Mt. 10:19–20).

The equipment which a Christian needs to be effective in his fight against the powers of evil consists, therefore, of integrity, total obedience to the will of God, the glad awareness of the happiness promised in his message, faith, salvation, and the word that God's Spirit can prompt him to speak. And all these are gifts which God will provide.

18. Following the description of the fighting equipment of the Christian, there follows a very strong emphasis on his need for **prayer.** His attitude must be one of prayer **in the Spirit,** not just at specified intervals but at all times. To **pray . . . in the Spirit** means to pray in that awareness of God which the Spirit brings, to be able to approach him in simple trusting confidence as a child to his father (Rom. 8:15–16); it means to pray in the knowledge that the Spirit 'helps our weakness' and even 'intercedes for us' (Rom. 8:26). It is an approach to God relying not on our own piety, but on the help which God in his Spirit offers to us. Such prayer includes both **prayer and supplication.** If the two are to be distinguished, **prayer** must mean the conscious awareness of God with a readiness to receive what he waits to give, whether he gives benefits or commands. In this kind of prayer no precise words need to be spoken. **supplication** on the other hand implies that we put requests to God, perhaps for ourselves, certainly for others and their needs.

If we are to be able to pray **at all times,** it will be necessary to **keep alert with all perseverence.** Such prayer is not something which human nature can do casually and carelessly. It does not come naturally. Till now the emphasis has all been on what God provides for the Christian. But at this point the need for the Christian's own self-discipline is stressed. He must provide watchful alertness against every approach of evil and not be taken off his guard, with his armour carelessly laid aside for comfort. There must be watchful alertness; and with it must go **perseverance.** He must resolutely wear the armour at all times, recognising how easy it is to grow tired and slack and thus expose himself to attacks for which he is unprepared and to which he may easily fall victim.

The supplication is **for all the saints.** Our prayers are required for all our fellow Christians. Prayer for them all without exception not only represents our concern for them, but also stimulates that concern. **also for me:** included among their fellow Christians, but with a special claim upon their prayers is Paul himself (6:19). This is one of the passages in the epistle where the writer seeks to emphasise the fact that he writes in Paul's name. 6:19-20 are largely dependent on Col. 4:2-4, where Paul writes as a prisoner. So here, too, Paul is represented as a prisoner (as also at Eph. 3:1), and in both Col. 4:2-4 and here he asks for their prayers (i) that he may be given words boldly to proclaim the message of the gospel; because (ii) this is something he ought to do; and (iii) it is the reason why he is in prison. Though the words used in the two letters at this point are not identical, the similarity of thought shows how close is their interdependence. The writer of Ephesians clearly has Col. 4:2-4 freshly in his mind at this point, but the way he reproduces the thought suggests that he does so from memory rather than by copying from the other letter verbatim.

19. Paul is represented as asking for their prayers that he may be given words (**utterance**) so as to make the gospel intelligible to his hearers. *RSV* uses the translation **proclaim,** but this is misleading. The Greek word used is not the ordinary one for preaching, but rather for elucidating a message to make sure it is understood. The word **boldly** is used frequently in different books of the *NT* to describe a Christian's conduct towards non-Christians, especially in relation to bearing witness. By derivation the word means 'with uninhibited speech', with a freedom unhampered by fear of what others may do or say, or by our own undue shyness or lack of confidence. *NEB* uses two English words for the one Greek word, 'boldly and freely', but this brings out the twofold meaning of the word accurately.

What he is to make known is **the mystery of the gospel.** The word **mystery** has already been prominent in Ephesians. Primarily it has been used of the unexpected way in which God's purpose has been worked out in the reconciliation of Jews and Gentiles within the Christian community. The acceptance of the gospel has achieved this. It is possible that something of this meaning of the word is present here also. It may, however, be used in its more general sense of 'the unbelievable truth' of the gospel.

20. Of this gospel Paul is described as **an ambassador in chains.** So too at 2 C. 5:20 Paul says: 'We are ambassadors for Christ,' his representatives in foreign territory. **in chains** represents the phrase 'on account of which I am in prison' (Col. 4:4). **as I ought to speak** also comes from Col. 4:4.

21-22. These verses present a curious problem—perhaps also a

valuable clue, if only we knew how to use it—in any attempt to
resolve the relationship between Ephesians and Colossians. Up to
this point the borrowing of Ephesians from Colossians, though
constant and considerable, has not suggested that the writer actually consulted a copy of Colossians lying in front of him and
reproduced passages from it word for word. Rather, it seems as
though the writer knew Colossians very intimately and was able to
reproduce the gist of it from memory—including many groups of
three to five consecutive words—but without any precise quotation of more than a few consecutive words. Here, however, is
something quite different: thirty-two consecutive words in Ephesians are identical with a similar number of words from Col. 4:7–8.
Quite clearly the writer of Ephesians has at this point turned to a
copy of Colossians and copied it out verbatim. The only slight
differences are that in Ephesians the phrase **what I am doing**
is additional to what is found in Colossians, and in Colossians
Tychicus is called 'a fellow servant' additional to the words
beloved brother and faithful minister which occur in both
Colossians and Ephesians. Goodspeed noticed that the reference
to Onesimus in the same sentence in Colossians (4:9) is omitted
from Ephesians, and interpreted this as one piece of evidence
favouring his theory that Onesimus was in fact the compiler of
Ephesians as well as the collector of the first Pauline corpus of
letters.

The writer of Ephesians clearly felt that it was important to
include this sequence of words in his letter. Perhaps **Tychicus**
was still alive and known to many of the first readers. He would
be able to vouch for the fact that the letter truly embodied the
essentials of Paul's message, since he had been closely associated
with Paul and himself the bearer of the letter Paul sent to the
Colossian church. He may even himself have been the writer of
Ephesians and uses these words from Colossians to remind the
readers of the complete trust which Paul his master had been
willing to place in him.

BENEDICTION 6:23–24

23–24. This benediction brings together several characteristically Pauline words—grace, faith, love, and peace. **Grace** and
peace were associated in the initial greeting at 1:2 (as also at

Phil. 1:2, Col. 1:2, 1 Th. 1:1, etc.). **Grace** is the word *par excellence* which for Paul emphasises the generous giving of God. **Peace** and **love** are its fruits in human life. **faith,** itself part of God's gift to the believer, is at the same time the believer's response to God's giving, his receptiveness towards the gift. **brethren** are the members of the Christian community who receive this letter (cf. the reference in 6:21 to 'brother'). Among Christians **brethren** by common custom became the standard word for fellow-believers. This widespread practice would arise very naturally because they all acknowledged **God, the Father** of their **Lord Jesus Christ,** as their own Father. They were members of the family of which God was Father and in which Jesus Christ was, as it were, the eldest brother (Rom. 8:29). The growth of the practice would find encouragement from the way in which their Lord himself had accepted his disciples as his real family (Mk 3:33-35). Even apart from this precedent which made the use of the word 'brother' so appropriate among early Christians, the word seemed the right one to express the warm sense of loyalty and love which members of the early Church felt for one another.

The writer's wish is that **peace, love,** and **faith,** all God's proffered gifts, will be appropriated and enjoyed by his readers, and the second benediction, which begins with verse 24 calls down God's **Grace** upon his readers. This is a common feature of the concluding greeting in several of Paul's letters (Gal. 6:18, Phil. 4:23, etc.). Those for whom God's grace is requested are, however, described in a phrase which some have felt to be un-Pauline: **all who love our Lord Jesus Christ.** This phrase does not in fact occur in any greeting in the Pauline letters, and some scholars insist that it cannot be regarded as a characteristic Pauline expression. They contend that Paul preferred to call Christians 'the saints' or 'believers' or 'those in Christ', and that he shrank from the phrase 'those who love God' as laying too much emphasis on man's attitude and too little on God's part in the relationship. It is certainly more characteristic of Paul's own use of the word **love** to apply it to God's love for man (as in Rom. 8:37; Gal. 2:20, etc.) and man's love for his fellows (as in Rom. 13:8-9; Gal. 5:14, etc.) rather than to man's love for God. This is broadly true, but Paul does in fact write occasionally of man's love for God (e.g., Rom. 8:28; 1 C. 2:2, 8:3), though it is not very frequently.

The Greek words translated by *RSV* as **with love undying** literally mean 'in (or "with") immortality' or 'incorruption'. It is not clear how they should be translated or to what other part of the sentence they should be related. *AV* translated them 'with sincerity'. *RV*, with its commendable determination to represent accurately and consistently the words in the Greek text, translated 'in incorruptness'. These both suggest that the phrase describes the Christian's love for Christ (so *RSV*). *NEB* recognises this as a valid possibility, but relegates it to a footnote: 'who love . . . Christ with love imperishable'. The other possibility is that it should be associated with God's grace. *NEB* regards this as the stronger alternative of the two and in the text translates: 'God's grace be with all who love our Lord Jesus Christ, grace and immortality' (literally 'grace with immortality').

If the concluding sentence should be thought of as summarising the main emphasis of the epistle as a whole, our preference also would be to regard this final phrase as a description of God's unlimited grace towards man. Grace has been the keynote of all the epistle—God's generous, courteous approach to man in his need and sinfulness. It is fitting that its final wish should be for this grace to be fully known to all who love Christ. The last words give the assurance that this grace will never fail them. It is **undying,** indestructible. It is not subject to change or decay. Neither man's stubborn resistance nor his callous ingratitude can finally defeat it. It knows no ending. It shares the very nature of God's eternity. If the emphasis in the earlier chapters was that this grace from God is 'unmerited and free', the note in this concluding verse is that it is also 'unalterably sure'.

INDEX OF AUTHORS

INDEX OF SUBJECTS

Historically, the only matter to determine is -- not whether Paul was the infallibly inspired writer (as Xians reverence see here) but whether the revelation he expresses! fr. which he draws conclusion is that; ! if it's a message for us.

Eph 7 Sermon 149
also Eph 3 page

42 Christology

'hump for', an urgent
Need picked up at natel
for sex, 2 think

p 13 on Eph 2:8-9

117 on (Paul) I Pet authorship
194 I Pet! Haustafeln
110 I Pet 2:1 sojourners
113 "cornerstone"
115
108 I Pet 2 "new race"
168 mt 5:37
202-3 I Pet 3:21

202 I Pet 3:
p 147 on I Pet 3:19
211 Ex 20:12 x